SAVORING
THE
SEASONS

OF THE NORTHERN HEARTLAND

SAVORING THE SEASONS

OF THE NORTHERN HEARTLAND

BETH DOOLEY & LUCIA WATSON

University of Minnesota Press

Minneapolis • London

Originally published in hardcover by Alfred A. Knopf as
part of the Knopf Cooks American series
First University of Minnesota Press edition, 2004

Published by the University of Minnesota Press
111 Third Avenue South, Suite 290
Minneapolis, MN 55401-2520
http://www.upress.umn.edu

Library of Congress Cataloging-in-Publication Data

Dooley, Beth.
Savoring the seasons of the northern heartland / Beth Dooley
and Lucia Watson.—1st University of Minnesota Press ed.
p. cm.
Originally published: New York : Knopf, 1994.
Includes index.
ISBN 0-8166-4574-4 (pb : alk. paper)
1. Cookery, American—Midwestern style. 2. Cookery—Middle West.
3. Middle West—Social life and customs.   I. Watson, Lucia. II. Title.
TX715.2.M53D66 2004
641.5977—dc22

2004013040

Printed in the United States of America on acid-free paper

The University of Minnesota is an
equal-opportunity educator and employer.

12 11 10 09 08 07 06 05 04   10 9 8 7 6 5 4 3 2 1

CONTENTS

Our Great Appreciation To:

Bonnie Blodgett, writer and agent, for her thoughtful reading of and valuable insights into our work (especially early on), and for her encouragement and support. John Borchert, author of *America's Northern Heartland,* for his help in defining this vast territory. Evelyn Birkby, author of *Neighboring on the Air,* for her memories of the KMA Radio Homemakers. Deborah Morris Kahn, author and historian, for her understanding of Northern Heartland history. Susan Poupore, caterer, for her recipes and memories of growing up in northern Minnesota. Eleanor Ostman, food writer and editor, *St. Paul Pioneer Press,* for her recipes and stories about the Iron Range. Beatrice Ojakangas, food writer and author of numerous cookbooks, including *The Great Scandinavian Baking Book,* for her insights into Scandinavian-American food and customs. Diana Boegemann of Roots & Fruits for her knowledge and her network of local produce and cheese suppliers. Nance Oleson for her splendid St. Lucia Day celebration. Nancy Carlson, children's book author and illustrator (who knows all about *rommegrøt*), and Marty Schneider, who helped with local sources. Christopher Cardozo, author of *Native Nations: First Americans as seen by Edward S. Curtis,* for sharing the Curtis prints. Doug Stenge, editor of *In-Fisherman,* for his fish stories and photos. Jim Kwitchak, Alice Hoolihan, Rose Block, Ann Sorenson, Florence Zarling, Daisy Samuelson, Hilda Kringstad, Jean Housey, and Elsie Oehler for sharing their memories, childhood stories, and recipes. Mary Doerr of Dancing Wind Farms, Mary Eichten and Ed Eichten of Eichten's Hidden Acres, Scott Erickson of Bass Lake Cheese Factory, Lucy Steinkamp of LaPaysanne, Nan Bailly of Alexis Bailly Winery, and Mac Graham of Star Prairie Trout Farm, Wally Johnson of Johnson Meats, and Hunk Schere of Schere Meats. Karal Ann Marling, author of *Blue Ribbon,* and Susan Puckett, author of *A Cook's Tour of Iowa,* for sharing photos and information. Eddie Lewis, author of *Ray Had an Idea About Love,* for his Rainy Lake insights into the final draft, and Matt Lewis for catching all those fish. Nach Waxman, Kitchen Arts & Letters, for his thoughts on the American food scene. Patty Hoolihan, author of *Small Miracles,* for her help proofreading. Gus Gustafson, Gerald Gustafson Photography, for photographing us. Leslie Bush, who read, tested, and retested recipes, and Caroline Glawe, Jane Tilka, and James Davies for testing recipes in their homes. Mike Reed, illustrator, and Tacy Rygmyr, video producer. Kevin Dooley, for reading and rereading this manuscript, and for his unfailing support and boundless enthusiasm...and Matt, Kip, and Tim Dooley...plus Mary-Katherine Meinkheim and Allison Ek, who provided a nurturing and steady home base. Mary Ann Clifford, Ann Schroeder, Susan Muskat, Beth Fisher, Julie Bloor, Anna Marie Rigleman, Mark Lokowich, and Gene Zarling, who tested and shared recipes, plus Al Updike of Lucia's Wine Bar who knows the local breweries...and the entire staff of Lucia's Restaurant. Judith Jones, our editor, from whom we have learned so much.

INTRODUCTION

The land is of beautiful lakes all communicating with each other by equally beautiful streams full of excellent fish and ducks of twenty Species, Swans & geese with abundance of rice for you & them. The boarders well furnished with grapes, plums, thorn apples and butternut. The Woods Swarming with Deers & Bears & beavers ...Whenever this country becomes settled how delightfully will the inhabitants pass their time.

—PAPERS OF GEORGE NELSON, MINNESOTA TRAPPER, 1803

This book of recipes and stories tells how generations of inhabitants in the Northern Heartland have delighted in the region's splendor, just as George Nelson predicted we would. We have gathered here a feast of harvest vegetables and fruit, native wild rice, succulent game, farmstead cheese, and firm fresh fish from the region. There are recipes for hearty soups and stews, wholesome breads, and rich cakes and fruit pies made to go with endless cups of coffee. All of these foods reflect the past and the way our eating habits have changed as the land was settled, as food industries developed, and as different waves of immigrants contributed their unique flavors to the Midwest's potluck.

As a geographic term, Northern Heartland defies state boundaries. It encompasses Minnesota, Iowa, Wisconsin, the Upper Peninsula of Michigan, and eastern North Dakota. What distinguishes cooking from this area is the dramatic climate, the surprisingly diverse ethnic heritage, and the nature of the land, as well as the ingredients themselves. These factors continue to influence the way we live and the way we cook today.

Weather has always been a regional preoccupation, especially when winter begins as early as Halloween and the windchill dips as low as 75 degrees below zero. It is still a much accepted theory that eating enhances one's ability to stay warm. Back in 1894, Sara Tyson Rorer, a noted Philadelphia cookbook author, lectured her Minneapolis audience, "Well-fed people never mind the weather. An inch of healthy fat on the body is worth more in keeping warm than a sealskin cloak."

Many of today's warming soups and stews were created to satisfy outdoor hunger, using ingredients from a meager winter's larder. What wasn't smoked, pickled, canned, or stashed away in the cellar by October simply wasn't eaten in January. Our refreshing chilled vegetable and fruit soups and crisp, colorful salads were originally created for the lighter appetites of summer's scorching days. June through mid-September, we feast on platters of golden corn, sliced tomatoes, and juicy berry and fruit pies.

Early explorers, voyageurs, and trappers learned from native Ojibway and Sioux tribes how to live off the land—to dry fish, harvest cranberries, and cook wild rice (Indian oats). These Native Americans taught the trappers how to weave gill nets that are still used in the fishing industry today.

The first settlers came from Scandinavia, Germany, Eastern Europe, Scotland, and Wales to homestead the abundant farmland. The East Europeans and the Scottish brought with them a hardy strain of spring wheat that flourished despite the harsh weather. Transplanted New Englanders Cadwallader C. Washburn and Charles Pillsbury, with the expertise of immigrant Hungarian millers, unlocked the mystery of milling the tough kernels into the world's finest flour. Companies such as the Washburn

Crosby Milling Company (which later became General Mills) and Pillsbury Flour Company were funded with flour capital and grew to become giant producers of cereal, processed vegetables, and packaged foods.

The Central Europeans, drawn to the region's rolling grasslands in the early 1900s, settled on farms and were soon turning their clover-sweet milk into fine butter and the cheeses of their homelands. They formed the nation's first dairy cooperatives that, within twenty years, grew into major concerns like Land O' Lakes, Minnesota, by shipping butter and cheese to ports as far-flung as Hong Kong.

The Germans brought their talent for animal husbandry to Iowa and their love of beer brewing and sausage making to Wisconsin. The Italians brought homeland cultures for making cheese. Those who came from agricultural backgrounds delighted in the bounty of their farms. The region's corn, potatoes, and crop vegetables, as well as our butter, cheese, beer, pork, and sausage, have long stocked the nation's larder.

In the early 1900s iron mines, logging camps, railroad yards, flour mills, and factories brought Norwegians, Finns, Germans, Hungarians, Poles, Russians, Czechs, Ukrainians, Romanians, and Serbs, Croats, and Slovenes (from the area once known as Yugoslavia) to Minnesota, Wisconsin, and the Upper Peninsula of Michigan, most of them young bachelors seeking a fortune. These men without wives sought lodging and comfort in the homes of friends and relatives, and these homes often developed into commercial boardinghouses, with new wings added on demand. The rambling structures offered dormitory-style rooms, three meals a day, and laundry.

Boardinghouse food was hearty with the flavors of the old country. "Cooking twenty to thirty pounds of meat was an everyday task for mother," recalls Frank Blatnik, son of a Croatian miner in Nashwauk, Minnesota. "She filled the miners' dinner pails with hot cabbage soup on the bottom so the *potica* (walnut pastry) on top stayed warm." When contracted brides from the old country started arriving, they brought their ethnic flavors with them. A Hungarian bride-to-be always had fine paprika as part of her dowry.

"It wouldn't be a wedding on the Iron Range without *sarma* (Croatian cabbage rolls), pasties (Cornish meat pies), *porketta* (Italian pork roast), or *pulla* (Finnish cardamom bread)," writes Eleanor Ostman, food editor for the St. Paul *Pioneer Press,* originally from Hibbing, Minnesota. "We all grew up with them no matter our ethnic heritage, because if our families didn't make them, our friends did. The Iron Range has often been called a 'melting pot.' It should be called a 'stewpot' for all the flavors that have been stirred together by those hearty families who came to work the iron mines and stayed to build the necklace of towns strung between the pits and the dumps."

The logging camps in Wisconsin and Minnesota were manned with farmers who worked through the winter and returned home to plant their crops. These men lived a secluded life in forest camps and cultivated a language of their own. At the "cook shack" (dining hall) they ate "stove lids" (sourdough pancakes), "logging berries" (prunes), "sow belly" (salt pork), "red horse" (corned beef), "pregnant women" (dried apple pie), and "Murphy's" (fried potatoes, so named for their association with an Irish diet of potatoes), washed down with plenty of "dish water" (coffee) or "swamp water" (tea).

In rural areas the vast distances between farms, the harsh, unpredictable weather, and the hard, lonely labor required of farmers have made cooperation and communication especially important. Threshing, barn raisings, wood chopping, quilting bees, hog killings, apple peelings, and other communal efforts punctuated the seasonal routine. Of all these, threshing to harvest the oats, wheat, and barley was perhaps the most demanding task of the year. The farm cook, with the help of her neighbors, would supply three or four meals a day to the thirty or so men hustling to "make hay while the sun shines." Cooking was competitive, for most people believed that the best food and fastest service drew the strongest crew. Midmorning and midafternoon lunches of roast beef or ham sandwiches, homemade sugar doughnuts, and coffee were delivered to the field by cart; noon dinner was a sit-down meal of roast beef or pork or a rich stew, homemade bread and butter, sliced fresh tomatoes and cucumbers, fresh cottage cheese, pickles, corn relish, fruit pie or plain cake and coffee—all served on china, with linen and glassware.

The Radio Homemaker shows, first aired in 1925 by KMA, Shenandoah, Iowa, were designed to bridge the vast distances between isolated farm women. "We started out at a time when there were many lonely people in the countryside," notes Evelyn Birkby, author of *Cooking with the KMA Radio Homemakers.* "We neighbored on the air. It was just like we were coming over for coffee." Devoted to recipes and cooking tips, programs such as *Kitchen Klinik,* full of chitchat and advice, were broadcast directly from the host's home, complete with yelling children, ringing doorbells, and banging pots and pans.

In the Northern Heartland a "coffee" has always meant more than the brew. "Neighbor women would just stop by and rap on the screen door, usually around four o'clock or so, before starting dinner chores," recalls Florence Zarling of Glencoe, Minnesota. "Of course, no one serves coffee without something sweet. My mother taught me to always have bars or a pound cake stashed in the cupboard ready for such visits."

The daily ritual of gathering over coffee, like so many other Northern Heartland traditions, is still very much alive today. A good deal of the research for this book was done over coffee, talking to men and women who remember grinding nutmeg for their grandmother's stollen, churning the weekly supply of butter, and "putting up" quarts of pickles. We sifted through old recipes calling for a handful of this and a teacup of that. And we tried to identify the values underlying this generous, openhanded cuisine that still govern the way we cook today.

One of us, Lucia Watson, is the proprietor and chef of Lucia's Restaurant, which opened in 1985 in one of Minneapolis's oldest neighborhoods. Lucia, a native Minnesotan, learned to cook from her grandmother Lulu, who used to bake bread in a wood stove in the family's summer cabin on Rainy Lake, near the Canadian border. Lulu proved a great source of inspiration to us in writing this book, and her name appears often in these pages, reminding us all of how things were done in the past. Lucia's restaurant kitchen also provided fertile ground for developing creative recipes. There the menu changes every week, adapting to whatever is available locally in the market and to how the weather affects appetites. From her customers Lucia has learned what kinds of dishes are particularly appealing to those seeking genuine regional flavors and new interpretations of traditional dishes.

The other one of us, Beth Dooley, is a transplanted Easterner who brings to the project a newcomer's enthusiasm and curiosity about what makes food special in this part of the country. In the fifteen years she has lived here, she has covered the fast-changing food scene for local companies, and she has been drawn to the rich histories of those fearless immigrants who left behind family and friends to begin new lives, and who still managed to maintain a connection to the past through the foods they held dear. As a home cook and cooking-school teacher, Beth has worked with Lucia to make sure that all of the ingredients are accessible and that the recipes can be made easily in one's own kitchen.

In selecting the recipes for the book, we always looked for foods that were representative of Northern Heartland traditions: the wholesome whole grain breads (honey cracked wheat) and rich holiday loaves (saffron-scented Saint Lucia Buns); Christmas cookies (gingery Pepparkakor), bars, and bubbly fruit pies. We sought simple comforting stews—a rich beef stew with caramelized onions and beer, or a pork loin braised in cider and apples until tender and succulent—that require little of the cook but patience as they simmer away. We focused on local ingredients in recipes such as a salad of roast duck and wild rice in a hazelnut vinaigrette. And we've revised a number of dishes for today's busy cooks with lighter palates, offering recipes like a chicken sauté with fresh seasonal vegetables and a seasoned flank steak for summer and winter.

Some local readers may be disappointed that we did not include step-by-step directions for making traditional Scandinavian *rommegrøt* (cream porridge), lutefisk (lye-treated, dried, reconstituted codfish), and lefse (flat potato bread). We do have stories about them, but we felt that these specialties, usually reserved for the holidays, are perhaps best learned from an experienced cook who can demonstrate when the lefse dough is ready for the griddle or when to stop stirring the *grøt*. They do not represent the way people around here are cooking at home today. We've also omitted many of the casseroles bound in canned soup often associated with Midwestern cooking. These are really more typical of the convenience-food cooking that pervades every region of the country.

Like those sturdy, innovative Northern Heartlanders of past generations, we cook in tune with the seasons. Inspired by the wealth of native ingredients, we've blended new flavors with traditional values in bold, imaginative ways. This food reflects our need to waste nothing, to savor all that we have, and to share the bounty.

SAVORING
THE
SEASONS

OF THE NORTHERN HEARTLAND

Old-fashioned Milk Bread

Honey Cracked Wheat Bread

Café Latte's Dakota Bread

Oatmeal Bread

Susan Poupore's Wild Rice Bread

Raised Corn Bread with Sweet Corn

Cottage Cheese Dill Bread

Potato Bread

Limpa Rye

Finnish Cardamom Coffee Bread

Cinnamon Rolls (with Raisin-Cinnamon Loaf Variation)

Christmas Bread

Saint Lucia Buns

Kolachke (Sweet Buns)

French Toast

Norwegian Toast

Pancakes

German Oven Pancake

Swedish Pancakes

Black Walnut Bread

Corn Muffins (and Corn Bread)

Pumpkin-Cranberry Muffins

Fry Bread

MILLING AND BAKING

BREADS, MUFFINS, AND GRIDDLE CAKES

Here then was the start! These few sacks of grain would not only supply [Per Hansa] and his family with all the wheat flour they needed for a whole year, but would raise many bright dollars as well, a great store of riches...and more than that, seed for the next year, seed again for the year after, and thus down through the years to come....And always greater and greater abundance of food for the poor the world over....

His wonder grew as he gazed at the kernels; there they lay, so inanimate, yet so plump and heavy, glowing with smouldering flame. It was as if each kernel had light within it—now asleep. He thrust his hand into the sack and took out a handful of grain; it weighed like lead. As his grasp tightened, the kernels seemed to soften under the warmth of his hand; they squirmed and twisted, slipping against one another; they seemed to be charged with a delicate life that was seeking release.

—O. E. RÖLVAAG, *GIANTS IN THE EARTH*

Baking day has always been a high note in the rhythm of the week. "Friday my mother baked," writes Patricia Hoolihan of Grand Rapids, Minnesota. "I loved being able to sift the flour into the dough and brush the butter across the top of the freshly baked loaves. She'd cut me a slice so warm the butter melted right off the knife. One of my mother's gifts was the smell of baking bread as we came in the door," Patricia

3

recalls. "The Thursday night before my grandmother died, she set out the pans, measuring cups, bowl, and flour for her weekly ritual."

Back in the 1850s bread was sometimes the only food on a settler's table. In this land of long winters and short growing seasons, the root cellar was empty long before spring, leaving a household with only flour, cornmeal, and salt. In years of drought or heavy rains, and during the grasshopper plague when the wheat crop failed, pioneer housewives ground flour from corn, buckwheat, and oats in their coffee mills.

For many immigrants, bread was a sturdy link to the past. I. O. Krohnke, a German settler from New Holstein, Wisconsin, planted rye, although it was unpopular. "The dear old black bread still tastes best, and in spite of the fact that we eat wheat bread, I prefer the rye bread," he wrote in a letter back home.

Beloved flavors that were impossible to duplicate with what could be grown here were sent for from the old country. The aroma of cardamom and almond identified a Norwegian kitchen; nutmeg and anise, a German; and caraway, a Bohemian. Hilda Kringstad recalls helping her mother and grandmother grind spices for their Norwegian Christmas breads: "There was for me an air of mystery and excitement in this ritual that I was too young to understand."

The fertile plains of the Northern Heartland, when planted with hard spring wheat, seeded the nation's milling industry. By 1900 the region had become the "breadbasket to the world." Today many entrepreneurial millers have returned to grindstone milling, providing bakers with a wide selection of fine organic flours.

In this chapter we've searched for traditional loaves, like Norwegian Limpa Rye, fragrant with anise, caraway, and fennel, that are as satisfy-

In the Northern Heartland, bread was eaten three times a day and often as a snack. Big city bakeries, like Charles Holtz and Company Bake Shop, St. Paul (1910), supplied bread for the wealthy who lived in mansions along Summit Avenue, as well as the harried home cook who needed a loaf quickly.

ing to knead, shape, and bake today as they were when they were made in the wood stoves of long ago. We've also created new recipes, such as Raised Corn Bread with Sweet Corn, that were inspired by native ingredients; dense and textured with fresh golden kernels, this corn bread is hearty and nutritious.

Throughout we've relied on principles that have guided generations of Northern Heartland bakers: good bread is made from scratch with wholesome, local ingredients, patience, and care.

OLD-FASHIONED
MILK BREAD

MAKES 2 LOAVES

Good bread makes the homeliest meal acceptable and the coarsest fare appetizing.

—*BUCKEYE COOKERY*, ST. PAUL, 1876

*T*his is our favorite white bread. The light, fine-textured loaf makes wonderful sandwiches, Chocolate Bread Pudding (page 358) or French Toast (page 38).

> 3 cups whole milk
> 2 packages (or 2 scant tablespoons) active dry yeast
> 2 teaspoons sugar
> 7½ cups unbleached all-purpose flour
> 1 tablespoon plus 1 teaspoon salt
> 1 stick (8 tablespoons) butter, softened, plus a little more
>   for greasing the bowl and bread pans

*S*cald the milk in a saucepan by bringing it just to a boil and quickly removing it from the heat. Cool to "baby bottle" temperature (105 to 115°F), pour it into a large bowl, add the yeast and sugar, and let it "proof" (become foamy on top) for about 5 minutes. Then add *3 cups* of the flour, the salt, and butter, and beat the dough until smooth. Add enough of the remaining flour to make a soft dough that pulls away from the sides of the bowl.

Turn the dough onto a lightly floured board and knead it until smooth and elastic, about 8 minutes, sprinkling with flour as needed. Then place the dough in a bowl lightly greased with butter, turning the dough so it is also lightly greased. Cover the bowl with a clean towel and allow the dough to rise for 45 minutes.

Punch the dough down and shape into 2 loaves. Place these loaves in lightly greased 9-inch bread pans and allow them to rise ½ inch above the pans, about 45 minutes. Bake the loaves in a preheated 400°F oven for about 45 minutes, or until the loaves sound hollow when tapped. Remove the bread from the oven, turn out of the pans, and cool on a wire rack.

A WORD ABOUT YEAST

Yeasted doughs are easy to work with. Don't let the rising times control you. If you need to leave before the dough has doubled, punch it down to start the process again. Or put the dough in the refrigerator until *you* are ready.

We call for active dry yeast, *not* the quick-rise yeast, because several slow risings give a loaf character and flavor. The yeast must be dissolved first in very warm liquid (105 to 115° Fahrenheit) to become active. After a few minutes the surface of the liquid should get foamy. This signals the yeast is fresh and ready for the other ingredients. (If the liquid does not get foamy, discard and start again.)

One package of active dry yeast contains 2¼ teaspoons, or 1 scant tablespoon.

HONEY CRACKED WHEAT BREAD

MAKES 2 TO 3 LOAVES

*C*racked wheat, milled from wheat berries that have been broken apart by a coarse grindstone, is high in protein, phosphorus, potassium, calcium, iron, thiamine, riboflavin, and niacin. In this recipe the cracked wheat adds a nutty flavor and texture to a wholesome loaf of bread.

> *1¾ cups boiling water*
> *¾ cup cracked wheat*
> *⅓ cup honey*
> *¾ cup warm water (105° to 115°F)*
> *2 packages (or 2 scant tablespoons) active dry yeast*
> *1 cup unbleached all-purpose flour*
> *1½ teaspoons salt*
> *3–4 cups whole wheat flour*
> *Vegetable oil for greasing the bowl and baking sheet*

*I*n a large bowl, mix together the boiling water, cracked wheat, and honey to soften the wheat; let cool, then add the warm water. The entire mixture should be "baby bottle" temperature (105° to 115°F). Stir in the yeast and let this stand about 5 minutes, or until the surface becomes foamy. Add the white flour and beat 100 strokes. Let this rest 45 minutes, then stir it down and add the salt and enough whole wheat flour to make a stiff dough. It should clean the bowl as you stir.

Turn the dough onto a lightly floured board and knead about 10 minutes, adding as much flour as necessary to keep the dough from sticking. When the dough is smooth and elastic, place it in a lightly greased bowl. Cover it with a towel and allow to rise until double in bulk, about 1 hour. Punch the dough down, cover it, and again allow it to rise until doubled, about 1 hour.

Punch the dough down once again. Turn it onto a lightly floured board and knead it several turns. Shape it into 2 or 3 oblong loaves and place them seam side down on a lightly greased baking sheet. Allow these to rise about 45 minutes.

Make diagonal slashes using a sharp knife on top of the loaves. Bake the loaves in a preheated 350°F oven for 35 minutes, or until they sound hollow when tapped. Remove the loaves from the oven and cool on a wire rack.

BACK TO THE GRINDSTONE

Not everyone was eager to embrace the new, pure white flour. Just as Washburn was building his "monster mill," Sylvester Graham, a Presbyterian minister from Philadelphia, was denouncing the roller millers for "putting asunder what God has joined together."

By the 1940s scientists confirmed the health benefits of whole wheat flour, and consumers pressured companies to refortify white flour with niacin, iron, and vitamins B_1 and B_2.

Today's entrepreneurial millers have returned to grindstone milling as a more nutritious, though more expensive, alternative to roller milling. When the wheat is milled by grindstone, the vitamins contained in the hard wheat germ remain intact. The bran is not sifted out, so the flour contains more fiber. Whole wheat flour, unlike white flour, is not bleached or aged with chemicals that would also affect vitamin content.

In this book we incorporate whole wheat flour into many of the bread recipes because it adds flavor, texture, and vitamins, and we also use unbleached all-purpose white flour because it helps make the bread fine and light.

THE WORLD'S BEST FLOUR

To make good bread, the nineteenth-century housewife had to know her flour. *Buckeye Cookery* provided the following guidelines: "Good flour adheres to the hand, and when pressed, shows the imprint of the lines of the skin. Its tint is pure white."

Until 1860 consumers were limited to a dull, often brownish product made from soft winter wheat. Spring wheat (grown in Minnesota, Wisconsin, and northern Iowa) produced a superior flour, but its kernels were tough to crack. The traditional grindstone method shattered the wheat berry, producing a flour full of bran and middlings—small, unprocessed clumps of endosperm. As farmer-owned community mills became commercial operations, millers invented ways to sift out the middlings and brazenly sold their flour as MADE IN ST. LOUIS to escape the local brand's poor reputation. The middlings were sold to the Indians as "red dog."*

Then in 1870 the Middlings Purifier was developed. It was a separator that combined a vibrating sifter with a blast of air to remove the bran from the wheat berry, which was then ground into flour, and the purifier became standard equipment in the "new process" mills. Though efficient, it created enormous amounts of hazardous dust. Accumulated in a storage room and carelessly ignited by a spark, this dust became the explosive that destroyed the world's largest "monster mill"—the Washburn A Mill, which covered five Minneapolis city blocks—in 1878, leveling six nearby mills in its thunderous wake.

* Ironically, the discarded middlings became grist for one of our oldest packaged cereals, Cream of Wheat, which was created by the head miller for Diamond Milling, Grand Forks, North Dakota. Tom Amidon, a Scotsman, saw the potential profit in the simple homemade "breakfast porridge" he fed his family made from this protein-rich part of the wheat, sifted out after the kernels were cracked. He dubbed the white grainy meal "Cream of Wheat." Within four years the product had become so successful, the mill became the Cream of Wheat Corporation and moved to Minneapolis. Now owned by Nabisco, Cream of Wheat celebrated its 100th anniversary in 1993.

The disaster provided Cadwallader C. Washburn, founder of the Washburn Crosby Milling Company (later to become General Mills), with the impetus for replacing the old cumbersome millstones with steel rollers, which had been newly developed by millers in Budapest, Hungary.* Soon Washburn and his rival, Charles A. Pillsbury of the Pillsbury Flour Company, adopted the Hungarian process in all their mills, and many immigrant Hungarian millers found employment there.

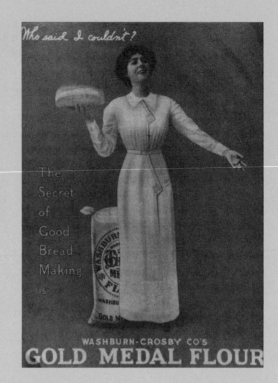

The new flour was eagerly accepted by cooks nationwide. Not only was it pure white, it contained less moisture than winter wheat flour, and so it enjoyed a longer shelf life. Its high gluten content made it easier to work with and produced a nicely textured loaf. It was soon dubbed "the world's best."

* *Washburn dispatched his head engineer, William de la Barre, to Budapest, to investigate the roller process used to mill the hard Hungarian wheat. The protective Hungarians refused this spy admission to their mills. De la Barre, however, befriended the night manager of his Budapest hotel, who got him a job under an alias in one of the newer mills. For a full month he worked the night shift, returning to his hotel room to sketch the rollers from memory. These sketches became the blueprints for Washburn Crosby's new A Mill, an amazing, fully automated roller-process mill.*

Meanwhile, Charles Pillsbury, working with an immigrant Hungarian miller, built the Pillsbury A Mill, which is still running today. He reportedly sneaked rollers out of Budapest.

CAFÉ LATTE'S DAKOTA BREAD

MAKES 2 LARGE OR 3 SMALL ROUND LOAVES

*C*afé Latte is a bustling cafeteria and bakery tucked into one of St. Paul's oldest neighborhoods, not far from the wide, elm-lined Summit Avenue where F. Scott Fitzgerald grew up. Here, in this renovated Victorian storefront, Café Latte owners Linda and Peter Quinn mill their own wheat, rye, and cornmeal for daily bread specials. Dakota Bread is Café Latte's best seller, and patrons often call a week in advance to reserve loaves. It is a light, nutty bread studded with sunflower and pumpkin seeds from North Dakota.

> *2 cups warm water (105° to 115°F)*
> *2 packages (or 2 scant tablespoons) active dry yeast*
> *¼ cup honey*
> *¼ cup vegetable oil*
> *½ cup cracked wheat*
> *1 tablespoon salt*
> *1 cup whole wheat flour*
> *5 cups unbleached all-purpose flour (or more for kneading)*
> *½ cup roasted, unsalted sunflower seeds*
> *⅓ cup hulled raw pumpkin seeds*
> *1 tablespoon poppy seeds*
> *1 tablespoon raw sesame seeds*
> *1 egg, beaten*
> *Vegetable oil for greasing the bowl and baking sheets*

*I*n a large bowl, combine the water, yeast, honey, oil, and cracked wheat and allow to proof about 5 to 10 minutes, or until the yeast is light and bubbly. Add the salt, whole wheat and white flours, and stir to combine.

Dump the dough out onto a well-floured surface and begin to knead, adding enough flour to make a nice soft dough. Knead about 10 to 15 minutes, sprinkling with more flour as necessary, or until the dough is smooth and elastic. You may want to use more flour depending on the dryness of the cracked wheat and the flours, as well as the general humidity.

Mix the seeds together and sprinkle them over the dough, reserving a few tablespoons to sprinkle over the loaves before baking. Then knead the seeds into the dough. Turn the dough into a greased bowl, cover with a dish towel, and set it in a warm place. Allow the dough to rise until double in bulk, about 1 hour. Punch the dough down. Let it rest for 5 minutes. Divide the dough and shape it into 2 large or 3 small round loaves, and place them on lightly greased baking sheets. Let rise 25 to 30 minutes. Brush the loaves with a beaten egg and sprinkle on any remaining seeds. Bake the loaves in a pre-heated 375°F oven for approximately 30 to 40 minutes, or until the loaves are nicely browned and sound hollow when tapped. Remove the loaves from the oven and cool on wire racks.

The whole family (and neighbors) brought in the sheaves at harvest time. The threshing machine moved from farm to farm throughout the season. This photo was taken in Dane County, Wisconsin, in 1875.

OATMEAL BREAD

MAKES TWO 8-INCH ROUND LOAVES

*T*oasting the oats first before adding them to the dough intensifies their flavor and adds some crunch. This bread makes a very good breakfast toast. Rely on your nose to tell you when the oats are toasted and the bread is baked. You'll notice a lovely, nutty smell.

> *1 cup boiling water*
> *1 cup buttermilk**
> *1 tablespoon honey*
> *1 package (or 1 scant tablespoon) active dry yeast*
> *2½ cups unbleached all-purpose flour*
> *1½ cups oatmeal (not instant)*
> *1 tablespoon salt*
> *1½–2 cups whole wheat flour*
> *Vegetable oil for greasing the bowl and baking sheet*
>
> **If you do not have buttermilk, add 1 tablespoon vinegar to 1 cup*
> *milk (preferably whole milk) and allow 30 seconds for it to sour.*

*I*n a large mixing bowl, stir together the boiling water and buttermilk so that the temperature of the liquid is "baby bottle" warm (about 105 to 115°F). Add the honey and yeast, stirring to dissolve the yeast, and let the liquid proof for 5 minutes, or until the surface becomes foamy. Add the white flour and beat 100 strokes, until the mixture is the consistency of mud. Cover the bowl and allow to rise 45 minutes, or until double in bulk.

Meanwhile, toast the oats by spreading them in an even layer on a cookie sheet and baking them for 10 minutes in a preheated 350°F oven, stirring occasionally so they toast evenly, until golden. Remove and allow to cool.

Stir down the dough. Add the salt, the toasted oatmeal, and enough of the whole wheat flour to make a smooth, elastic dough. Turn the dough onto a lightly floured surface and knead 5 to 10 minutes, or until it is smooth. It will be a bit sticky.

Oil a large bowl and place the dough in it, turning it several times to coat it with the oil, cover with a towel, and let rise in a warm place about 45 minutes, or until double in size. Punch the dough down and shape into 2 round loaves and place them on a greased baking sheet. Let the dough rise for 30 minutes, or until nearly double in size. Slash the tops with an X using a sharp knife and bake in a preheated 375°F oven for 45 to 50 minutes, or until the loaves sound hollow when tapped. Remove the loaves from the oven and cool on a wire rack.

OATMEAL HILL

Hunter's Park, in Duluth, Minnesota, is nicknamed "Oatmeal Hill" for its large Scottish population. Oats were first planted by Scottish settlers in the 1890s, and they took easily to Midwest soil. To this day oats not only survive brutal winters but store well in silos for about a year. Minnesota, Wisconsin, Iowa, and South Dakota are the world's largest producers of oats.

Jean Nichols of Duluth, who grew up near Oatmeal Hill, remembers: "My grandmother made oatmeal bread. She'd hold that large stoneware mixing bowl on one hip with one arm, stir with the other, and quote the poetry of Robert Burns."

SUSAN POUPORE'S
WILD RICE BREAD

MAKES 3 LOAVES

*R*ich, moist, and just a little sweet, this recipe was developed by Duluth caterer Susan Poupore for the Minnesota Wild Rice Council. It is among her most popular and most requested recipes.

> 2 cups water
> 1 cup oatmeal (not instant)
> ½ cup molasses
> ½ stick (4 tablespoons) butter
> 2½ teaspoons salt
> ½ cup cold water
> ¾ cup nonfat dry milk powder
> 1 package (or 1 scant tablespoon) active dry yeast
> ½ cup warm water (105° to 115°F)
> 7½ cups unbleached all-purpose flour
> 2 cups cooked wild rice
> 1 egg, beaten
> ¼ cup sesame, poppy, or sunflower seeds (alone or
>   in combination)
> Vegetable oil for greasing the bowl and cookie sheet

*B*ring the water to a boil and stir in the oatmeal; cook for 1 minute, then remove from heat. Stir in the molasses, butter, salt, cold water, and dry milk. Allow the mixture to cool until lukewarm. Dissolve the yeast in ½ cup warm water (105 to 115°F) and add to the oat mixture. Add *4 cups* of the flour to the oat mixture and beat it well. Stir in the wild rice and the remainder of the flour. Let the dough rest for 10 minutes.

Turn the dough out onto a lightly floured surface and knead it until it is smooth, about 5 to 10 minutes, adding more flour as necessary. Place the dough in a greased bowl and then turn it so it becomes lightly greased. Cover the bowl and allow the dough to rise until double in bulk.

Turn the dough out onto a lightly floured surface and divide it and shape into 3 round loaves, or cut into 3 strands and braid them into 1 large loaf. (The braid may also be shaped into a circle.) Place the bread on a lightly greased cookie sheet, brush with the beaten egg, and sprinkle with the seeds. Let the bread rise about 30 minutes, then bake in a preheated 350°F oven for about 40 to 45 minutes for the smaller loaves and about 50 minutes to 1 hour for the large loaf. Remove the bread from the oven and cool on a rack.

Members of the Ojibway tribe in northern Minnesota continue to harvest rice by hand using the tools of their forefathers.

BEST USES FOR STALE BREAD

Not so long ago, homemade bread was served three times a day and also as a snack. Not one heel was ever thrown away; the bread was turned into croutons, rusks, stuffing, or French toast and used in countless other ways.

Rebecca Trumpy Gillings of Redgranite, Wisconsin, remembers: "After school we would pour a little coffee over a slice of day-old bread, top it with thick cream from the bowl in the pantry, and sprinkle it with sugar." Mrs. Robert Sanford of River Falls, Wisconsin, recalls her evening snack after milking the cows was "a bowl of leftover bread and milk with raw onions."

After all the work of making fragrant loaves, it's hard to see them become stale. Take heart: stale bread makes wonderful rusks, croutons, bread pudding, and stuffing.

CROUTONS: Cube the bread and toss in melted butter and/or olive oil. Spread the cubes on a cookie sheet and bake at 350°F until toasty. (Cut slices into rounds for soups.)

RUSKS: Lightly butter both sides of sliced bread and place in a low oven (200°F) until thoroughly dried. You can use any bread, including sweet quick breads, to make these rusks.

STUFFING: Toast the bread first before adding stuffing ingredients (see page 68).

BREAD PUDDING: Sweet yeasted coffee bread and breads with nuts, whole grains, or rice, leftover muffins, and quick breads make especially good bread pudding (for Chocolate Bread Pudding, see page 358).

FRENCH TOAST: Try Susan Poupore's Wild Rice Bread (page 16) or Finnish Cardamom Coffee Bread (page 24) to make French Toast (page 38).

TOASTED BREAD CRUMBS: For dry bread crumbs, toast the stale bread lightly, then process in a blender or food processor fitted with a steel blade. Use bread crumbs to top hot dishes, casseroles, and hot buttered noodles. (The bread crumbs may be stored in the freezer.)

RAISED CORN BREAD
WITH SWEET CORN

MAKES 2 LOAVES

*I*n August the focus of our dinner conversations is how sweet the corn is and where to find the best. (In January we fix on the windchill factor.) During the short growing season we just can't find enough ways to use sweet corn.

This golden loaf catches the flavor of late harvest. Fresh uncooked corn kernels add an almost sweet surprise. It makes marvelous French Toast (page 38) and stuffing for pork or game (page 69).

> *1 package (or 1 scant tablespoon) active dry yeast*
> *2 cups warm water (105° to 115°F)*
> *1 tablespoon sugar*
> *2½–3½ cups unbleached all-purpose flour*
> *1 tablespoon salt*
> *1 cup cornmeal*
> *Fresh corn kernels from 2 ears of corn (about 1 cup)*
> *Vegetable oil for greasing the bowl and baking sheet*

*I*n a large bowl, dissolve the yeast in the warm water with the sugar and wait about 5 minutes to see that the surface becomes foamy. Add *2½ cups* of the flour and beat 100 strokes. Cover the bowl and allow the dough to rise 45 minutes. Stir it down and add the salt, cornmeal, and corn kernels. Stir in enough of the remaining flour to make a stiff dough.

Turn the dough onto a lightly floured board and knead 8 to 10 minutes, or until it is smooth and elastic. Place the dough in a lightly greased bowl, cover with a clean towel, and allow to rise until double in bulk, about 1 hour. Punch the dough down.

Turn the dough once again onto a lightly floured board and knead it several turns. Divide the dough in half, shape into 2 oblong country-style loaves, and place them on a lightly greased baking sheet. Make several horizontal slashes in the tops, using a sharp knife, and allow to rise 30 minutes. Bake in a preheated 350°F oven for 45 minutes. Remove the bread from the oven and cool on racks.

COTTAGE CHEESE DILL BREAD

MAKES 1 LOAF

*A*nn Schroeder, a chef at Lucia's Restaurant, developed this recipe, which was inspired by the memory of her grandmother's cottage cheese bread. She added her own touch of dill. Serve this bread warm from the oven or slice it for turkey, roast beef, or ham and Cheddar sandwiches.

> *1 package (or 1 scant tablespoon) active dry yeast*
> *¼ cup warm water (105° to 115°F)*
> *2 tablespoons sugar*
> *1 cup cottage cheese*
> *4 tablespoons dill seed or ¼ cup chopped fresh dill*
> *1 stick (8 tablespoons) butter, softened*
> *1 teaspoon salt*
> *¼ teaspoon baking soda*
> *1 large egg*
> *3½ cups unbleached all-purpose flour*
> *Vegetable oil for greasing the bowl and loaf pan*

*S*tir together the yeast, water, and sugar in a small bowl (Ann's grandmother used a coffee cup) and allow to proof 5 minutes, or until the surface becomes foamy. In a large bowl, beat together the cottage cheese, dill, butter, salt, baking soda, and egg. (The mixture may be lumpy.) Stir in the yeast mixture.

Add the flour to the batter 1 cup at a time, mixing in each cup before adding the next, up to 3 cups. Turn out the dough onto a floured board and knead for 10 minutes, adding enough flour to keep the dough from sticking. The dough will be soft because of the cottage cheese, butter, and egg.

Put the dough into a medium-sized greased bowl and cover loosely with a towel. Let it rise in a warm place about 1½ hours, or until double in size.

Punch the dough down and let it rest 10 minutes. Shape and place it in a lightly greased 8- or 9-inch loaf pan. Allow the dough to rise 30 minutes. Bake the bread in a preheated 350°F oven for about 40 minutes, or until it sounds hollow when tapped. Take the bread from the oven and allow it to cool in the pan for 10 minutes, then turn it out onto a wire rack to cool.

POTATO BREAD

MAKES 1 LARGE OR 2 SMALL LOAVES

*T*his traditional loaf has a delicate flavor and soft texture, wonderful for hot turkey sandwiches with gravy and cranberries.

>*1 package (or 1 scant tablespoon) active dry yeast*
>*1 tablespoon sugar*
>*½ cup warm water (105° to 115°F)*
>*1 cup potato-cooking water*
>*1½ cups mashed potatoes*
>*4–6 cups unbleached all-purpose flour*
>*2 teaspoons salt or to taste*
>*Vegetable oil for greasing the bowl and baking sheet*
>   *or loaf pans*

*I*n a large bowl, dissolve the yeast and sugar in the warm water and let proof 5 minutes, or until the surface becomes foamy. Add the potato-cooking water, mashed potatoes, and *2 cups* of the flour, and beat until the mixture is the consistency of mud. Cover the bowl and allow the dough to rise 45 minutes.

Taste the dough before adding the salt. (The amount will vary depending on how salty the mashed potatoes are.) Add enough of the remaining flour to make a stiff dough that no longer clings to the sides of the bowl. (The amount of flour will vary depending on the starch in the potatoes.)

Turn the dough onto a lightly floured board and knead about 5 minutes. Put the dough in a greased bowl and turn it so that the dough is lightly greased; cover the bowl and allow the dough to rise until double in bulk, about 1 hour. Punch the dough down and shape it into 1 or 2 round loaves and place on a lightly greased baking sheet or into 2 lightly greased 9-inch loaf pans. Allow the dough to rise again until doubled, about 45 minutes. Bake in a preheated 350°F oven for 50 minutes to 1 hour, or until the loaves sound hollow when tapped. Remove the loaves from the oven and allow to cool on wire racks.

POTATO BREAD

"My mother died when I was twelve. By then my two older sisters were married and living on farms of their own. I took over the household duties on my father's farm. Monday was wash day. Tuesday we went to town for supplies. On Friday my father boiled potatoes for his noon dinner. I'd save the potato water to start bread for Saturday's baking. If we were lucky, there would be leftover potatoes, too. Nothing makes a lighter, fluffier bread than mashed potatoes. We always used those light and tender loaves first."

—FLORENCE ZARLING OF GLENCOE, MINNESOTA

LIMPA RYE

"My old folks," said Tiny Soderball, "have put in twenty acres of rye. They get it ground at the mill, and it makes nice bread. It seems like my mother ain't been so homesick, ever since father's raised rye flour for her."

—WILLA CATHER, *MY ÁNTONIA*

What distinguishes limpa from other rye bread? Beatrice Ojakangas, second-generation Finn and author of *The Great Scandinavian Baking Book* and many other cookbooks, explains: "The combination of fennel, caraway, and anise create a distinct fourth flavor, unique to Scandinavian baking. All my family's holiday breads use the three together, perhaps in Christian symbolism." In Finland, according to Bea, a special version of limpa that includes orange zest is baked during the Christmas holidays—*Jululimppu.*

LIMPA RYE

MAKES 2 LOAVES

*O*range zest infused in warm milk heightens the flavors of anise, caraway, and fennel in this dense, flavorful bread. Rye breads will keep a long time covered in plastic wrap and refrigerated. This recipe is easily doubled, and the bread freezes well.

> *1 package (or 1 scant tablespoon) active dry yeast*
> *1 tablespoon sugar*
> *¾ cup warm water (105° to 115°F)*
> *2¼ cups milk*
> *Zest of 1 orange, finely chopped*
> *¾ cup molasses*
> *3 tablespoons butter, melted*
> *1 tablespoon salt*
> *3 tablespoons caraway seeds*
> *1 tablespoon fennel seeds*
> *1 tablespoon anise seeds*
> *3½ cups unbleached all-purpose flour*
> *4½ cups rye flour*
> *Vegetable oil for greasing the bowl and baking sheet*

*I*n a large bowl, dissolve the yeast and sugar in the warm water and wait 5 minutes, or until the surface becomes foamy. Meanwhile, scald the milk by bringing it just to a boil, then immediately removing it from the heat. Add the orange zest and cool to room temperature.

Combine the milk with the yeast mixture, molasses, butter, salt, caraway, fennel, and anise seeds. Beat in *½ cup* of the white flour, all the rye flour, then enough of the remaining white flour to make a stiff dough.

Turn the dough out onto a lightly floured board and knead 8 to 10 minutes, or until smooth and elastic. Place it in a well-oiled bowl and turn the dough to coat it. Cover the bowl with a towel or plastic wrap and allow to rise until double in size, about 3 hours.

Limpa Rye (continued)

Punch the dough down and shape it into 2 round loaves. Place them on a lightly greased baking sheet and let rise until doubled, about 45 minutes.

Bake the loaves in a preheated 425°F oven for 10 minutes, then brush with ice water and reduce the oven to 325°F. Continue baking for 40 to 45 minutes more, or until the loaves sound hollow when tapped. Remove the bread from the oven and cool on wire racks before slicing.

FINNISH CARDAMOM COFFEE BREAD

MAKES 1 LARGE OR 2 SMALL LOAVES

*H*ere we add freshly ground coffee and the traditional cardamom to this old-fashioned Finnish loaf. Susan Barrott, head baker at Café Latte, created this fragrant bread. Try it lightly toasted or as French Toast (page 38).

> 1⅓ cups warm water (105° to 115°F)
> 2 packages (or 2 scant tablespoons) active dry yeast
> ¼ cup maple syrup
> ¼ cup honey
> 2 eggs
> 2 teaspoons salt
> 1 tablespoon vanilla extract
> 6–8 cups unbleached all-purpose flour
> 1½ cups toasted chopped pecans
> 1½ tablespoons ground cardamom
> 2 teaspoons ground cinnamon
> 1 tablespoon finely ground dark-roast espresso coffee beans
> 1 egg yolk beaten with 1 tablespoon milk
> Vegetable oil for greasing the bowl and baking sheet

*M*ake sure all ingredients are at room temperature. In a large bowl, mix together the water, yeast, maple syrup, and honey, and proof about 5 to 10 minutes, or until the surface is foamy. Stir in the eggs, salt, and vanilla.

Stir in enough flour to pull the wet ingredients together into a soft mass. Dump this dough out onto a well-floured surface. (Be sure to scrape off the sides of the bowl and the spoon, too.) Knead the dough, working in more flour as you go. Keep the dough as soft and loose as possible. It should be a very elastic dough that remains sticky as you knead. Use just enough flour to keep it rolling.

When the dough is smooth and becomes glossy, add the pecans, cardamom, cinnamon, and coffee, sprinkling them over the top while continuing to knead until mixed in. Transfer the dough to a greased bowl, cover with a clean towel, and let rise in a warm place until double in size, about 1 hour.

Punch the dough down and let it rest 5 minutes. Shape it into 2 loaves or cut into 3 strands and braid them into 1 large loaf. Place on a greased baking sheet and allow to rise again until double in bulk, about 30 minutes. Brush the tops of the loaves with the egg-and-milk mixture. Bake in a preheated 375°F oven for approximately 30 minutes for smaller loaves, 45 minutes for a large loaf, or until the loaves sound hollow when tapped. Remove the bread from the oven and cool on wire racks.

THE HEARTH

A typical fireplace of early Swedish- and Norwegian-Americans provided warmth and served as an oven. A lefse grill rested on 4-inch tripods or stones (making lefse was back-breaking labor). The round-ended tool here made a ring cake, and the flat-ended tool made waffles. The long-handled pan is a bed warmer.

CINNAMON ROLLS
(WITH RAISIN-CINNAMON
LOAF VARIATION)

MAKES 24 BUNS OR 2 LOAVES

*T*he dough for this recipe, re-created from Lucia's grandmother Lulu's notes, makes gooey sticky buns or swirled cinnamon-raisin loaves. To have fresh rolls early in the morning, make the dough and shape the rolls the night before and put them in the refrigerator overnight, then pop them into the oven first thing. The sweet smell of cinnamon will drift through the house, drawing everyone into the kitchen.

DOUGH

1 cup milk
3 tablespoons butter
½ teaspoon vanilla extract
1 package (or 1 scant tablespoon) active dry yeast
2 cups warm water (105° to 115°F)
2 tablespoons brown sugar, light or dark
5½–6½ cups unbleached all-purpose flour
2 eggs
1 tablespoon salt

FILLING

1 cup brown sugar, light or dark
1 teaspoon ground cinnamon
¼ cup raisins or more to taste (optional)

GLAZE

2 cups brown sugar, light or dark
½ cup honey
½ stick (4 tablespoons) butter
⅓ cup chopped pecans
1 tablespoon water

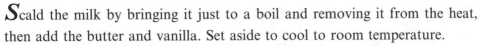

*S*cald the milk by bringing it just to a boil and removing it from the heat, then add the butter and vanilla. Set aside to cool to room temperature.

In a large bowl, proof the yeast by dissolving it in the water with brown sugar for 5 minutes, or until the surface is foamy. Add *2 cups* of the flour, beating it until the mixture reaches the consistency of mud. Beat 100 strokes. Cover the bowl and let the dough rise 30 minutes.

Add the milk mixture, eggs, and salt, and stir until smooth. Add enough of the remaining flour to form a smooth dough. Turn onto a lightly floured board and knead 8 to 10 minutes, sprinkling with flour to keep the dough from sticking. Place the dough in a lightly greased bowl, cover with a towel, and allow to rise until double in size, about 30 minutes.

CINNAMON ROLLS

*W*hile the dough is rising, prepare the filling by mixing all of the ingredients together in a small bowl.

Prepare the glaze by stirring together all the ingredients in a saucepan set over low heat and bring the sauce to a simmer for about 1 minute.

Punch the dough down and turn it onto a lightly floured board. Cut the dough in half and roll each out into a long, 9 × 13-inch rectangle and sprinkle on the filling. Starting with the long side, roll the dough up into a log.

Pour the glaze into two 9-inch-round or 9-inch-square cake pans. Slice the log into rolls about 2 inches thick. Place the rolls on one of the cut sides down, on top of the honey mixture. Let them rise again for 15 to 20 minutes. (Or cover with a large plastic bag and refrigerate overnight, then allow to come to room temperature before baking.) Bake them in a preheated 350°F oven for 40 to 50 minutes, or until golden brown and the tops sound hollow when tapped. Remove from the oven and serve warm.

IOWA CINNAMON ROLLS

"*Y*ou know you're in a genuine Iowa small-town café when the cinnamon rolls are homemade and are about half the size of your head. Iowa is the cinnamon roll capital of the entire universe."

—PAT DENATO OF THE DES MOINES *SUNDAY REGISTER*

Cinnamon Rolls (continued)

RAISIN-CINNAMON LOAF

*W*hile the dough is rising, prepare the filling by mixing together all of the ingredients in a small bowl. You won't need the glaze for this loaf. Punch the dough down and turn it onto a lightly floured board. Cut it in half and roll each half out into a rectangle about 9 inches wide and sprinkle with half the filling. Repeat with the other rectangle. Beginning with the short side, roll each rectangle up and place in well-greased 9-inch loaf pans. Allow the dough to rise 15 to 20 minutes. (Or cover with a large plastic bag and refrigerate overnight, then allow to come to room temperature before baking.) Bake in a preheated 350°F oven for 50 minutes to 1 hour, or until golden brown and the tops sound hollow when tapped. Remove from the oven, turn the loaves out of the pans, and cool on wire racks.

THE LAST SHEAF AND THE SOWING LOAF

The early Swedish-American farmers, according to tradition, always saved the last sheaf of grain from the harvest. It was believed that all the life-generating force and energy lay hidden in this sheaf—that it embodied the spirit of fertility. In some homes it was saved until Christmas and then given to the cattle as thanks for their milk; in others it was placed outside the house to bless those within and those who came to visit. Sometimes it was attached to an apple tree for an abundant crop the following season, or braided and brought inside to bless the house, then set outside as thanks to the birds.

The flour milled from the grain of the last sheaf was made into *sakaka*, a rich braided loaf very much like the Christmas breads described on the next page. *Sakaka* decorated the table through the Christmas season and was then stashed away until spring. The day before planting, the hard, dry loaf was broken into pieces, soaked in homemade beer, and fed to the family and farm animals to provide strength, vigor, and well-being for the year. Crumbs were mixed with seed corn and wheat kernels and planted with visions of burgeoning crops.

CHRISTMAS BREAD

MAKES 1 LARGE BRAIDED LOAF

*S*wedish *Julbrød,* Austrian *Vanocka,* Norwegian *Julekage,* Czech *Houska,* and German *Stollen*—all are traditional Christmas breads that differ primarily in their shapes, seasonings, and fillings; their doughs are quite similar. *Julbrød* is a cardamom-scented braided loaf. Along with this recipe are several different ethnic variations.

JULBRØD

2 packages (or 2 scant tablespoons) active dry yeast
½ cup warm water (105° to 115°F)
¾ cup warm milk (105° to 115°F)
½ cup sugar
1 teaspoon salt
1 stick (8 tablespoons) butter, melted
3 eggs, beaten
2 teaspoons ground cardamom
2 teaspoons almond extract
6–7 cups unbleached all-purpose flour
Vegetable oil for greasing the bowl and baking sheet or
  cake pan
Melted butter and confectioners' sugar for finishing the
  loaf (optional)

ICING (OPTIONAL)

1 cup confectioners' sugar
3 tablespoons milk
1 teaspoon almond or vanilla extract

2 tablespoons sliced almonds for topping

*I*n a large bowl, dissolve the yeast in the warm water. Add the milk and sugar and let stand about 5 minutes, or until the surface becomes foamy. Stir in the salt, butter, eggs, cardamom, almond extract, and *3 cups* of the flour, then

Christmas Bread (continued)

beat until very smooth. Add enough of the remaining flour to form a soft dough. Turn the dough onto a lightly floured board and knead for about 5 to 8 minutes. Place the dough in a lightly greased bowl and turn it to coat the entire surface. Cover the bowl with a towel and allow the dough to rise until double in volume, about 1 hour.

Turn the dough out onto a lightly floured board and divide it into thirds. Using the palms of your hand, roll each of these thirds out into ropes about 20 inches long. Braid the ropes together and lift the braid onto a lightly greased baking sheet to form a wreath, pinching the ends together to seal them. Roll the trimmings into strands, then make curls to decorate the top of the braid. Let rise in a warm place about 45 minutes to 1 hour.

Bake the braid in a preheated 350°F oven for about 40 minutes to 1 hour, or until it sounds hollow when tapped. Place the loaf on a wire rack to cool. Make the icing by mixing together all the ingredients in a small bowl. Drizzle the icing on the cool braid and sprinkle on the almonds.

AUSTRIAN VANOCKA

My grandfather made the Vanocka. He started with a five-strand braid of dough for the bottom layer; then four, then three, and then he made two doves for the top. Most Vanocka were not so large or elaborate, but heavens, he needed it for his twelve kids. The breads were taken to the baker who baked them in outdoor ovens.

—BLANCH MENDL OF DEERBROOK, WISCONSIN

*S*ubstitute freshly grated nutmeg for the cardamom.

Add 3 tablespoons grated orange rind to the batter.

When kneading the dough, add *1 cup each,* light and dark raisins plus 1 cup slivered almonds until thoroughly incorporated.

To shape the Vanocka *after the first rising:* Turn the dough onto a lightly floured board and divide into thirds. Divide each of the thirds into thirds again, and using the palms of your hands, roll out 9 ropes for 3 separate braids of graduating sizes (the largest should be 20 inches long). Lay the longest braid down on a lightly greased baking sheet. Lay the next longest braid on top of that. Lay the shortest braid down on that. Let rise about 45 minutes to 1 hour.

Bake the loaf in a preheated 350°F oven for about 50 minutes to 1 hour, or until it sounds hollow when tapped. Remove from the oven and allow to cool before drizzling with icing, then sprinkle with the almonds.

NORWEGIAN JULEKAGE

*W*hen kneading the dough, add *1 cup each,* toasted slivered almonds and light raisins to the dough until thoroughly incorporated.

To shape the Julekage *after the first rising:* Turn the dough out onto a lightly floured board and divide it in half. Shape each half into a smooth, flat round and place in a lightly greased 9-inch-round cake pan, or shape into a smooth, flat loaf, and place on a lightly greased baking sheet. Let the loaves rise until double in size, about 1 hour.

Bake in a preheated 350°F oven for 35 to 45 minutes, or until the loaves sound hollow when tapped. Place the loaves on a rack to cool. Drizzle on the icing; sprinkle with the almonds.

Christmas Bread (continued)

CZECH HOUSKA

*D*ecrease the amount of cardamom to 1 teaspoon and add 1 teaspoon freshly grated nutmeg.

Add 3 tablespoons grated orange rind to the batter.

When kneading the dough, add 2 cups light raisins until thoroughly incorporated into the dough.

To shape the Houska *after the first rising:* Turn the dough out onto a lightly floured board and divide it in half. Divide each half into thirds. Using the palms of your hand, roll each of these thirds out into the shape of a rope about 20 inches long. Braid 3 ropes together for the bottom braid and place this on a lightly greased baking sheet. Braid the remaining 3 ropes and place them on top of the first (or you may simply bake the 2 braids separately). Pinch the top and bottom together. Brush the loaves with butter and sprinkle with confectioners' sugar. Let the dough rise another hour.

Bake the braid(s) in a preheated 350°F oven for about 45 minutes to 1 hour (about 35 to 45 minutes for the single braids). Place the loaf or loaves on a rack and brush with melted butter and dust with confectioners' sugar. Make the icing by mixing together all the ingredients in a small bowl. Drizzle the icing over the cool braid(s) and sprinkle on the almonds.

GERMAN STOLLEN

In November when the sun sets and the sky turns red,
Chriskindl is heating his oven to make Christmas Stollen.

—GERMAN-AMERICAN SAYING

*S*ubstitute 2 teaspoons ground nutmeg for the cardamom.

Add 3 tablespoons grated orange rind to the batter.

When kneading the dough, add *1 cup each,* light and dark raisins plus 2 cups toasted slivered almonds to the dough until thoroughly incorporated.

To shape the Stollen *after the first rising:* Turn the dough out onto a lightly floured board and divide it in half. Pat each half into a round, flat circle and place on a lightly greased baking sheet. Brush the loaves with melted butter and sprinkle with confectioners' sugar. Fold each of the circles almost in half, so that the top does not quite meet the bottom but leaves about 2 inches exposed. Brush the loaves again with butter and sugar. Bake in a preheated 350°F oven for 35 to 45 minutes, or until the loaves sound hollow when tapped. Place the loaves on a rack and brush with melted butter and dust with confectioners' sugar. Let them cool and dust with additional confectioners' sugar. Omit the icing.

SAINT LUCIA DAY

According to the old Swedish calendar, December 13 (*Lusse*) was the longest and darkest night of the year. Saint Lucia became the symbol of light and hope, the promise of Christ and the end of the darkest season. Here in the Northern Heartland, where winter begins as early as Halloween, the return of sunlight is worth some fuss, Swedish or not.

Nance Oleson, an actress living in Minneapolis, has been celebrating Saint Lucia ever since she was a little girl, and continues the tradition in her own home. Well before dawn, friends brave the breath-catching cold and gather in the Olesons' living room, lit only with candles. At 6:00 a.m. Nance and three other women, dressed in the traditional white robes (for purity) with red sashes (for martyrdom), don candlelit wreaths and descend the stairs, singing the Swedish Santa Lucia hymn. They are followed by the star bearers—children also in white robes carrying candles.

To the hushed crowd Nance recounts the legends of Lucia, a wealthy Roman woman who became a Christian and gave away her dowry to the poor, enraging her jealous nobleman fiancé, who had her burned at the stake. It's also told that this martyred saint appeared off the coast of Sweden in the 1400s during a winter famine in a ship blazing with light, delivering gifts of food and spirits.

Nance then invites guests to the buffet, loaded with traditional foods brought by friends: herring, fruit soup, rye breads, smoked white fish (netted and smoked in Bayfield, Wisconsin), hard-boiled eggs, Swedish coffee bread, and, of course, the traditional Saint Lucia buns.

SAINT LUCIA BUNS (LUSSEKATTER)

MAKES 20 TO 24 BUNS

*T*he Swedish name *Lussekatter* means "Lucia's cats," from the pagan belief that Lucia's light helped send off the evil spirits who, disguised as cats, lurked in dark corners on bleak winter nights. The stylized shape of these open-cross buns is thought to ward off the devil. The dough is also shaped into a braid made to hold candles and used as a centerpiece on the Saint Lucia Day table.

Toasting the saffron threads before steeping them in hot milk gives the bread its intense flavor and rich color.

> *⅔ cup milk*
> *2 teaspoons toasted saffron threads**
> *2 packages (or 2 scant tablespoons) active dry yeast*
> *½ cup sugar*
> *½ cup warm water (105 to 115°F)*
> *1 stick (8 tablespoons) butter, softened*
> *1 egg*
> *1 teaspoon salt*
> *5–6 cups unbleached all-purpose flour*
> *Vegetable oil*
> *Raisins for garnish*
> *Melted butter for brushing the tops of the buns*
> *1 egg beaten with 1 tablespoon water*
> *2 tablespoons sugar*
>
> **Place the saffron in a dry, heavy skillet and toast over medium-high heat for several seconds, stirring with a wooden spoon, until the threads become slightly darker.*

*S*cald the milk in a small pan by bringing it just to a boil and removing it from the heat; then set it aside, add the saffron threads, and allow to cool to lukewarm. Dissolve the yeast and sugar in the warm water. In a large bowl, combine the milk, yeast, butter, egg, salt, and *3 cups* of the flour. Beat the mixture until smooth. Stir in enough of the remaining flour to make a soft dough. Turn the dough onto a lightly floured surface and knead it until smooth. Place the dough in a greased bowl, cover, and allow to rise until double in bulk, about 1 hour.

Punch the dough down and divide it into 24 parts. To make Lucia Buns, lightly form each piece into a rope; place one rope on top of another to form an X (or any of the shapes shown in the illustration below). Place a raisin at the end of each X. Put the buns on a greased cookie sheet. Brush the tops with melted butter and allow them to rise until doubled.

Brush the egg-and-water mixture lightly over the buns. Sprinkle the buns with the sugar and bake them in a preheated 350°F oven for 15 to 20 minutes. Remove from the oven and cool on wire racks.

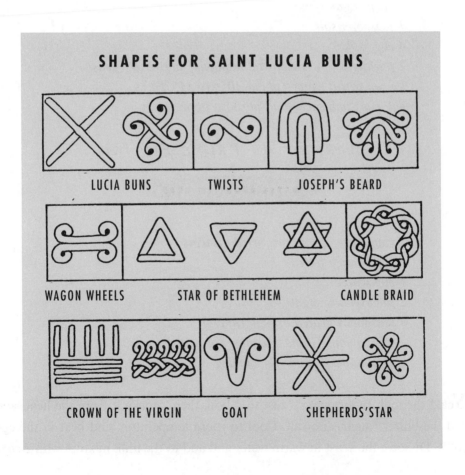

SHAPES FOR SAINT LUCIA BUNS

LUCIA BUNS   TWISTS   JOSEPH'S BEARD

WAGON WHEELS   STAR OF BETHLEHEM   CANDLE BRAID

CROWN OF THE VIRGIN   GOAT   SHEPHERDS' STAR

KOLACHKE (OR KOLACHE) (SWEET BUNS)

MAKES ABOUT 24 BUNS

*C*laimed by Czechs and Poles, these sweet buns are served with morning and afternoon coffee. Fillings of prune, apricot, poppy seed, or cottage cheese are folded into an envelope of dough and baked until golden brown, then sprinkled with confectioners' sugar.

> *½ cup milk*
> *1¼ sticks (12 tablespoons) butter, softened*
> *½ cup sugar*
> *1 teaspoon salt*
> *4 egg yolks*
> *2 packages (or 2 scant tablespoons) active dry yeast*
> *½ cup warm water (about 105° to 115°F)*
> *4½ cups unbleached all-purpose flour*

APRICOT OR PRUNE FILLING

MAKES ABOUT 1¾ CUPS

> *2 cups pitted prunes or dried apricots*
> *1 cup orange juice*
> *1 cup water*
> *2 tablespoons sugar*
> *3 teaspoons grated orange rind*
> *2 tablespoons Grand Marnier (or orange juice)*
> *Confectioners' sugar for dusting*

*S*cald the milk by bringing it just to a boil, then remove it from the heat, and add the butter, sugar, and salt. Cool to room temperature and beat in the egg yolks. Dissolve the yeast in warm water and add to the milk mixture with *2 cups* of the flour. Beat this for 5 minutes, until smooth. Stir in enough of the remaining flour to make a very soft dough. Cover the dough with a towel and allow it to rise in a warm place until double in volume, about 1 hour.

Meanwhile, make the filling. Chop the fruit and mix with the orange juice, water, and sugar in a medium-sized saucepan over medium-low heat until the mixture becomes thick, about 15 minutes. Cool, then stir in the orange rind and liqueur (or orange juice). Pour this into a food processor fitted with a steel blade and pulse until the fruit is coarsely chopped.

Stir the dough down with a wooden spoon. Turn it out onto a lightly floured board and knead it with floured hands for several minutes. Divide the dough in half. Cut each half into 12 pieces. Lightly roll or pat each piece into a small rectangle and place on a greased baking sheet about 2 inches apart. Place a dollop of filling on each rectangle, then fold each corner up toward the center to cover the filling, but allow some of it to peep through. Let these rise about 45 minutes, or until double in size. Bake in a preheated 350°F oven for 15 minutes, or until golden brown. Remove from the oven, dust with confectioners' sugar, and serve warm.

POSSIBLY THE BEST *KOLACHKE*

"Tucking the napkin into the neck of my sunsuit and folding my hands in my lap, I waited for our hostess to be seated. The warm *kolachke* which nearly covered the plate sent up messages of buttery flakiness and sweet oozing of prune filling that were painful to ignore. But when you were being so finely served, you must have the character to respond in kind.

"I held my head over the plate for fear of spilling prune filling on the beautiful napkin. This was the best *kolachke* I had ever tasted, possibly the best that had ever been produced. When I had devoured every morsel and only the severest self-control had restrained me from licking all my fingers, my hostess beamed, 'More?' "

—FAITH SULLIVAN, *THE CAPE ANN*

FRENCH TOAST

SERVES 4 (RECIPE IS EASILY DOUBLED OR TRIPLED.)

*T*he French Canadians are credited with French Toast or *pain perdu,* meaning "lost bread," but Polish, German, and Swedish settlers had similar recipes for reclaiming stale bread. The Poles would add ground poppy seeds to the batter and serve it for meatless dinners, and the Germans, shunning maple syrup, would top theirs with lemon juice and confectioners' sugar.

The seasonal variations for French Toast are endless: Susan Poupore's Wild Rice Bread (page 16), Finnish Cardamom Coffee Bread (page 24), Old-fashioned Milk Bread (page 6), or Raised Corn Bread with Sweet Corn (page 19) with toppings of sour cream or Thickened Cream (page 87) and berries, Blueberry-Honey Sauce (page 367), Old-fashioned Apple Butter (page 283), Vanilla Poached Fruit (page 286), and, of course, warm maple syrup.

1 cup milk
5 eggs
8 pieces bread, sliced ½–1 inch thick
Butter for the skillet

*I*n a large bowl, beat together the milk and eggs. Put the bread in the bowl and allow it to absorb the batter. Melt some butter over medium heat and fry the bread a few slices at a time, being careful not to crowd the skillet, until the bottom is lightly browned. Flip the bread with a spatula and fry the other side until lightly browned. Serve hot with one of the suggested toppings.

NORWEGIAN TOAST

MAKES 1 LOAF (RECIPE IS EASILY DOUBLED.)

*T*his sweet cardamom-scented quick bread is sliced and baked again into toasty rusks that keep for weeks in airtight containers. The recipe, from a friend's Norwegian grandmother, is one Lucia used in her early catering days for Sunday brunch.

> *1 stick (8 tablespoons) butter*
> *¾ cup sugar*
> *1 egg*
> *2 cups unbleached all-purpose flour*
> *½ teaspoon baking soda*
> *½ teaspoon ground cardamom*
> *½ teaspoon ground mace*
> *½ cup buttermilk**
>
> ** If you do not have buttermilk, add 1½ teaspoons vinegar to*
> *½ cup milk (preferably whole milk) and allow 30 seconds for*
> *it to sour.*

*C*ream together the butter and sugar, then beat in the egg. Sift together the dry ingredients. Add the dry ingredients to the egg-and-butter mixture alternately with the buttermilk, and stir until just combined. Do not beat.

Turn the batter into a lightly greased 9-inch loaf pan and bake in a preheated 350°F oven for 35 to 40 minutes, or until the loaf tests done with a toothpick.

Remove the loaf from the oven and cool in the pan for about 5 minutes. Turn the loaf from the pan and finish cooling on a wire rack. Slice the loaf into ½- or ¼-inch slices. (If the bread is still too warm, the slices will crumble.)

Lay these slices on a lightly greased cookie sheet and bake 10 minutes per side at 350°F. Remove the slices from the oven, cool on a rack, then store in an airtight container.

LEFSE

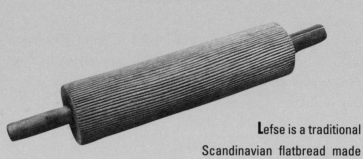

Lefse is a traditional Scandinavian flatbread made of mashed potatoes, soft and thin as a tortilla. It is served either warm or at room temperature, spread with butter and sometimes sugar or jam, with meals, or as a snack. It is also eaten wrapped around herring, lutefisk and potatoes, meatballs, or gjetost (a semifirm light brown, slightly sweet cheese made of goat's milk and cow's milk, nicknamed Norwegian peanut butter).

Making lefse requires patience, perseverance, skill, lots of practice, the right equipment, and Scandinavian genes. It is impossible to learn without the assistance of someone who knows how smooth and what temperature the mashed potatoes should be (cool but not cold) and how much flour to add based on the feel of the dough (depending on humidity). Lefse requires a special grooved rolling pin that keeps the dough from sticking and gives it a pattern and a flat, wooden "lefse stick" to lift and place the dough on a hot, dry griddle and flip it to brown both sides.

Like lutefisk (reconstituted cod) and *rommegrøt* (cream pudding), lefse is reserved for the holidays. In some homes lefse-making is still practiced by cooks dedicated to keeping Scandinavian traditions alive. Others purchase their yearly supply from bakeries and specialty shops throughout the region.

LEFSE RECIPE
(FROM MEMORY)

"Every day we polished our wonderful big wood-burning cook stove in our farm kitchen. Twice a week, we made lefse. I would mash the boiled potatoes until there were no lumps—adding some heated milk and a little melted butter to make it very smooth—then adding flour to make it doughy. I would let it stand to cool overnight in the "cold pantry." The next morning after firing up the stove, I would roll the dough out on a floured board into circles about 12 inches round. With the lefse stick, which every Scandinavian household had—usually made by the husband or hired hand—I'd toss the round onto the top of the hot stove, then would flip it over after it was browned on the one side, then brown on the other side. We kept piles of them wrapped in flour-sack dish towels in the cool pantry—and served the lefse warmed—with butter and sugar spread on them and rolled up. The smell of fresh lefse is lovely."

—ANNIE HUSTAD, LUCIA'S MATERNAL GRANDMOTHER,
AS TOLD TO ANN HUSTAD WATSON, LUCIA'S MOTHER

PANCAKES

MAKES 24 PANCAKES

*I*n the logging camps of Wisconsin and Minnesota, pancakes were called "flannel cakes" because their texture was like that of the flannel shirts worn by loggers. A griddleful of cakes was called a "string of flats" after the open cars used by railroads to ship lumber. Round cakes were called "sweatpads," the name inspired by the perspiration pads women wore under their dresses.

Pancakes make easy use of leftover mashed potatoes, sour milk, sweet corn, and wild rice. They are sometimes made with buckwheat (known as pig-weed because it was fed to the pigs), rye, or graham flour.

Elinor Watson, Lucia's aunt, remembers: "We ate pancakes just about every morning on the farm with thick-cut bacon or ham. But I liked leftover pancakes best for an after-school snack. We'd take the morning cakes, butter and stack them in a bowl, sprinkle them with sugar and douse them with cream."

> *1¼ cups unbleached all-purpose flour*
> *½ teaspoon baking soda*
> *2 teaspoons baking powder*
> *½ teaspoon salt*
> *1 tablespoon sugar*
> *2 cups buttermilk**
> *1 egg*
> *2 tablespoons vegetable oil*
> *Vegetable oil for skillet*
>
> ** If you do not have buttermilk, add 1 tablespoon vinegar to 1 cup milk (preferably whole milk) and allow 30 seconds for it to sour.*

*M*ix the dry ingredients together. Add the wet ingredients and beat to a thin batter. Heat a griddle or large skillet to medium-high and lightly grease it with about 1 tablespoon of the oil. Pour about ¼ cup of batter per pancake onto the griddle or skillet and cook until bubbles form on the top. Flip the pancake and continue cooking until the bottom side is golden brown.

VARIATIONS

Buckwheat Cakes: Substitute ½ cup buckwheat flour plus ¾ cup white flour for the unbleached all-purpose flour.

Corn Pancakes: Substitute ½ cup cornmeal plus ¾ cup white flour for the unbleached all-purpose flour and add ½ cup sweet corn kernels to the batter. Serve with Blueberry-Honey Sauce (page 367).

Berry Pancakes: Add 1–2 cups fresh berries to the batter or individually to each pancake after it is first poured onto griddle.

Wild Rice Pancakes: Substitute ¾ cup unbleached all-purpose flour plus ½ cup cooked wild rice for the flour. Substitute 2 tablespoons maple syrup or light or dark brown sugar for the white sugar. Serve topped with warm maple syrup and toasted pecans.

Oat Pancakes: Substitute ¾ cup white flour plus ½ cup oatmeal for the unbleached all-purpose flour. Add 2 tablespoons sunflower seeds to the batter and serve with bananas or sautéed apples.

Light Pancakes: Beat 2 egg whites until stiff and fold into the batter.

Loggers relied on pancakes (also called "griddle cakes," "flannel cakes," or "flats") for a hearty breakfast before heading out into the snowy woods.

GERMAN OVEN PANCAKE
(PFANNKUCHEN)

SERVES 4

"*W*e like our *Pfannkuchen* just a little custardy," notes Lucille Mauermann, a dairy farmer in Brodhead, Wisconsin, who shares her recipe. "These can be made lighter by omitting one egg."

Serve this puffy, golden shell drizzled with lemon juice and sprinkled with confectioners' sugar, or topped with berries and whipped cream, Old-fashioned Apple Butter (page 283), Vanilla Poached Fruit (page 286), or Blueberry-Honey Sauce (page 367).

> ½ stick (4 tablespoons) butter
> 4 eggs
> ¾ cup milk
> ¾ cup unbleached all-purpose flour
> 1 teaspoon vanilla extract

*M*elt the butter in a medium-sized skillet over high heat. Remove from the heat. In a medium-sized bowl, whisk together the eggs and the milk. Whisk in the flour, a little at a time, then whisk in the vanilla and *2 tablespoons* of the melted butter. Allow the batter to stand about 10 minutes. Heat the skillet again so that the remaining butter is hot, and swirl it around the pan to coat the sides. Pour the batter into the pan. Bake the pancake in a preheated 400°F oven for about 15 minutes. Reduce the heat and continue baking another 10 to 15 minutes more, or until the pancake is puffy and the edges are golden. Remove from the oven and slip the pancake onto a large platter. Serve immediately.

SWEDISH PANCAKES
(PLATTAR)

**MAKES ABOUT THIRTY-TWO 6-INCH PANCAKES
OR SIXTY-FOUR 3-INCH PANCAKES**

*S*wedish Pancakes are a traditional Thursday night dinner for those of Swedish heritage. Ann Sorenson of Minneapolis remembers: "First we had pea soup with a big ham bone in it for dinner, and then the pancakes with lingonberries (tiny cousins of our cranberries) and sour cream. My mother did not have a spatula but flipped the pancakes with a silver knife and used two round iron griddles (*platts* in Swedish) at the same time." The pancakes were called *plattar*.

The secret to making pancakes, says Ann, is in keeping the batter as flat and airless as possible. Do not overbeat the eggs, and stir the batter gently. Let the batter sit two days in the refrigerator until it is truly flat.

> *4 eggs*
> *4 cups milk*
> *2½ cups unbleached all-purpose flour (unsifted)*
> *½ cup sugar*
> *¼ teaspoon salt*
> *1 stick (8 tablespoons) butter, melted*

*L*ightly beat the eggs together and add the milk, flour, sugar, and salt, gently stirring until blended completely. Stir in the melted butter. Cover the batter and allow it to sit at least overnight (2 days is best) in a cool room (64°F is ideal) or the refrigerator.

Heat a lightly greased griddle over a hot flame, preferably a wood stove. Pour a thin stream of batter in a circle onto the griddle to make a 3- or 6-inch pancake. The pancakes should be very very thin. Cook 20 seconds, flip, and cook another 20 seconds until done.

Serve right away with sour cream and blueberries (or, lingonberries; see Sources), or sour cream, butter, and light or dark brown sugar.

BLACK WALNUT BREAD

MAKES 1 LOAF (RECIPE IS EASILY DOUBLED.)

*W*alnut oil enhances this quick bread's rich walnut flavor, as does toasting the nuts before grinding. Sniff the walnuts before using them to be sure they aren't rancid, dry, or stale.

This nutty bread goes well with soft cheese or unsalted butter as an accompaniment to a salad of bitter greens or fresh fruit.

> *1¼ cups whole wheat flour*
> *1¼ cups unbleached all-purpose flour*
> *2 teaspoons baking powder*
> *½ teaspoon baking soda*
> *½ teaspoon salt*
> *2 eggs*
> *⅓ cup honey or maple syrup*
> *⅓ cup molasses*
> *1 cup buttermilk**
> *3 tablespoons walnut oil*
> *1½ cups walnuts, toasted, then ground*
>
> **If you do not have buttermilk, add 1 tablespoon vinegar to 1 cup milk (preferably whole milk) and allow 30 seconds for it to sour.*

*S*tir together the dry ingredients. In a separate bowl, beat together the eggs and mix in the honey, molasses, buttermilk, and oil. Stir in the dry ingredients and add the nuts. Turn the batter into a lightly greased 9-inch loaf pan. Bake in a preheated 350°F oven for 1 hour, or until a straw inserted in the center comes out clean. Remove from the oven and cool the bread in the pan for 10 minutes. Turn the loaf from the pan and cool on a rack. This bread freezes well.

A TOUGH NUT TO CRACK

Black walnuts have a rich, strong, pure flavor and are not bitter. Black walnut trees thrive in Wisconsin, Minnesota, and Iowa, providing wonderful shade with their wide-spreading leaves. Their hard round nuts have thick shells with greenish-brown husks that must be dried to a dark brown—this takes about three weeks—before they can be shucked. We recommend using a flatiron to crack the nuts. The shells shatter easily, but the meat is difficult to pick out, and one's hands become badly stained. It's tedious work but worth it.

The nuts should be stored in a cool, dry place or refrigerated.

CORN BREAD

". . . [But] for supper Grandma made hasty pudding. She stood by the stove, sifting the yellow corn meal from her fingers into a kettle of boiling, salted water. She stirred the water all the time with a big wooden spoon, and sifted in the meal until the kettle was full of a thick, yellow, bubbling mass. Then she set it on the back of the stove where it would cook slowly. . . . At supper time Pa and Grandpa came in from the woods . . . Pa and Grandpa had brought the syrup from the big kettle in the woods . . . Grandma made room for a huge brass kettle on the stove. Pa and Grandpa poured the syrup into the brass kettle, and it was so large that it held all the syrup from the four big buckets . . . everybody ate the hot hasty pudding with maple syrup for supper."

LAURA INGALLS WILDER, *THE LITTLE HOUSE IN THE BIG WOODS*

Explorer and mapmaker Jonathan Carver visited the Green Bay, Wisconsin, area in 1766 and found that the members of the Ojibway tribe made a delicious bread of fresh corn formed into small cakes, wrapped in basswood leaves, and cooked in hot embers. "A better flavored bread I never ate in any country," he wrote.

On the frontier the style of corn bread served was a good indication of the family's prosperity. A simple bread could be made from a blend of cornmeal, water, and salt, and a rich, sweet bread from a thick batter enriched with eggs, sugar, and milk or cream.

CORN MUFFINS
(AND CORN BREAD)

MAKES 12 MUFFINS OR 12 PIECES OF CORN BREAD

*I*n the summer add fresh berries and in winter add dried herbs or shredded cheese to this rich batter. Leftovers make wonderful stuffing (page 18). We often make a double batch and freeze one just to have on hand.

> 1 cup cornmeal
> 1 cup unbleached all-purpose flour
> ½ cup sugar
> 1 tablespoon baking powder
> ¼ teaspoon salt
> 1 cup buttermilk*
> 1 large egg
> ⅓ cup (5½ tablespoons) butter, melted
>
> *If you do not have buttermilk, add 1 tablespoon vinegar to 1 cup milk (preferably whole milk) and allow 30 seconds for it to sour.*

*S*ift the dry ingredients into a medium-sized bowl. Add the remaining ingredients and stir with a wooden spoon until the dry ingredients are just moistened. (Do not overmix or the muffins will be tough.)

Spoon the batter into muffin tins that have been lightly greased or filled with paper liners. Fill each about two-thirds full with the batter.

Bake in a preheated 375°F oven for 15 to 20 minutes, or until the centers of the muffins feel firm to the touch and a toothpick inserted in the center comes up clean. (Watch that they don't become too brown.) Remove from the oven, cool 5 minutes before turning from the muffin tin, and serve warm.

For variety, fold these ingredients into the batter just before filling the muffin cups:

- *Berry Muffins:* 1 cup fresh or frozen raspberries or blueberries
- *Cheese Muffins:* ½ cup grated Cheddar cheese
- *Herb Muffins:* 1 tablespoon dried or ¼ cup chopped fresh dill or sage

Corn Muffins (continued)

CORN BREAD VARIATION

MAKES 12 SQUARES

*F*ollow directions for corn muffins. If you're planning to use the corn bread for stuffing, reduce the sugar to ¼ cup. Pour the batter into a lightly greased 8- or 9-inch pan and bake in a preheated 350°F oven for 20 to 30 minutes, or until the edges are light brown and a toothpick inserted into the center comes out clean. (Watch that it doesn't become too dark.) Remove the pan from the oven and cool 5 minutes before cutting into squares. Serve warm.

ONE GOOD TEST FOR DONENESS

Nineteenth-century cookbooks such as *Buckeye Cookery* and *Maria Parola's New Cookbook* for the Washburn Crosby Milling Company gave readers lots of helpful general advice about cooking and homemaking. Instead of exact cooking or baking times, the authors guided cooks in what to see, smell, feel, and taste when following a recipe. Maria Parola's test for a bread's doneness is timeless:

"Lay the hand on the bottom of the loaf and if the escaping steam is too hot to bear, it shows that the interior needs more cooking. When safe to handle, it is safe to take out."

PUMPKIN-CRANBERRY MUFFINS

MAKES ABOUT 2 DOZEN MUFFINS

*T*hese chewy, moist muffins may be made with puréed winter squash (try delicata or acorn) or canned pumpkin if fresh is not available. You need about 2¼ pounds of pumpkin or squash for about 1½ cups of purée.

> ½ cup honey
> 2 eggs
> 1 cup milk or ½ cup each, milk and orange juice
> 1½ cups pumpkin or squash purée, or one 16-ounce
>   can pumpkin
> 1 cup vegetable oil
> 1½ tablespoons grated orange rind
> 3 cups unbleached all-purpose flour
> 1 cup sugar
> 1 tablespoon plus 1 teaspoon baking powder
> 1 teaspoon salt
> ½ teaspoon ground nutmeg
> 1 teaspoon ground cinnamon
> ½ cup cranberries, chopped and tossed with
>   2 tablespoons sugar

*I*n a medium bowl, beat together the honey, eggs, milk (or milk and juice), pumpkin or squash purée, oil, and orange rind. Sift the dry ingredients into a large bowl. Fold the wet ingredients into the dry ingredients and stir just until combined. Fold in the sweetened cranberries. Spoon the batter into muffin tins that have been lightly greased or lined with paper liners, and bake in a preheated 350°F oven for 20 to 25 minutes. Remove the muffins from the oven, cool for about 5 minutes before turning them out of the pan, and serve warm.

POWWOW

Fry bread is among the traditional Native American foods eaten at a Pow-wows, such as this Mesquakie Native American celebration in Iowa.

FRY BREAD

MAKES 12 SMALL OR 6 LARGE PIECES

*F*ry bread is sold by members of the Ojibway tribe at late-summer festivals, such as the Applefest in Bayfield, Wisconsin, and it is served sprinkled with sugar or topped with maple syrup. At powwows, such as the annual Ni-Mi-Win (meaning "come and dance") near Duluth, Minnesota, the bread is split and filled with hamburger or sprinkled with salt to accompany wild rice or moose-meat soup.

It's also delicious sprinkled with lots of cinnamon sugar and served with coffee.

> *2 cups unbleached all-purpose flour*
> *3 teaspoons baking powder*
> *1 tablespoon sugar*
> *1 teaspoon salt*
> *⅔ cup water*
> *Vegetable oil for frying*

Stir together the dry ingredients in a medium-sized bowl. Add the water and stir to make a stiff dough. Turn the dough out onto a lightly floured board and knead for about 3 minutes. Cover the dough with plastic wrap and let it stand at room temperature for about 1 hour.

Divide the dough into 12 small or 6 large pieces and flatten each piece into a round. Cover these with plastic wrap while you heat the oil.

Pour 2 inches of oil into a fryer or skillet and heat to about 350°F. (If the oil gets too hot, the middle of the fry bread will not cook.) Fry the dough in batches, being careful not to crowd the skillet. Allow about 1 to 2 minutes per side, or until they are lightly browned. Drain the rounds on paper towels. Sprinkle with cinnamon sugar, or drizzle with maple syrup, or sprinkle with salt and serve immediately.

Roast Chicken with Four Seasonal Variations

Basil-Roasted Chicken with Garlic Sauce

Maple-Glazed Hen with Mushroom Stuffing

Lemon-Herb Turkey Breast with Caper Butter

Corn Bread Stuffing

Chicken in Gin with Juniper

Buttermilk Oven-Fried Chicken

Chicken Salad with Apples, Walnuts, and Maple-Mustard
  Vinaigrette

Chicken or Turkey Breast Sauté with Seasonal Variations

Chicken Liver Pâté

Roast Goose with Corn Bread Stuffing

Wisconsin Cheddar Spoon Bread

Omelets

Fresh Ricotta Cheese

Thickened Cream

Blue Cheese Coins

Corn Blintzes

Ricotta-Parmesan-Herb Blintz Filling

Sweet and Savory Butters

Baked Wisconsin Goat Cheese on Croutons

Dumplings

Spaetzle (Tiny Noodles)

Noodles with Zesty Italian Cheese and Fresh Tomato Sauce

HENHOUSE AND DAIRY

CHICKEN, EGGS, AND CHEESE

Today lean, quick-cooking cuts of chicken and turkey are tremendously popular for everyday meals. But not long ago "chicken every Sunday" was a mark of affluence for immigrant settlers who had left poorer farms behind. Most families said thanks to God before a big Sunday supper, especially when the preacher came to call. "Even during the Depression, we always had fine eggs from our henhouse, chicken for Sunday dinner, and wonderful cream from our cow," recalls Barb Olson of Ames, Iowa. "First we had to catch the chicken," adds Susan Anes of Spearfish, North Dakota. "I can still see my grandmother chasing a big hen, swearing to herself in Norwegian."

Back then, the age of a hen and the season determined the method of preparation. In early June young and tender "spring chickens" were fried crisp and golden, sautéed, or poached for chicken salad. When January's wind made snowdrifts high as the barn door, fat hens ("old clucks") were slowly cooked in a fricassee or stewed. Anything else became soup.

With a wide variety of poultry available year-round, today's cooks are influenced primarily by the weather and fresh local ingredients when planning chicken dinners. For this chapter we've created master recipes for a

55

light sauté, and roast chicken with four distinct seasonal variations. We've also revised regional favorites, such as the Buttermilk Oven-Fried Chicken that avoids the mess, as well as the fat and calories of deep-fat frying, but the chicken is still old-fashioned crispy good.

Raising chickens, gathering eggs, milking, churning butter, and making cheese were household chores—the work of women and children. "My mother's 'egg money' came from more than eggs," says Jim Kwitchak of Anoka, Minnesota. "She sold her spring chickens, eggs, cheese, and butter to buy ribbons and sweets."

Today small cheesemakers are thriving, despite competition from corporations like Kraft (Illinois) and Land O' Lakes (Minnesota) that produce most of the nation's dairy products. Handmade traditional Colby, European-style cheese made of goat's milk and sheep's milk, and Italian cheeses that are started with old-world cultures are very much in demand. Our recipes for Corn Blintzes with Ricotta-Parmesan-Herb Blintz Filling and Noodles with Zesty Italian Cheese and Fresh Tomato Sauce were inspired by these local ingredients.

ROAST CHICKEN WITH FOUR SEASONAL VARIATIONS

SERVES 2 TO 4

*R*oast chicken is always in season. In the spring, pile the roasting pan with new leeks; in summer, toss in tomatoes and fragrant herbs. In autumn, use the harvest of hard squash and fresh sage, and in winter, when windows are thick with frost, turn to onions and mushrooms.

For crisp skin and tender chicken, blast the chicken first in a hot oven to sear the skin and seal in the juices; rotate the chicken to distribute the juices, basting frequently to keep the meat moist. Here is a simple guide to roasting chicken with seasonal accompaniments.

> *1 chicken (about 2½–3 pounds)*
> *1–2 tablespoons butter, softened*
> *Salt and freshly ground pepper*
> *Dried herbs (marjoram, rosemary, sage, thyme, or poultry*
>   *seasoning)*
> *4 cloves garlic, peeled*
> *1 cup cooking liquid (homemade Chicken Stock,* wine,*
>   *water, and lemon—see Seasonal Variations)*
>
> **For homemade Chicken Stock, see page 141, or use low-salt canned broth.*

*R*emove the fat, neck, gizzards, and liver from the body cavity, and rinse and pat the chicken dry. Rub the chicken all over with the softened butter, and sprinkle with salt and pepper and dried herbs. Put the garlic in the body cavity and place the chicken, breast side down, in a large roasting pan. Pour the cooking liquid into the pan and roast in a preheated 400°F oven for 20 minutes. Reduce the heat to 350°F. Turn the chicken breast side up and brush again with the pan juices. Continue to roast for 40 to 50 minutes, basting occasionally, until the juices run clear when the thickest part of the thigh is pierced. Remove to a platter and allow the chicken to rest about 5 minutes before carving.

SEASONAL VARIATIONS

FALL

1 chicken (about 2½–3 pounds)
1–2 tablespoons butter, softened
Salt and freshly ground pepper
4 cloves garlic, peeled
6–8 sprigs fresh sage or 1 tablespoon dried
1 acorn squash, peeled, seeded, and cut into 2–3-inch
*   chunks (or any other winter squash, to equal 2–3 cups)*
1 medium onion, peeled and cut into 3-inch chunks (about
*   1–1½ cups)*
½ cup dry white wine
½ cup homemade Chicken Stock*
½ cup toasted pumpkin seeds or walnuts for garnish

*For homemade Chicken Stock, see page 141, or use low-salt
canned broth.

*R*emove the fat, neck, gizzards, and liver from the body cavity, and rinse and pat the chicken dry. Rub the chicken all over with the softened butter and sprinkle with salt and pepper. Put the garlic and a few of the sprigs of fresh sage into the body cavity of the bird or sprinkle with the dried sage. Fill the roasting pan with the squash and the onion chunks. Lay the remaining sage sprigs over the vegetables or sprinkle with the dried. Add the wine and the stock. Place the chicken, breast side down, on the vegetables. Roast the chicken according to the directions on page 57.

Carve the chicken and serve it on top of the vegetables, drizzled with the pan juices and garnished with the toasted pumpkin seeds or walnuts.

WINTER

1 chicken (about 2½–3 pounds)
1–2 tablespoons butter, softened
Salt and freshly ground pepper
1 tablespoon dried thyme
4 cloves garlic, peeled
1 pound large mushrooms (any kind), cut into quarters
2 medium onions, peeled and cut into 2-inch chunks (about
2–3 cups)
½ cup homemade Chicken Stock*
½ cup Marsala or dry sherry

*For homemade Chicken Stock, see page 141, or use low-salt canned broth.

Remove the fat, neck, gizzards, and liver from the body cavity, and rinse and pat the chicken dry. Rub the chicken all over with the softened butter and sprinkle with salt and pepper and dried thyme. Put the garlic inside the body cavity of the chicken. Fill the roasting pan with the vegetables and add the stock and wine. Place the chicken, breast side down, on top of the vegetables. Roast according to the directions on page 57.

Carve the chicken and serve it on top of the vegetables, drizzled with the pan juices.

"WE ALL ATE GARLIC"

"**W**hen we were at my Czech grandmother's house, we all ate garlic . . . in everything," recalls Jim Kwitchak. "She hung a big rope of garlic heads knotted together on the back of the kitchen door. In the morning she'd pull a head off, break up some cloves, and chop them for our scrambled eggs. She'd bake garlic into her bread and throw whole cloves into the potato pot. Chicken, roasted or stewed, was loaded with garlic. If someone had a cold, she made a poultice of garlic to spread on his chest."

—JIM KWITCHAK OF ANOKA, MINNESOTA

FREE RANGE

Free-range farmers throughout the Northern Heartland supply local farm markets, co-ops, butcher shops, and supermarkets with fresh and frozen free-range birds. (They will also ship, see Sources, page 372.)

Unlike most commercially raised birds kept in indoor pens, free-range turkeys and chickens roam around the farmyard pecking on mixtures of corn and soy (often certified organic feed). They are not fed antibiotics or hormones. Free-range chickens have bigger thighs and slightly smaller breasts and are slaughtered at four to six pounds, free-range turkeys at eight to twelve pounds.

Is there a difference in taste? "My kids won't eat a grocery-store chicken. Free-range chickens have a firm, not mushy, texture. They taste better . . . like chicken," says Marge Nussbaum, a free-range turkey-and-chicken grower in Princeton, Minnesota.

SPRING

1 chicken (about 2½–3 pounds)
1–2 tablespoons butter, softened
Salt and freshly ground pepper
4 cloves garlic, peeled
2 large leeks
½ cup dry vermouth or white wine
½ cup homemade Chicken Stock*
¼ cup chopped chives for garnish
Chive flowers for garnish, if available

*For homemade Chicken Stock, see page 141, or use low-salt canned broth.

Remove the fat, neck, gizzards, and liver from the body cavities, and rinse and pat the chicken dry. Rub the chicken all over with the softened butter and sprinkle with salt and pepper. Put the garlic into the body cavity of the bird. Trim the "whiskers" from the leeks, slice them horizontally, then wash them thoroughly under cold running water. Slice the leeks 1 inch thick, starting with the white bulb and moving up to 2 inches of the green leaves. Spread the leeks on the bottom of the roasting pan. Add the vermouth and stock, and place the chicken, breast side down, on top of the leeks. Roast the chicken according to the directions on page 57.

Carve the chicken and serve with the leeks spooned on top. Drizzle with the remaining pan juices and garnish with chopped chives and chive flowers.

SUMMER

1 chicken (about 2½–3 pounds)
1–2 tablespoons butter, softened
Salt and freshly ground pepper
Large bunch of fresh garden herbs (thyme, marjoram,
    basil, or some of each)
4 cloves garlic, peeled
4 young carrots
2 stalks celery
10–12 new potatoes or Finnish potatoes
⅓ cup lemon juice
⅔ cup homemade Chicken Stock*
Herbs and lemon slices for garnish

*For homemade Chicken Stock, see page 141, or use low-salt canned broth.

Remove the fat, neck, gizzards, and liver from the body cavities, and rinse and pat the chicken dry. Rub the chicken all over with the softened butter and sprinkle with salt and pepper. Place a few sprigs of herbs inside the body cavity along with the garlic cloves. Gently lift the skin from the breast of the chicken without detaching it from the breastbone and push the remaining herbs between the skin and flesh of the breast. Cover the roasting pan with the vegetables and add the lemon juice and stock. Place the chicken, breast side down, on top of the vegetables and roast according to the directions on page 57.

Carve the chicken and serve it on top of the vegetables, drizzled with the pan juices and garnished with more fresh herbs and lemon slices.

BASIL-ROASTED CHICKEN
WITH GARLIC SAUCE

SERVES 8 (RECIPE IS EASILY CUT IN HALF.)

*I*n this recipe plenty of garlic roasts along with the chicken and is puréed into a rich, brown, and slightly sweet sauce.

> *2 chickens (about 2½–3 pounds each)*
> *½ stick (4 tablespoons) butter, softened*
> *¼ cup chopped fresh basil*
> *¼ cup chopped fresh parsley*
> *½ teaspoon salt*
> *¼ teaspoon freshly ground pepper*
> *1 cup small fresh basil leaves or other fresh herbs*
> *30 large cloves garlic, unpeeled*
> *¼ cup lemon juice*
> *2 cups homemade Chicken Stock (page 141) or low-salt*
>   *canned broth*
> *Salt and freshly ground pepper to taste*
> *Fresh basil leaves for garnish*

*R*emove the fat, neck, liver, and gizzards from the body cavity, and then rinse and pat the chicken dry. Gently separate the skin from the flesh, running your fingers from the front to the back of the chicken and along the leg and thigh, being careful not to rip the skin or detach it from the bird.

Mix the butter, chopped basil and parsley, salt, and pepper together in a small bowl. Rub half of the butter mixture under the loosened skin and then tuck ½ of the whole basil leaves under the loosened skin of one chicken; be sure to get it under the skin around the leg and thigh. Repeat with the second chicken.

Put 4 of the garlic cloves into the body cavity of each chicken and scatter the rest in the roasting pan. Add the lemon juice and stock. Place the chickens, breast side up, on top of the garlic and stock. Roast in a preheated 350°F oven, basting occasionally with the pan juices for 1 hour, or until the juices run clear when the thickest part of the thigh is pierced. Transfer the chickens to a heated platter and tent with aluminum foil to keep warm.

Pour the juices with the garlic cloves into a blender and purée the mixture. (The garlic skins will remain whole.) Strain the purée through a sieve into a medium-sized saucepan, pressing on the garlic skins with the back of a spoon. Bring the liquid to a simmer over medium heat, stirring occasionally, about 3 minutes, and add salt and pepper to taste. Carve the chickens and serve them drizzled with the sauce and garnished with fresh basil leaves.

Up until the mid-1900s most Midwestern families relied on their backyard chickens for eggs and meat. This photo was taken in southern Minnesota in 1905.

MAPLE-GLAZED HEN
WITH MUSHROOM STUFFING

SERVES 6

*N*ative Ojibway hunters would roast wild game birds over an open fire and brush them with a maple sapling branch dipped in maple syrup.

In this recipe we roast the small hens, glazing them with maple syrup and red wine, until they are a deep golden brown. The rich mushroom stuffing absorbs some of the glaze and the flavor of the roasted meat. These are delicious served on a bed of sautéed chard, escarole, and arugula. The deep bitter greens make a nice counterpoint to the sweet glaze.

6 Cornish game hens

STUFFING

1 medium onion, peeled and quartered
1 stalk celery, trimmed
1 pound mushrooms, rinsed and patted dry
3 tablespoons butter
2 tablespoons dry sherry (optional)
1 tablespoon chopped fresh thyme or 2 teaspoons dried
¼ cup chopped fresh parsley
½ loaf homemade-type white bread, cut into small cubes
  (about 4–5 cups)*
*About ¾ cup homemade Chicken Stock (page 141) or
  low-salt canned broth*
Salt and freshly ground pepper to taste

**Try Old-fashioned Milk Bread (page 6) or Cottage Cheese
Dill Bread (page 20).*

GLAZE

1 cup maple syrup
½ cup red wine or ¼ cup lemon juice

*R*inse the hens and pat dry. Finely mince the onion, celery, and mushrooms. (You may do this in a food processor fitted with a steel blade.) In a large skillet, melt the butter over medium heat and cook the minced vegetables until they are soft and all the moisture has evaporated. Add the sherry. Turn the mixture into a large bowl and toss in the thyme, parsley, and bread. If the mixture is too dry, moisten with chicken stock, several tablespoons at a time, up to ¼ *cup*. Cool completely. Taste and season with salt and pepper.

Gently fill each bird's cavity with the stuffing, being sure not to pack it too full. (Cook any leftover stuffing in a separate dish, moistened with a little stock and covered with aluminum foil.) Pour the remaining ½ cup stock into the roasting pan.

In a small dish, make the glaze. Mix together the maple syrup and red wine. Brush the hens with the syrup and roast in a preheated 400°F oven for 20 minutes. Reduce the heat to 350°F, baste with the pan drippings, and cook for another 25 to 30 minutes, brushing the birds with the glaze every 10 minutes.

"SPRING CHICKEN" AND "OLD CLUCK"

Back when most families raised their own chickens, the terms "spring chicken" and "old cluck" were used to describe the age and eating quality of a hen. The chicks were hatched in February, and by spring they were two-pound pullets, strong enough to go outside.

Jim Kwitchak of Anoka, Minnesota, who was born some sixty years ago on a farm, remembers: "They were spry and fast, pecking and scratching in the grass, chasing each other, making all kinds of noise. They made real good eating, tender and juicy. Mother would butcher some for fried chicken and chicken salad, and sell some in town; fifty cents apiece—a very good price. By June we'd move the rest of the flock to the henhouse for the laying season. When they reached five pounds, their laying slowed down. We'd place a glass egg under these hens to trick them into laying more.

"Old clucks just sat there clucking away, tough old birds. We'd butcher them through the winter for soup. My grandmother would clean and skin the chicken feet for stock because she said they had the most flavor."

LEMON-HERB TURKEY BREAST
WITH CAPER BUTTER

SERVES 6 TO 8

*M*arinated in lemon juice overnight and lightly cooked, this turkey breast is extremely tender and juicy. Slice the meat diagonally and serve it with noodles and a bright trio of sautéed sugar snap peas, carrots, and red cabbage.

> *1 whole boned turkey breast (about 2 pounds), with*
> *   skin on*
> *½ cup fresh lemon juice*
> *1 cup olive oil*
> *1 cup fresh basil or ½ cup fresh sage and ½ cup fresh basil*
> *2 teaspoons grated lemon zest (discard bitter white pith)*
> *1 clove garlic, crushed*
> *Freshly ground pepper*
>
> *CAPER BUTTER*
>
> *½ stick (4 tablespoons) butter*
> *2 tablespoons chopped shallots*
> *1 tablespoon capers*
> *2 tablespoons chopped fresh chives*
> *1 teaspoon lemon juice*
> *Fresh chive flowers for garnish, if available*
> *Fresh opal basil for garnish*

*M*arinate the turkey, breast side down, in the lemon juice and olive oil overnight. Just before cooking, chop the herbs and mix together with the grated lemon zest, garlic, and a few grinds of pepper. Using your hands and a dull knife, gently lift up the skin of the breast, being careful not to tear it, then force the herbs between the skin and flesh of the breast.

Roast the breast in a preheated 375°F oven, basting occasionally with pan juices and remaining marinade for about 18 minutes per pound. The meat will be slightly rare and very tender.

To prepare the caper butter, melt the butter in a small skillet over medium heat and sauté the shallots until translucent. Turn off the heat and add the capers, chives, and lemon juice. Slice the turkey horizontally.

We suggest serving it on a bed of pasta with sautéed sugar snap peas, sliced carrots, and red cabbage. Drizzle the caper butter over all and garnish with chive flowers and opal basil leaves. (Opal are nice, if available. If not, regular fresh basil is fine.)

A blue-ribbon turkey—early 1900s

DRESSING A BIRD

Years ago, when farm-raised chickens had leaner breasts and meatier legs and thighs than today's birds, farm wives would stuff their chickens and turkeys to plump up the breast and stretch the number of people one bird might serve. Today we use stuffing to add flavor and texture, tucking fresh herbs under the skin and tossing together dressings of garlic and homemade bread crumbs.

You'll need about ½ cup of stuffing for each pound of bird for either the neck or body cavity or under the skin stuffing. Do not pack the body cavity too full or force too much under the skin, because the stuffing will expand as it cooks.

Be careful. A warm body cavity and stuffing ingredients make a fertile breeding ground for salmonella. Never use raw meat in stuffing. The stuffing mixture should be cool before filling the bird. Roast the bird as soon as it's stuffed; never allow it to sit more than 1 hour before cooking (even if refrigerated). After cooking, remove the stuffing from the body cavity and store both the bird and the stuffing separately in the refrigerator.

As an alternative, the stuffing may be cooked alongside the bird in a separate container and basted with the pan juices. Reheat the stuffing in a 325°F oven, covered, for about 30 minutes and toss with a little melted butter if it is dry.

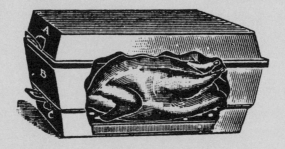

CORN BREAD STUFFING

MAKES ABOUT 4 CUPS

*T*his versatile stuffing is good inside a turkey or under the skin of a roasting chicken. When the corn is ripe and sweet, add ½ cup of fresh kernels to the stuffing. We like to serve it with Cranberry-Leek Compote (page 287).

1 recipe Corn Bread (page 49) or an 8-inch pan, crumbled
  into large chunks (about 4½–5 cups)
5 strips good-quality bacon
3 ribs celery, chopped
1 scallion or green onion, trimmed and chopped
¼ teaspoon crumbled or rubbed sage
2 eggs, beaten
¼–½ cup buttermilk*
Dash of cayenne pepper or Tabasco sauce
Salt and freshly ground pepper to taste

*If you do not have buttermilk, add 1 tablespoon vinegar to 1 cup milk (preferably whole milk) and allow 30 seconds for it to sour.

*P*lace the corn bread on a baking sheet in a 300°F oven for about 20 minutes, or until it is dried out. Fry the bacon and save the fat. Crumble the bacon and set aside. Crumble the corn bread again into a large mixing bowl. Sauté the celery and scallion in the reserved bacon fat until tender. Add the sage, celery, and scallion, the crumbled bacon and the eggs, and toss together, adding just enough buttermilk to moisten the stuffing. (It should be moist but not soggy.) Season with a dash of cayenne pepper and salt and freshly ground pepper to taste.

CHICKEN IN GIN
WITH JUNIPER

SERVES 4

*T*he combination of gin and juniper gives this chicken a wonderful sharp flavor. Serve with wild rice, or Wild Rice Pilaf with Dried Cherries and Walnuts (page 279), and a side of Overnight Coleslaw (page 264). For a more mellow-tasting dish, substitute an equal amount of red wine for the gin.

> *1 chicken (about 2–3 pounds), cut into pieces*
> *3 tablespoons vegetable oil*
> *2 medium onions, chopped*
> *1 clove garlic, chopped*
> *2 tablespoons unbleached all-purpose flour*
> *½ cup plus 2 tablespoons gin*
> *1 cup homemade Chicken Stock**
> *6 juniper berries, crushed*
> *2 teaspoons–1 tablespoon chopped fresh thyme*
> *1 bay leaf*
> *Salt and freshly ground pepper to taste*
> *1 tablespoon chopped fresh chives, parsley, or thyme for*
> *   garnish*
>
> **For homemade Chicken Stock, see page 141, or use low-salt canned broth.*

*R*inse and pat the chicken dry. Heat the oil in a large skillet and brown the pieces on all sides. Remove the chicken and set aside.

Add the onions and garlic to the skillet and cook over moderate heat, tossing for about 8 minutes, or until soft and just browned. Sprinkle the flour over the skillet and stir it in thoroughly to absorb the fat. Cook for about 1 minute. Add ½ cup of the gin and all the stock, stirring until the flour is absorbed. Add the remaining ingredients, except the 2 tablespoons of gin, and the dark-meat pieces of chicken. Cover the skillet, reduce the heat to a low simmer, and cook for about 20 minutes. Add the white-meat pieces, cover, and cook an additional 10 minutes, or until the chicken is tender. Pull out all of the chicken and cook the liquid for 3 to 5 minutes, or until it thickens slightly. Turn off the heat and adjust the salt and pepper to taste. Add the remaining 2 tablespoons gin. Put the chicken on individual plates or a large platter, along with wild rice or pilaf, and pour the sauce over all, then garnish with the chopped fresh herbs.

JUNIPER

A low-growing evergreen, the juniper is native to Europe and North America. German, Finn, Swedish, and Norwegian settlers dried the small, round, bitter berries and then crushed them for seasoning. The Hungarians especially liked the berries in cabbage dishes, and the Germans put them in their sauerkraut. Juniper berry is also used in marinades for game birds, venison, and pork. Juniper is the dominant flavoring in gin and is sometimes used in homemade beer.

BUTTERMILK
OVEN-FRIED CHICKEN

SERVES 4

*T*his recipe was inspired by Mary Williams, a KMA Radio Homemaker and an editor of the *Kitchen-Klatter Magazine*. The chicken soaks in buttermilk overnight to make it especially tender before being dusted with seasoned flour. It's baked in a hot oven to a crispy brown. Honey-Lemon Sauce adds a sweet touch. Serve with Fresh Corn Pudding (page 262) and a big plate of thickly sliced fresh tomatoes when they're in season.

>   *1 chicken (about 2–3 pounds), cut into pieces*
>   *2 cups buttermilk, see note, page 73*
>   *1 cup unbleached all-purpose flour*
>   *1 teaspoon salt*
>   *½ teaspoon freshly ground pepper*
>   *1 teaspoon dried thyme*
>   *1 teaspoon dried oregano*
>   *¼ teaspoon cinnamon*
>   *Vegetable oil*

*R*inse the chicken and pat it dry. Place the pieces in one layer in a shallow dish and cover with the buttermilk. Cover the dish with plastic wrap and soak the chicken overnight in the refrigerator, turning several times. Mix together the remaining ingredients in a paper bag. Remove the chicken from the buttermilk and shake each piece individually in the paper bag to coat it with the seasoned flour. Lightly oil a shallow pan. Place the chicken, skin side up, in the pan and bake in a preheated 400°F oven for 30 to 40 minutes, or until it is tender and the thigh juices run clear when pricked. Serve with the Honey-Lemon Sauce passed separately.

HONEY-LEMON SAUCE

½ stick (4 tablespoons) butter
¼ cup lemon juice
¼ cup honey

*I*n a small saucepan, melt together the butter, lemon juice, and honey. Be careful not to boil the sauce.

BUTTERMILK

"The best thing about churning butter was the buttermilk. Once a week I'd crank that old wooden churn until it wouldn't turn anymore. Then I'd pop the cork out of the bottom and put my mouth right up to it and drink. It was tangy with lots of pieces of butter in it. You can't buy that kind of buttermilk in stores. We'd keep it good and cold in glass jugs in the springhouse. I could finish a quart in no time after a hot and dusty day in the field."

—JIM KWITCHAK OF ANOKA, MINNESOTA

CHICKEN SALAD WITH APPLES, WALNUTS, AND MAPLE-MUSTARD VINAIGRETTE

SERVES 4 TO 6

*T*his recipe has some of the ingredients of an old-fashioned chicken salad, but we have lightened it and sharpened the different textures and flavors. It makes a colorful light entrée or first course: tart apples, toasted walnuts, and juicy chicken in a sweet and sharp Maple-Mustard Vinaigrette (page 253). This chicken salad is good served on bitter greens, garnished with Spicy Nuts (page 296). Try it with smoked turkey or chicken.

> *1–1½ pounds skinless, boneless poached chicken or turkey*
> *breast meat, cut into ½-inch chunks (or leftover turkey*
> *or chicken to equal about 2½–3 cups)*
> *1 cup diced celery*
> *2 large tart apples, cored, skinned, and cut into ½-inch*
> *chunks*
> *¾ cup lightly toasted, chopped walnuts or Spicy Nuts*
> *(page 296)*
> *Fresh greens*
> *⅓–½ cup Maple-Mustard Vinaigrette (page 253)*

*C*ut the chicken or turkey breast meat into chunks and set aside in the refrigerator.

Toss together the celery, apples, and walnuts with just enough dressing to lightly coat all, and refrigerate until cold. When ready to serve the salad, place the chicken or turkey on a bed of fresh greens and drizzle with additional vinaigrette.

NOT JUST FOR THANKSGIVING

"Fresh turkey isn't just for Thanksgiving anymore," claims Jerry Jerome, president of Jerome Foods, Barron, Wisconsin, which calls itself "the turkey capital of the world." Turkey growers throughout Wisconsin, Minnesota, and North Dakota supply Jerome (the world's largest fresh turkey processor) with turkeys all year long. Big toms are processed into fresh cuts: breast meat slices, tenderloins, roasts, and ground turkey. The meat is vacuum-packed and then chilled to 31 degrees Fahrenheit to keep it fresher longer than meat held at the conventional 35 degrees, yet not so cold as to be damaged by ice crystals that form when meat freezes.

Lean and quick-cooking, fresh turkey cuts make a low-fat alternative to beef and pork and an economical substitute for veal. Be careful not to overcook fresh turkey cuts. They quickly become dry and tasteless. Breast meat and ground turkey are done when the internal temperature reaches 160 degrees Fahrenheit on a meat thermometer. A breast roast is ready at 165 degrees and dark meat at 175 degrees (not 180 to 185 degrees, as is suggested in many older cookbooks). See page 190 for a Holiday Roast Wild Turkey (or domestic).

CHICKEN OR TURKEY BREAST SAUTÉ WITH SEASONAL VARIATIONS

SERVES 2 (RECIPE IS EASY TO DOUBLE.)

*I*n these quick and easy skillet recipes, we cut the meat into strips to shorten the cooking time. This way the vegetables and chicken are both ready in minutes to serve over cooked rice, pasta, or potatoes.

> *¾–1 pound chicken or turkey breast meat*
> *1 tablespoon olive oil or butter (or a combination of both)*
> *2 cups prepared fresh vegetables (see Seasonal Variations)*
> *¼–½ cup cooking liquid (homemade Chicken Stock,**
> *white wine, red wine, lemon juice, vegetable stock)*
>
> **For homemade Chicken Stock, see page 141, or use low-salt canned broth.*

*C*ut chicken into strips, approximately 2 inches wide by 4 inches long. Heat the oil and/or butter in a skillet over medium-high heat. Throw in the chicken and start adding the vegetables (see suggested variations, pages 77–9). Toss the vegetables and chicken with a fork to cook evenly over medium-high heat for about 1 to 3 minutes. When the outside of the chicken is cooked, add the liquid and continue cooking for about 1 to 2 minutes, or until the chicken is cooked through and the vegetables are tender-crisp. Serve the chicken and vegetables on a bed of rice or pasta or with steamed potatoes.

SEASONAL VARIATIONS

FALL

1 medium acorn squash, peeled, seeded, and cut into 1-inch chunks (or enough of any other winter squash to equal about 2 cups)

1 tablespoon walnut or olive oil

¾–1 pound chicken or turkey breast meat, cut into 2 × 4-inch strips

1 small onion, peeled and chopped

1 clove garlic, peeled and chopped

¼ cup orange juice

¼ cup dry white wine or homemade Chicken Stock*

1 tablespoon chopped fresh rosemary or 1 teaspoon dried

Grated zest of 1 orange

¼ cup chopped red pepper for garnish (optional)

¼ cup grated smoked mozzarella cheese for garnish (optional)

2 tablespoons toasted chopped walnuts for garnish (optional)

*For homemade Chicken Stock, see page 141, or use low-salt canned broth.

Blanch the squash by immersing it in rapidly boiling water for about 5 minutes, or until it is tender, then drain. Heat the oil and sauté the chicken and vegetables according to the directions on page 76. Add the orange juice, wine, rosemary, and orange rind, and cook for about 2 minutes. Serve over rice or pasta and garnish with chopped red pepper, grated smoked mozzarella cheese, and lightly toasted, chopped walnuts.

WINTER

1 tablespoon olive oil or butter (or a combination of both)
¾–1 pound chicken or turkey breast meat, cut into 2 × 4-inch strips
1 clove garlic, peeled and chopped
¼ cup peeled, chopped onions
½ cup sliced carrots
¼ cup broccoli florets
¼ cup cauliflower florets
¼ cup red wine
¼ cup homemade Chicken Stock*
1 tablespoon chopped fresh oregano or 1 teaspoon dried
½ cup cooked red pinto beans, drained
¼ cup diced smoked ham
¼ cup grated sharp Cheddar cheese for garnish (optional)

*For homemade Chicken Stock, see page 141, or use low-salt canned broth.

*H*eat the oil and/or butter and sauté the chicken and vegetables according to the directions on page 76. Add the wine and stock and cook about 2 minutes. When the vegetables are tender, add the oregano, beans, and ham, and toss until warm. Serve over rice, garnished with shredded Cheddar cheese.

SPRING

1 tablespoon olive oil or butter (or a combination of both)
¾–1 pound chicken or turkey breast meat, cut into 2 × 4-inch strips
¼ cup sliced carrots
¼ cup sliced leeks or scallions
¼ cup sliced morel mushrooms or any other mushroom
3 tablespoons lemon juice
2–3 tablespoons sherry or homemade Chicken Stock*
¼ cup peas
2 tablespoons chopped fresh chives for garnish

Chive flowers for garnish, if available
1 tablespoon grated lemon rind for garnish

*For homemade Chicken Stock, see page 141, or use low-salt
canned broth.

*H*eat the oil and/or butter and sauté the chicken and vegetables according to the directions on page 74. Add the lemon juice and sherry and cook about 2 minutes, or until the vegetables are tender; then toss in the peas. Serve over pasta and garnish with chopped chives, chive flowers, and lemon rind.

SUMMER

¾–1 pound chicken or turkey breast meat, cut into 2 × 4-
inch strips
1 tablespoon olive oil or butter (or a combination of both)
1 clove garlic, peeled and minced
¼ cup sliced red and/or yellow cherry tomatoes
1 cup chopped red, yellow, and green sweet peppers
(or whatever is available), mixed
1 cup summer squash, cut into 1-inch pieces
1 tablespoon chopped fresh rosemary or 1 teaspoon dried
2 tablespoons balsamic vinegar or lemon juice
2–3 tablespoons homemade Chicken Stock*
2 tablespoons grated Parmesan cheese or crumbled feta
cheese for garnish (optional)
2 tablespoons chopped black olives for garnish (optional)

*For homemade Chicken Stock, see page 141, or use low-salt
canned broth.

*S*auté the chicken and vegetables according to the directions on page 74. Add the rosemary, vinegar, and stock, and continue cooking another 1 to 2 minutes. Serve over pasta garnished with Parmesan or feta cheese and olives.

BEYOND TURKEY SANDWICHES

Leftover roast turkey in your refrigerator is like having a treasure—it can be used in so many creative ways. Here are a few simple suggestions:

🦃 Toss chunks of diced turkey with the Maple-Mustard Vinaigrette (page 253), diced celery and apples, and serve on a bed of lettuce, then sprinkle with Spicy Nuts (page 296).

🦃 Make an omelet filling of finely diced turkey meat mixed with Thickened Cream (page 87) and Sweet and Hot Pepper Jelly (page 283).

🦃 Use sliced leftover white and dark turkey meat in the recipe for Casserole of Caramelized Onions and Leftover Meat (page 182).

🦃 Toss diced turkey meat into the recipe for Noodles with Zesty Italian Cheese and Fresh Tomato Sauce (page 102).

🦃 For a simple skillet meal, cut turkey meat into matchstick-sized strips and toss into the recipe for Morels, Asparagus, and Sunchokes in Brown Butter with Toasted Hazelnuts (page 245) and serve over wild rice.

🦃 For a main-dish salad, toss chunks of turkey into the Wild Rice, Cranberry, Walnut, and Vegetable Salad (page 278).

🦃 Add chunks of turkey to the Wild Rice Pilaf with Dried Cherries and Walnuts (page 279) for an easy hot dish.

🦃 Mix Rhubarb Chutney (page 292) or Green Tomato Mincemeat (page 295) with mayonnaise when making your favorite turkey salad sandwich.

CHICKEN LIVER PÂTÉ

MAKES 2 CUPS (ENOUGH FOR A PARTY OF 12)

*T*his easy, delicious appetizer is made of the livers that come packed in whole chickens. It's great on crisp homemade Croutons (page 18). The recipe can easily be doubled for a buffet.

¾–1 pound chicken livers
Milk to soak the livers
1 clove garlic
1 tablespoon fresh rosemary or 1 teaspoon dried
1 tablespoon fresh marjoram or 1 teaspoon dried
1 tablespoon fresh thyme or 1 teaspoon dried
¼ pound diced bacon or ⅛ cup goose fat, if available
¼ pound mushrooms, chopped
2 shallots, peeled and chopped
2–3 tablespoons brandy or red wine
Salt and freshly ground pepper to taste
¼–½ cup heavy cream

*S*oak the chicken livers in milk for about 30 minutes, then drain and discard the milk. In a large bowl, toss the chicken livers with the garlic, herbs, bacon, mushrooms, and shallots, and turn it all into an ovenproof skillet. Cook in a preheated 350°F oven for about 15 to 20 minutes, or until the livers are cooked but still pink inside. Add the brandy and salt and pepper to taste. In a food processor fitted with a steel blade, purée the liver mixture in batches while still warm, adding enough cream to make the mixture very smooth and creamy. Chill before serving.

ROAST GOOSE
WITH CORN BREAD STUFFING

SERVES 2 TO 4

*T*o cook a plump domestic goose, prick it gently with a fork or sharp knife, penetrating just the layer of skin and fat (do not poke through to the flesh) before putting it in the oven. This will release the fat, and the bird will baste itself while it cooks.

In the late fall stuff the goose with Corn Bread Stuffing (page 69) and serve it with Braised Red Cabbage with Apples and Bacon (page 271).

Roast Goose with Corn Bread Stuffing (continued)

> *1 goose (about 8–10 pounds)*
> *Salt and freshly ground pepper*
> *1 recipe Corn Bread Stuffing (page 69)*
> *¼–½ cup brandy or orange juice*

*R*inse the goose and pat dry, then sprinkle it liberally inside and out with salt and freshly ground pepper. Stuff the goose lightly with stuffing.

Using a sharp knife point or the tines of a fork, lightly prick the skin just to the fat layer. Tuck the wing tips behind the back and tie the drumsticks across the body cavity. Place the goose, breast side up, on a rack in a roasting pan.

Roast the goose in a preheated 400°F oven for 1 hour, sprinkling it occasionally with the brandy, and continue to prick it lightly with the knife point or a fork. Drain and save the fat during the roasting. Reduce the temperature to 325°F and continue roasting for another hour to 1½ hours, or until the juices run clear.

"NOODLED" GOOSE

Most farm families counted a few fat geese and several puddle ducks among their livestock. German and English settlers especially prized roast goose at Christmas. Its thick layer of fat provided shortening for cooking and also for medicinal rubs. Dark bread spread with goose fat was a much-loved snack.

In Watertown, Wisconsin, German farmers force-fed, or "noodled," geese to enlarge their livers for foie gras. While commercial foie gras operations have long since closed, a few farm families still continue the practice for their own special occasions. Foie gras is usually made into pâté, but it is also delicious sautéed with apples and onions.

WISCONSIN CHEDDAR
SPOON BREAD

SERVES 6 TO 8 AS A SIDE DISH OR 4 AS A MEAL

*T*his easy spoon bread puffs up like a soufflé, then falls. It makes a hearty main dish served with a tossed green salad and a lovely side dish with the Cider-Soaked and Brown-Sugar-Glazed Ham (page 116).

> 2¼ cups water
> 1 teaspoon salt
> 1 cup cornmeal
> ½ teaspoon white pepper
> 2 tablespoons butter
> 1 cup milk
> 4 large eggs, well beaten
> 1½ cups shredded sharp Cheddar cheese
> 3 tablespoons chopped scallions

*B*utter a 1½-quart casserole and set aside. In a large saucepan, bring the water to a boil. Add the salt and lower the heat to a simmer. Slowly add the cornmeal, stirring to keep lumps from forming. (A wire whisk works well.) When all the cornmeal has been added, continue cooking, stirring constantly for about 1 to 2 minutes. The mixture should be completely smooth.

Remove the pan from the heat and stir in the pepper and butter and then the milk. When the mixture is smooth, stir in the eggs, beating well until everything is very smooth. Stir in the cheese and the chopped scallions. Pour the mixture into the casserole and bake in a preheated 400°F oven for 40 minutes, or until a toothpick inserted in the center comes up clean. This will be puffy and light.

OMELETS

MAKES 1 OMELET

"Sometimes they were served at breakfast and sometimes at supper; sometimes we ate them plain and sometimes with butter and jam and sometimes with shredded cheese," recalls Ervin Zahn of Shawano, Wisconsin. "We called them egg cakes, but they're the same as omelets—crisp on the edges, buttery inside—and we loved them."

These easy omelets make a filling brunch or simple dinner entrée. Vary our suggested fillings with ingredients you already have on hand.

It's best to make one 2-egg omelet at a time. A perfect omelet is soft and creamy in the center, enveloping a warm filling. (If you are using cheese, it should be melted through.)

> *2 eggs*
> *Salt and freshly ground pepper to taste*
> *1 tablespoon butter*
> *¼ cup filling*

*I*n a small bowl, beat the eggs with salt and pepper until they are just blended. Melt the butter in an 8-inch nonstick skillet, and when it is foamy, pour in the eggs. Shake the skillet back and forth to coat the pan with the eggs. Use a spatula to pull up a little of the edge of the omelet, tip the skillet, and allow the eggs to run under; continue shaking the pan. When the pan is thoroughly coated with the eggs and the center of the egg mass is soft and just barely starting to cook, spread the warmed filling across the center of the omelet. Using a spatula or a fork, roll one third of the omelet over itself, then turn it onto the plate, so that it folds once more. You may also simply fold the omelet in half and slip it onto the plate.

FILLINGS

Use about ¼ cup per omelet. Have the filling warm and ready before you begin to cook.

◢ Smoked trout with cream cheese and watercress

◢ Morel mushrooms, lightly sautéed in butter, with smoked Gouda cheese and chopped fresh chives

◢ Brie cheese and chopped pears

◢ Sautéed mushrooms with ham and Colby cheese

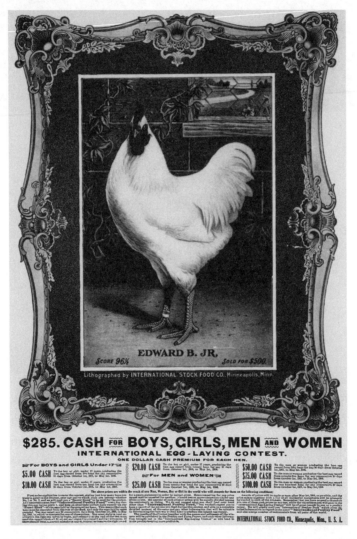

Poster for an international egg-laying contest sponsored by the International Stock Food Company, 1905. The best egg-laying chickens commanded a great price.

FEEDING   CAT BY HE WAY

FRESH RICOTTA CHEESE

MAKES 1 CUP

My grandmother kept a bowl of sour milk on the back of
the stove and a bag of cottage cheese on the clothesline.
Sometimes, instead of letting the whey drip into the ground,
she would put a dishpan under the bag so the ducks could
feed on it.

—BARB OLSON, AMES, IOWA

*T*his is a traditional recipe for fresh ricotta that is very easy to make. It has
a delicate, light flavor and is delicious sprinkled with salt and pepper, chopped
fresh herbs, and a little olive oil. Spread it on homemade Croutons (page 18).
It's best eaten within a week.

1 quart whole milk
½ cup heavy cream
Juice of ½ lemon

*I*n a large saucepan, bring the milk and cream to a boil over high heat. As it reaches a rolling boil, add the lemon juice. As soon as the milk separates (within about 10 seconds), remove the pot from the stove and pour the liquid through a fine sieve lined with a double thickness of cheesecloth. Discard the clear watery whey that drips through. Allow the curds to drain until cooled to room temperature. Turn into a bowl or plastic container, cover, and keep refrigerated until ready to use.

THICKENED CREAM

MAKES 2 CUPS (RECIPE IS EASILY DOUBLED.)

"*M*y mother used to scoop out the thick cream that rose to the top of our milk and put it in a dish and let it sit a day or more. It would get a little tangy but not too thick, and we'd pour it over fresh berries or homemade applesauce," recalls Daisy Samuelson of Oxlip, Minnesota.

The sour cream we buy in the store today is much thicker than that made from fresh milk on the farm. The closest we can come in taste and texture is the following cultured cream that keeps two weeks in the refrigerator. It's delicious on stewed fruit, blended into salad dressings, and used to thicken soups, sauces, and stews. Unlike cream, it will not break down in a sauce and may be heated without much care.

> *2 cups heavy cream (not ultrapasteurized)*
> *2 tablespoons buttermilk*

*H*eat the cream to "baby bottle" temperature (105° to 115°F). Add the buttermilk. Pour it into a jar with a lid and set in a warm spot on top of the refrigerator or near the stove for about a day, or until it is thick. Keep it covered and store in the refrigerator.

BUTTER SCULPTURE

Since the early 1900s, golden Minnesota butter has been carved into elaborate sculptures to promote the state's rich resource.

In 1901 fairgoers at the Buffalo Exposition marveled at Minnesota's exhibit of an eleven- by five-foot replica of the new state capitol in St. Paul, carved from a giant block of butter.

In 1904, Minnesota took first prize for an astonishing life-size tableau of Father Louis Hennepin stepping ashore at St. Anthony Falls, in Minneapolis (shown below). Here we also see the priest, his Indian guide, a voyageur with a paddle, their canoe, and the bush to which it was tethered, plus the rippling waters—all are carved from butter.

MINNESOTA STATE FAIR—
PRINCESS KAY OF THE MILKY WAY

In recent times a young woman is selected every year by the Minnesota dairy industry from over 24,000 dairy farms to be its spokesperson. Princess Kay of the Milky Way and her ten-member court are each carved from a sixty-eight-pound block of butter. The princesses, swaddled in goose-down jackets, sit in a refrigerated rotating glass cube as the sculptor hones their likenesses. Passersby, who linger to watch, sample scraps of butter from the carving. The sculptures remain in the Dairy and Meat Products Building throughout the two-week run of the state fair; then they are sent to the princesses' hometowns to reign over displays in the cheese shop or deli.

BLUE CHEESE COINS

MAKES 40 ROUNDS

*T*hese whimsical snacks are based on a recipe for Cheese Pennies from the *Family Friend Cookbook,* published by the Ladies of the Ascension Church in Stillwater, Minnesota, in 1853. We shape the dough into tiny rounds to float on soup or toss into salads.

> *3 tablespoons butter*
> *3 ounces blue cheese*
> *1 cup unbleached all-purpose flour*
> *1 egg yolk*
> *⅛ teaspoon nutmeg*
> *Salt and freshly ground pepper to taste*

*C*ream together the butter and blue cheese, then mix in the remaining ingredients to make a stiff dough. Shape the dough into 2 logs with diameters about that of a quarter. Wrap the rolls in plastic wrap and refrigerate overnight.

Slice the rolls into coins and place them on very lightly greased cookie sheets. Bake in a preheated 350°F oven for about 10 minutes. Watch to be sure the coins become golden but not too brown. Remove and cool on racks before serving or wrapping to freeze. Store in airtight containers.

CORN BLINTZES

MAKES ABOUT 8 TO 12 BLINTZES

*R*ussian blintzes, Polish *palacinkes,* Swedish pancakes, simple thin pancakes, filled with cottage cheese or cream cheese or sour cream, made quick meatless meals for many a busy farm wife.

The batter is rich and nicely textured with fresh sweet corn. Be sure to let it sit a while (best overnight) before using it so that all the air bubbles rise to the top. This keeps the batter thin and even on the griddle.

We make small blintzes for appetizers, filling them with the Ricotta-Parmesan-Herb Blintz Filling (page 91). For entrées we make them a bit larger and add fresh sautéed peppers or blanched asparagus to the filling.

> *½ cup unbleached all-purpose flour*
> *½ cup half-and-half*
> *2 eggs*
> *½ teaspoon salt*
> *Freshly ground pepper to taste*
> *2 tablespoons butter, melted*
> *1 cup fresh corn kernels*
> *Vegetable oil for the skillet*

*I*n a blender or food processor fitted with a steel blade, blend together the flour, half-and-half, eggs, salt, pepper, and butter. Add the corn and blend for about 30 seconds more, until the corn is coarsely puréed. Allow the batter to rest at least 15 minutes or overnight.

Heat a griddle or large skillet over medium-high heat until beads of water dance across it. Lightly grease the skillet with oil, using a paper towel. Pour 2 tablespoons to ¼ cup batter at intervals onto the skillet, leaving space between—do not crowd the skillet. When bubbles begin to form on top, gently flip each blintz over and continue to cook until lightly browned. Remove each blintz from the skillet and immediately place about 1 to 2 tablespoons of the filling in the center. Then roll the pancake up and place it seam down on a cookie sheet. When all are done, put the blintzes into a 350°F oven to warm the filling through, about 15 to 20 minutes. (If you're planning to hold the blintzes more than 20 minutes, cover them with aluminum foil so they do not dry out.)

To make these several hours or even a day ahead, stack the cooked blintzes between waxed paper, wrap in plastic wrap, and refrigerate. Before serving, fill the blintzes, place them on a cookie sheet, cover with aluminum foil, and put them into a 350°F oven to warm through.

RICOTTA-PARMESAN-HERB BLINTZ FILLING

**MAKES ABOUT 1½ CUPS
(ENOUGH FOR 8 TO 10 BLINTZES)**

*T*ry substituting Gouda or Cheddar cheese for the Parmesan. The filling will keep a day, covered with plastic wrap, in the refrigerator.

> *1 cup ricotta cheese or Fresh Ricotta Cheese (page 86)*
> *½ cup grated Parmesan cheese*
> *1 egg*
> *2 tablespoons chopped fresh basil*
> *1 teaspoon nutmeg*
> *Salt and freshly ground pepper to taste*

*C*ombine all of the ingredients and add salt and freshly ground pepper to taste.

BUTTER—THE HEARTLAND'S GOLD

A SIMPLE LUXURY

Butter is a luxury few Northern Heartlanders have ever done without. Early settlers traveled west with their simple belongings and a cow tethered to the back of the wagon, milk churning itself in a barrel along the way. Fresh butter in a supper of porridge cooked over the campfire made a filling meal.

Through the mid-1800s almost every family in Wisconsin, Minnesota, and Iowa had at least one cow, whether or not they lived on a farm. It wasn't

until 1910 that cities like Virginia, Minnesota, passed ordinances forbidding livestock in the street.

Housewives would make butter at least once a week, using a dasher, paddle, or crank butter churn. Warm milk was strained and cooled, and the cream was skimmed from the top and put into the churn, turned by the children or, in some homes, the family dog hooked to a treadmill. Washed, salted, and packed into wooden tubs or earthenware crocks, the butter was stored in the cool springhouse.

When cows "went dry" or when the milk lacked enough fat, superstitious farmers believed evil spirits were at work. To ward off witches, Swedes would tie a mountain ash branch to the churn; the Germans would pray to Saint Aneca.

A SUBSTANCE OF COUNTERFEIT

By the 1850s Northern Heartland dairy cooperatives were supplying the country (indeed, much of the world) with their butter, so when the French introduced oleomargarine to this country, the Wisconsin Dairymen's Association rallied to protect a treasured natural resource. Declared "a substance to counterfeit an article of food" by state legislatures, the first margarines were heavily taxed and regulated. Until 1979, retailers needed a license to sell margarine in Wisconsin, and Minnesota and Iowa required it to be sold lard-white. (Packages included a tube, bag, or tablet with yellow coloring that could be kneaded into the fat by hand.)

Today most margarine is made by butter companies and marketed as a healthy, lower-cost alternative to butter. However, claims of "no cholesterol" soy, corn, and cottonseed oil products are misleading because they contain tans-fatty acids, from the hydrogenation process, that are as harmful to one's health as the cholesterol in butter.

Margarine brands may promise "honest-to-butter flavor," but nothing melts into a slice of home-baked bread or enriches a sauce like pure golden butter. Butter will always be the standard by which others are judged.

SWEET AND SAVORY BUTTERS

*W*e like to use herb butters to flavor a grilled chicken breast or poached fish. Sweet and spicy butters melt wonderfully into hot English muffins, waffles, and muffins.

All of these recipes make a quarter pound of butter and are easily doubled. Shaped into logs and wrapped in plastic wrap, they freeze well.

CHARDONNAY BUTTER

1 shallot, peeled and chopped
1 stick (8 tablespoons) butter, softened
2 tablespoons Chardonnay
1 tablespoon chopped fresh herbs (like oregano, basil, marjoram, rosemary) or 1 teaspoon dried

*I*n a small saucepan, lightly sauté the shallot in *2 teaspoons* of the butter. Turn off the heat and add the wine and herbs, then cool. Beat in the remaining butter and shape into a log with your hands or pat into one large butter crock or several small ones. Refrigerate before serving. This butter is delicious on grilled fish, grilled chicken, and roasted vegetables.

ROASTED GARLIC BUTTER

1 large head garlic
1 teaspoon olive oil
1 stick (8 tablespoons) butter, softened
Salt and freshly ground white pepper to taste

*C*ut off the top of the garlic, exposing the cloves, and drizzle the olive oil over and into the garlic. Put the garlic on a baking sheet and roast it in a pre-heated 250°F oven for 1 hour. Squeeze out the roasted garlic cloves and beat them into the butter. Add salt and freshly ground white pepper to taste. Shape the butter into a log or press into one large crock or several small ones. Refrigerate before serving. Great with hot crusty bread, grilled steak, and baked potatoes.

LEMON-SPICE HONEY BUTTER

1 tablespoon honey
2 teaspoons grated lemon rind
1 teaspoon lemon juice
½ teaspoon ground cardamom
1 teaspoon grated fresh gingerroot (optional)
1 stick (8 tablespoons) butter, softened

*B*eat all of the ingredients into the butter. Shape the butter into a log or press into one large crock or several small ones. Refrigerate before serving. This butter is delicious over grilled pork chops, as well as with bread and muffins.

MAPLE-ALMOND-PECAN OR SPICY-NUT BUTTER

2 tablespoons maple syrup
2 tablespoons ground pecans or Spicy Nuts (page 296)
½ teaspoon almond extract
1 stick (8 tablespoons) butter, softened

*B*eat all of the ingredients into the butter. Shape the butter into a log or press into one large crock or several small ones and refrigerate before serving. Serve with Pancakes (page 42) or on grilled pork chops (page 115).

NORTHERN HEARTLAND CHEESE

Cheese-making in the Northern Heartland dates back to the mid-1800s when farmers formed the first dairy cooperatives. As the wheat fields of Minnesota and Wisconsin became depleted and were turned into grasslands, the Scandinavian settlers continued west in search of better soil. Newly arrived Swiss, German, East European, and Italian immigrants, who were used to a life "tied to a cow," began producing cheese for the nation and eventually for markets as far away as Hong Kong.

Today independent cheesemakers continue to thrive throughout the region, despite dramatic industry consolidation over the last seventy years. While large corporations dominate supermarket shelves with consistent products, entrepreneurs have found growing markets in co-ops and specialty shops for a wide variety of farmstead and raw-milk European-style cheese. Here's a quick guide to notable Northern Heartland cheese available throughout the country. (For more complete information on individual factories, see Sources, page 372.)

COLBY: Of the one hundred different kinds of cheese made in Wisconsin, only Colby is considered native to the area. It was developed in 1885 by Joseph Steinwald, whose father, Ambrose, had opened a Cheddar cheese factory in the town of Colby three years before. Colby is lower in acid than Cheddar, and it is eaten fresh, not aged. Its curds are often pressed into round cylinders for long-horn Colby.

MAYTAG BLUE: This creamy, pungent blue cheese was developed by Frederick Maytag, grandson of the washing-machine mogul, to make use of the milk from his father's prize-winning Holstein cows. Maytag, with researchers from Iowa State University, developed a mold from whole wheat bread crusts and built man-made curing caves. The big, well-ripened wheels are divided into wedges with special cutters fashioned from old washing machines.

RAW-MILK CHEDDAR AND GOUDA: The area's clover-sweet milk makes Northern Heartland cheeses distinct, especially those made with unpasteurized milk. Pasteurization kills all the milk's bacteria, some of which give cheese its unique flavor. Under U.S. law, raw-milk cheeses must be aged at least sixty days because any impurities will surface during that period. As in Europe, each batch of raw-milk cheese is unique, owing its personality to differences between the cows and what they ate.

🐦 GOAT'S MILK CHEESES: For the past ten years, regional cheesemakers have been producing chèvre (a fresh cheese), goat's milk brie, Colby, and Monterey Jack. Goat's milk is easier to digest and lower in cholesterol and calories than cow's milk, and it is high in potassium, vitamin A, thiamin, and niacin. Goat's milk cheeses melt quickly and tend not to separate in cooking.

🐦 SHEEP'S MILK CHEESES: The country's first sheep's milk cheese factory, La Paysanne, was founded by Lucy Steinkamp, a Parisian, who learned the art from her grandmother. The tiny factory in Hinckley, Minnesota, produces over twenty different varieties (from crumbly feta to aged Romano). Unlike cow's milk, sheep's milk is lactose free and contains mostly polyunsaturated or monounsaturated fats. It is especially rich in calcium and phosphorus. The low melting point of sheep's milk cheese makes it a good choice on pasta and toasted sandwiches.

🐦 TRADITIONAL ITALIAN CHEESES (Parmesan, Gorgonzola, Romano, provolone, fontina, Asiago, mascarpone): Drawn to cheap land, good labor, and excellent milk, Italian cheese companies opened factories in pastoral Wisconsin in the early 1900s. Companies like Tolibia and Auricchio continue to use one-hundred-year-old cultures and recipes to make their traditional cheeses.

BAKED WISCONSIN GOAT
CHEESE ON CROUTONS

SERVES 6

*F*or this simple salad we marinate the young goat cheese in olive oil to enhance its creamy texture and mellow flavor. (The marinated cheese will keep a week in the refrigerator.) We serve the baked croutons with greens tossed with Shallot Vinaigrette (page 252).

> *6–8 ounces goat cheese*
> *1 cup good-quality olive oil*
> *1 clove garlic, crushed*
> *2 tablespoons fresh herbs, like basil, tarragon, thyme,*
> *marjoram (alone or in combination)*
> *4–6 slices white bread for croutons, cut into desired shapes*

*M*arinate the goat cheese in olive oil, garlic, and herbs at least 1 hour or overnight. Brush the bread slices with some of the olive oil, then lightly toast them in a preheated 450°F oven for a few minutes. (Be careful that they don't burn.) Spread equal amounts of the cheese over the croutons and "blast" them in the hot oven for 1 to 2 minutes, until the cheese is hot but not melted or gooey.

DUMPLINGS

SERVES 6 TO 8

"*M*y Polish grandmother made her pierogi big and filled them with cabbage or kraut, served them with melted butter and lots of bread. That would fill you up after a day in the field," recalls Ellen Carlson of North Oaks, Minnesota.

The Czechs do not fill their pierogi, but serve them with butter and cheese. The Germans grate shredded cheese over their *knofli,* a companion to sauerkraut, served alongside a roast. Bread dumplings, cracker-meal dumplings, farina dumplings, and raw or cooked potato dumplings—everyone has a favorite recipe, and no two are quite alike.

The dough for these dumplings is easy to make. They are good served sprinkled with grated Parmesan cheese and chopped fresh herbs as a light dinner or first course. Or poach them in broth for a light soup. They are best eaten right away.

> *1 cup milk*
> *1 stick (8 tablespoons) butter*
> *¼ teaspoon salt*
> *1 cup unbleached all-purpose flour*
> *4 eggs*
> *¼ cup Parmesan cheese, plus a little more for garnish*

*I*n a large saucepan, bring the milk to a boil and add the butter. Then add the salt and flour, beating the dough with a wooden spoon until it becomes a paste that pulls away from the sides of the pan and forms a rough dough. Keep stirring for 30 seconds, then remove from the heat.

Beat the eggs into the dough one at a time, beating well after each addition. Stir in the Parmesan cheese. Cover the dough with plastic wrap and chill about 20 to 30 minutes. Bring a large pot of lightly salted water to a rolling boil, and with a teaspoon, scoop up portions of the dough and drop them into simmering salted water, being careful not to crowd the pot. The dough should puff up and float to the surface within a minute or so. Poach the dumplings about 6 to 8 minutes. They should feel firm and look white and light when done.

NOODLES AND DUMPLINGS

In the days when both men and women worked long and hard in the fields, the biggest share of the day's calories came from carbohydrates. Noodles, dumplings, and cornmeal dishes, all nutritious starches, were a large part of every cook's repertoire. Especially on meatless days, noodles and dumplings teamed up with cheese and eggs or were tossed with lots of butter and served with vegetables and bread. Noodles baked with sour cream or simply tossed with butter and honey also made a simple dessert.

What our ancestors knew instinctively, we have documented scientifically—that carbohydrates are a quick and salutary source of energy. Many traditional recipes for German spaetzle, Polish gnocci, and Czech dumplings are surprisingly fast and easy. Toss with fresh, seasonal vegetables and a bit of shredded cheese.

Pauline Mueller of St. Paul using an innovative spaetzle maker (a ricer) to produce quantities of the tiny noodles.

SPAETZLE
(TINY NOODLES)

SERVES 4 TO 6

*S*paetzle, meaning "little sparrow" in German, is traditionally served with roast meat and gravy, or by itself, well buttered and tossed with lots of grated Swiss cheese.

These tiny dumplings can be tricky to make. The experienced cook deftly works the sticky dough off the end of a spoon with his or her thumb—this takes lots of practice. It's a bit easier to press the dough through a colander with the back of a spoon or rubber spatula or squeeze it through a ricer. The dough will become easier to work with as it warms over the simmering water or stock.

> 2 cups unbleached all-purpose flour
> 2 eggs
> 1/2 cup heavy cream
> 1/4 cup milk
> 1/4 teaspoon each, salt and freshly ground pepper
> 1/8 teaspoon nutmeg
> 1 tablespoon chopped fresh parsley
> Salted water or broth

*M*ix together the flour, eggs, cream, milk, salt, pepper, nutmeg, and parsley in a medium-sized bowl until the dough is smooth. The dough should be elastic enough to stretch about 6 inches.

Fill a large kettle with water or broth and bring to a boil, then lower the heat to simmer. Rinse your utensils (potato ricer or colander) in cold water before they come in contact with the dough. Working in batches, take 1/4 cup of the dough and press it through a colander or ricer directly into the simmering water. Simmer the spaetzle for about 2 minutes, then remove with a slotted spoon, drain, and place in a serving dish and cover. Repeat with the remaining dough. The spaetzle may be kept warm in the oven for about 10 to 15 minutes before serving.

NOODLES WITH ZESTY ITALIAN
CHEESE AND
FRESH TOMATO SAUCE

SERVES 6 TO 8

*T*his dish tastes best when fresh tomatoes are at their peak. The slightly acidic flavor balances the rich creamy sauce. Off season, try good-quality Italian plum tomatoes (drained) and increase the amounts of garlic and onion.

CHEESE SAUCE

2 tablespoons butter
2 tablespoons unbleached all-purpose flour
2 cups milk
1 cup grated sharp Italian cheese (such as Asiago and/or fontina)
1 teaspoon salt
1½ teaspoons freshly ground pepper
Pinch nutmeg

1 pound wide noodles

FRESH TOMATO SAUCE

½ large red onion, peeled and diced
1 clove garlic, minced
1 tablespoon olive oil
2 tablespoons red wine (optional)
4–5 fresh tomatoes, peeled, seeded, and diced
Salt and freshly ground pepper to taste
2 tablespoons chopped fresh basil

¼ cup grated Parmesan cheese
Cracked black pepper
Fresh opal basil leaves (purple) for garnish

*T*o make the cheese sauce, melt the butter over low heat and blend in the flour, stirring for 3 to 5 minutes, until well blended. Slowly add the milk and simmer, stirring the sauce with a wire whisk until it has thickened and is smooth and hot. Stir in the cheese or cheeses until they have melted and the sauce is thick and creamy. Add the salt, pepper, and nutmeg. Set aside and cover to keep warm.

Meanwhile, to make the tomato sauce, lightly sauté the onion and garlic in the olive oil over medium heat until soft. Add the wine and the fresh tomatoes and toss together. Cover and cook about 3 minutes on low. Season with salt and pepper to taste. Remove the pan from the heat and add the chopped fresh basil.

Bring a large pot of salted water to a rolling boil and cook the noodles about 8 to 10 minutes (or according to package directions), until they are just done but still firm to the bite.

Toss the noodles with the cheese sauce and serve on individual plates or a large platter with the fresh tomato sauce on top. Garnish the dish with grated Parmesan cheese, cracked black pepper, and fresh basil leaves.

BARNYARD AND SMOKEHOUSE

FARMHOUSE MEATS

Like the harvest of corn in late summer or fresh greens in the spring, fall butchering brought a welcome change to the diet. It promised not only wonderful meals but a round of family dinners and neighborly exchange. "Just before the freeze, when it was cool enough that the meat wouldn't spoil, we'd plan a week of butchering with our families and friends," recalls Hunk Schere of Plymouth, Minnesota. "We Germans always celebrated with Oktoberfest. The kraut was ready, and there was nothing like those fresh spareribs and sausage," says Hunk. Today, towns like New Ulm, Minnesota, hold Oktoberfest celebrations with German oompah bands and bratwurst "feeds."

From the time the first pioneers settled, hogs were welcome in the barnyard. They took up little space and were cheap to feed with leftovers, scraps, and garbage. The meat—fresh, smoked, salted, and in sausages—provided meals of great variety, plus lard for baking and frying, and tallow for candles. Nothing was wasted in the immigrant kitchen, where people prided themselves on using "everything but the squeal."

Making sausages was a way of using up all of the butchering scraps (see the Communal Pot chapter); dishes like Swedish meatballs, Croatian *sarma* (cabbage rolls), and various meat loaves were inspired by leftover cuts. Today these recipes are easily duplicated with packaged ground meat.

Beef butchered from the family cow, too old to produce milk and raised on grass, was sure to be tough and lean. It was stewed or braised a long time, allowing busy cooks to attend to other household chores. Flavorful ethnic dishes, such as sauerbraten (marinated German pot roast), were always appreciated in this part of America, and they remain appealing today for their rich flavor and because they are so easy to prepare ahead.

Before refrigeration, meats were kept chilled or frozen during the long, cold winters, and smoking was a common practice on most farms. Sausages, hams, and bacon hung in the smokehouse, beef was corned, and lamb was sometimes dried—all ready to make into a quick meal or flavor a hearty soup.

Today, because of our concern about fat and cholesterol, we are eating less fresh and smoked meat, balancing our plates with vegetables, noodles, potatoes, and rice. Farmers are raising lean pigs and grass-fed beef and bison. In this chapter we've collected some old family favorites such as *porketta,* a traditional Iron Range pork roast infused with garlic and fennel, slowly cooked until succulent and juicy. We've created lighter recipes such as Veal Chop with Shiitake Mushrooms and Pears, which was inspired by wild mushrooms from the damp woods and sweet orchard pears. And we've selected marinades and basting sauces that flavor lean cuts of meat and are delicious on grilled poultry and vegetables, too.

PORK TENDERLOIN
WITH DRIED CHERRIES

SERVES 4 TO 6

*T*his simple (albeit rich) dish makes a delicious and impressive entrée when entertaining. The pork is tender and the dried cherries add a wonderful sweet-tart flavor to the sauce. If dried cherries are not available, substitute chopped dried apricots.

> ½ cup dried cherries*
> ¾ cup Madeira
> 1 whole pork tenderloin (1¼–1½ pounds)
> ½ teaspoon dried thyme
> ½ teaspoon crushed juniper berries
> ½ cup unbleached all-purpose flour
> Salt and freshly ground pepper
> ½ stick (4 tablespoons) butter
> ¾ cup white wine
> 1 cup homemade Chicken Stock†
> ¾ cup heavy cream (or Thickened Cream, page 87)

> *Dried cherries are available in most supermarkets (near the raisins and dried fruit), co-ops, and specialty shops. Chopped dried apricots may be substituted (or see Sources, page 372).*

> †*For homemade Chicken Stock, see page 141, or use low-salt canned broth.*

*I*n a small saucepan, combine the dried cherries with the Madeira and bring to just under a boil; then remove from heat and let the cherries steep until they are plump.

Cut the pork into thin slices (about ½ inch thick) and lightly pound between parchment paper or plastic wrap until not quite flat. Sprinkle the slices with the thyme and juniper and allow to rest for about 10 minutes.

Season the flour with salt and pepper. Dip each slice of pork into the

Pork Tenderloin with Dried Cherries (continued)

flour, shaking off the excess. Melt the butter in a large skillet and sauté the pork (about 30 seconds per side) until it is browned and cooked through. Remove the slices from the pan, set them on a warm plate, and tent with aluminum foil to keep warm.

Pour out any excess butter and immediately return the skillet to high heat. Deglaze the pan by pouring the white wine into it and scraping with a fork or spatula to loosen any of the browned bits of meat. Continue cooking over medium-high heat and reduce the wine to a syrupy consistency. (It should be thick enough to just coat the back of a spoon.) Then add the Madeira and cherries and the chicken stock, and reduce again. Add the cream and continue cooking and stirring until the sauce thickens.

PORKETTA
(GARLIC-FENNEL PORK ROAST)

SERVES 8 TO 10 (OR LESS, DEPENDING ON HOW MANY LEFTOVERS YOU'D LIKE)

*P*orketta is of Italian origin, but this garlic-studded, fennel-flavored long-cooked roast has been adapted by everyone—Finn, Norwegian, and Cornish alike—who grew up on the Iron Range, the iron-mining area of northern Minnesota. Its very mention will elicit tender declarations from even the most stoic north woodsman.

This recipe was inspired by Margaret Erjavec of Virginia, Minnesota, who contributed it to *The Old Country Cookbook.** You may want to adjust the seasonings according to your own tastes. The meat must be cooked until it falls apart when touched with a fork. *Porketta* should not be sliced, but pulled apart. It is wonderful served with roasted potatoes at supper, and is even better the next day or the day after, when eaten between slices of homemade Old-fashioned Milk Bread (page 6).

> 1 boneless pork butt roast (6 pounds)
> 2 teaspoons salt
> 2 tablespoons freshly ground black pepper
> 10 cloves garlic, coarsely chopped
> 1 cup chopped fresh parsley
> ½ cup fennel seeds
> ¼ cup olive oil
> 1 large fennel bulb, finely chopped
> 6 new potatoes, cut into large chunks
> 2 stalks celery, cut into chunks
> 6 carrots, cut into chunks
> 2 medium onions, peeled and cut into chunks

*C*ut the roast in half lengthwise and open it like a book. Combine all of the seasoning ingredients with the olive oil and rub it over both sides of the meat, pressing the fennel seeds and garlic into the meat. Spread the chopped fennel bulb over the meat, then fold the meat back together or roll it up and secure with a string. Place the meat in a roasting pan, cover, and bake in a preheated 325°F oven for 3 to 4 hours. Toward the last 30 minutes of cooking, scatter the vegetables on the bottom of the roasting pan and continue cooking the roast until it falls apart when touched with a fork.

Remove the roast from the pan and allow it to sit about 5 minutes before pulling it apart to serve with the vegetables.

*For more information, see Sources (page 372).

PORK LOIN WITH APPLES AND CIDER SAUCE

SERVES 6 TO 8

*I*n the apple-growing states of Minnesota, Wisconsin, and Iowa, apples, along with fresh, tart cider and brandy or applejack, find their way into a variety of pork recipes.

1 boneless pork loin (about 3⅓ pounds), rolled and tied
Brine for pork roast (page 111)
2 tablespoons butter
2 tablespoons vegetable oil
2 scallions, chopped
4 apples, peeled, cored, and chopped
2 carrots, chopped
1 onion, chopped
¼ cup brandy or applejack
3 cups apple cider
3 cups homemade Chicken Stock (page 141), or low-salt
   canned broth
4 fresh thyme sprigs, or 1 tablespoon dried
Bay leaf
8 peppercorns
¼–½ cup good-quality mustard (depending on taste)
Salt and freshly ground pepper to taste
Sautéed apple slices for garnish

*P*lace the pork loin in a noncorrosive bowl and add the brine solution, then refrigerate overnight. Drain the pork loin and pat it dry.

Heat a large, deep pan or flameproof casserole over medium-high heat. Add the butter and oil and sear the pork loin on all sides. Remove the meat from the pan, then add the scallions, apples, carrots, and onion, and sauté in the remaining fat. When the vegetables are soft, add the brandy and reduce the liquid by boiling for 1 minute. Add the cider, chicken stock, thyme, bay leaf, and peppercorns.

Return the pork to the pan with the vegetables and bring to a simmer; cover and then place it in a preheated 350°F oven and braise for about 2¼ to 2¾ hours, or until the internal temperature reaches 160°F on a meat thermometer. Juices should run clear. Take the loin from the pan, set it on a platter, and tent the meat with aluminum foil to keep it warm.

Strain the cooking liquid through a sieve, pressing with the back of a wooden spoon. Return the liquid to the pan and boil vigorously, skimming frequently. Beat in the mustard with a whisk, and season to taste.* Serve the pork garnished with sautéed apple slices and additional fresh thyme sprigs.

For a thicker sauce, turn the vegetables with the pan juices into a blender and purée. Serve alongside the pork.

BRINE

MAKES 4 GALLONS

Brining is an age-old method of preserving meat or preparing it for the smokehouse that also makes the meat more tender and succulent. The brine is made with enough salt and sugar to "float an egg."

4 gallons water
2 bay leaves
2 cups salt
2 cups sugar
1 teaspoon allspice berries
2 teaspoons dried thyme

Bring all the ingredients to a boil in a stockpot. Cool before soaking the meat in the brine.

COUNTRY SPARERIBS
AND SAUERKRAUT

SERVES 6 TO 8

*N*ew Ulm, Minnesota (like Green Bay, Wisconsin, and Amana, Iowa), reserves the third weekend in October for an autumn feast—Oktoberfest. It is a celebration of the harvest: the pigs are slaughtered, and the kraut is nicely soured in its big barrel. Oompah bands parade down Main Street, and the dancing lasts all weekend.

One of the region's oldest breweries, August Schell (founded in New Ulm in 1860) releases its Schell Bock and Oktoberfest in time for the celebration. Special dark, malty-sweet Oktoberfest beer complements the traditional *schlactplat:* huge platters of pork ribs, sausage, and sauerkraut. Serve this dish with boiled potatoes, Braised Red Cabbage with Apples and Bacon (page 271), or Country Sauerkraut (page 268), rye bread, and fresh applesauce.

4 teaspoons dried thyme
4 teaspoons freshly ground pepper
1 teaspoon salt
½ teaspoon rubbed sage
2 tablespoons Dijon mustard
1 tablespoon horseradish (grated fresh, if available)
2 tablespoons caraway seeds
4 pounds country-style spareribs
2 tablespoons vegetable oil
2 large onions, peeled and thinly sliced
4 cloves garlic, chopped
One 12-ounce bottle dark beer (amber lager)
2 cups homemade Dark Stock (page 142), or low-salt
   canned broth
3 bay leaves
2 large apples, cored and thinly sliced
6–8 bratwurst or knockwurst sausage (optional)

Boiled potatoes
Fresh parsley for garnish
Braised red cabbage or sauerkraut (optional)

*I*n a small bowl, stir together *2 teaspoons* of the thyme, *2 teaspoons* of the pepper, salt, sage, mustard, horseradish, and caraway seeds, then spread evenly over the ribs. Heat the oil in a large Dutch oven or heat-proof casserole, add the onions and garlic, and cook until the onions are a light brown. Add the beer and stock, along with the remaining teaspoons of thyme and pepper, the bay leaves and apple slices, and stir, turning the apples, until thoroughly combined. Place the spareribs on top of the onion mixture. Cover the casserole and put it in a preheated 350°F oven. Bake for 1 hour and then remove the cover. If including sausage, add it to the casserole and continue baking another 30 to 40 minutes, until the ribs are tender. Serve the ribs (and optional sausage) on a large platter surrounded by boiled potatoes garnished with parsley, or with braised red cabbage or sauerkraut, if desired.

A prizewinning hog, Minnesota State Fair, 1926

HOOSIER PORK

In the pioneer days, when pigs were left to forage in the woods for food, hoosier pork was a treat. Hoosiers were self-supporting hogs whose snouts were so long they could poke through a fence and root up a row of potatoes. Today hogs are scientifically raised lean, and some cuts actually match skinless chicken and turkey in calories and fat. Iowa leads the country in individual hog operations, producing over 25 percent of the pork eaten in the United States over the past several years.

Thanks to advances in raising and processing technology, commercially sold pork is free of trichinosis, and it is no longer necessary to overcook pork until it is tough and dry.

Here are a few suggestions for cooking low-fat pork that will help to keep it moist and tender:

🐖 Soak pork in brine (page 111) several hours or overnight in the refrigerator before cooking.

🐖 Use low, not high heat, and cook pork slowly.

🐖 Keep about 1 inch of liquid (stock, wine, or water) in the roasting pan.

🐖 Don't overcook pork. Pork should be cooked just until the internal temperature is 160 degrees Fahrenheit for flavor, tenderness, and juiciness. (A meat thermometer is the best guide.)

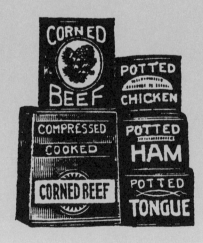

IOWA CHOPS
WITH SAVORY RUB

SERVES 4

*T*he Iowa Chop is not just any old pork chop. Ester Vermeer, a pork producer in Leighton, Iowa, explains: "A true Iowa chop is a lean center-cut loin or rib chop that's an inch and a quarter to an inch and a half thick. I don't think I've ever served an Iowa chop to anyone who hasn't liked it."

The dry rub in this recipe is made with spices and salt that penetrate the meat with flavor. It's also delicious used to flavor larger cuts of beef, pork, and lamb.

> *2 bay leaves*
> *1 tablespoon freshly ground pepper*
> *3 cloves garlic, peeled*
> *1 tablespoon dried thyme or ¼ cup chopped fresh*
> *2 teaspoons ground cloves*
> *1 tablespoon ground nutmeg*
> *1 teaspoon ground cinnamon*
> *½ teaspoon ground cardamom*
> *4 thick premium loin pork chops (10 ounces each)*
> *1 tablespoon olive oil*
> *1 tablespoon each, butter and olive oil or just olive oil*

*I*n a coffee grinder, spice mill, or blender, process the bay leaves, pepper, garlic, thyme, cloves, nutmeg, cinnamon, and cardamom until completely blended. (The bay leaves will not be totally crushed.) Rub the chops with the olive oil, then rub the spice blend over all of the chops. Cover and set aside for about 30 minutes to 1 hour at room temperature.

Sear the chops in the butter/oil in a heavy skillet over high heat about 3 to 4 minutes per side, until they are golden brown. Place the chops on a cookie sheet and bake in a preheated 400°F oven for about 30 minutes, or until the juices run clear.

CIDER-SOAKED AND BROWN-SUGAR-GLAZED HAM

SERVES 20 FOR DINNER OR 40 FOR SANDWICHES AND SNACKS

*T*he Easter ham evokes strong memories for those who remember those meatless Lenten meals when families ate mostly eggs—fried, scrambled, poached, and deviled. Rose Block of Pierz, Minnesota, recalls: "After church, we dyed eggs with red onion skins, and they turned a lovely shade of reddish brown, while mother put that ham in the roaster until it was warm and juicy. We'd feast on homemade bread with chokecherry jelly, and lettuce salad dressed with cream."

This ham makes a simple but tempting centerpiece to a holiday buffet table, with leftovers for the busy season. Have the butcher saw off the hock to use in soup.

> *1 bone-in country ham (about 9–10 pounds)*
> *1 gallon apple cider*
> *20–30 whole cloves*
> *1 cup brown sugar, light or dark*
> *1 tablespoon good quality mustard*

*S*oak the ham in the cider overnight. (It's easiest to place the ham in a large kitchen-size plastic bag and then add the cider and tie the bag at the top. This way, the entire ham is covered with the cider.)

Remove the ham and reserve about 3 cups of the cider. Stud the ham with cloves and place in a large roasting pan, then add the reserved cider. Bake the ham in a preheated 350°F oven, allowing about 15 minutes per pound, basting every 30 minutes with the cider in the pan.

Pour ¼ cup of cider from the pan into a small saucepan and add the brown sugar and mustard. Bring to a boil over medium heat. About 20 minutes before removing the ham from the oven, baste the ham with the brown sugar mixture several times so that it becomes shiny and glazed.

Remove the ham from the oven and allow to stand 10 minutes before slicing.

DAYS AFTER THE HOLIDAY HAM

Leftover ham is a bonus for creative cooks with a seasonal cadre of relatives and friends to feed. Here are a few easy suggestions:

🐖 Wrap thinly sliced ham around blanched asparagus, green beans, or broccoli spears and serve with a mustard mayonnaise.

🐖 Make sandwiches of thinly sliced ham, cream cheese, and chutney.

🐖 Stuff artichokes with sautéed mushrooms, chopped ham, and cream sauce.

🐖 Toss matchstick-size pieces of ham with blue cheese and walnuts into a salad of romaine lettuce and dress with Maple-Mustard Vinaigrette (page 253).

🐖 Make a casserole of creamed mushrooms, olives, chopped ham, and mustard and top with our Biscuit Crust (page 170).

🐖 Cube the ham and toss into omelets and scrambled eggs.

RULLE POLSE
(SCANDINAVIAN MEAT ROLL)

SERVES 10 TO 12

*T*his recipe makes flavorful use of an inexpensive cut of meat that, with proper seasoning and care, is a festive addition to the cold section of the holiday table. Lucia's mother remembers that her mother made this at Christmas using a special wooden press that helped extract the excess moisture so that the meat could be sliced very thin.

Serve this cold, on dark bread with coarse mustard.

Rulle Polse *(continued)*

> *1 beef flank steak (about 1¼ pounds)*
> *2 tablespoons Dijon mustard*
> *½ pound pork sausage*
> *1 cup peeled, finely chopped onions*
> *¼ teaspoon ground cloves*
> *¼ teaspoon ground allspice*
> *¼ teaspoon salt*
> *¼ teaspoon freshly ground pepper*
> *Cotton string*
> *½ cup red wine*
> *4 quarts homemade Dark Stock (page 142), or low-salt*
> *   canned broth, or half water/half stock*
> *12 whole peppercorns*
> *12 allspice berries*
> *12 whole cloves*
> *2 bay leaves*

*B*utterfly the flank steak. Use a long, thin, sharp knife and start cutting through the center of the meat at the long end, working up so that you leave a "living hinge" at the flank's edge (or have the butcher do it); the steak will open like a book. Trim off the ragged edges to make an even rectangle. Place the steak cut side up on a worktable. Rub the the steak with mustard. Mix together the pork sausage with the onions, cloves, allspice, salt, and pepper, and spread over the rectangle, leaving bare a 1-inch flap along the top of the flank.

Roll (*rulle*) the flank steak into a sausage (*polse*), jelly-roll style, starting at the long end. Roll it tightly until you have an even log, and secure the roll with cotton string tied in three places (on both ends and in the middle).

In a large stockpot, bring the red wine and stock to a rolling boil and add the whole peppercorns, allspice berries, whole cloves, and bay leaves. Place the roll into the stock, reduce the heat, and simmer for about 1 hour.

Remove the roll, draining off as much liquid as possible. (Save the liquid for soup such as Yellow Split Pea Soup, page 150). Place the roll in a large baking pan, or press, and cover it with aluminum foil. Then place a plate on top of that and weight it down with a heavy book or rock. Refrigerate this overnight. When ready to eat, slice the steak thin and serve with mustard and dark bread.

MIXED KEBABS WITH ORANGE-HONEY MARINADE

SERVES 4 TO 6 (MARINADE MAKES 2½ CUPS.)

*T*his simple marinade helps tenderize the meat and give it a light fresh taste, and the honey forms a glaze as it grills. Try it on chicken and fish, too.

MARINADE

Grated zest of 2 oranges
1½ cups fresh orange juice
¼ cup balsamic vinegar
2 tablespoons honey
1 tablespoon soy sauce
1 tablespoon crushed garlic

1½–2 pounds kebab meat (pork, beef, lamb combination)*

*For kebab meat, use boneless center-cut pork, leg of lamb, and top sirloin of beef.

*W*hisk together the marinade ingredients and pour over the meat. Marinate the meat at least 1 hour at room temperature or longer in the refrigerator. String the meat onto kebab skewers and cook about 5 to 10 minutes over medium-high coals, basting frequently with the marinade, until the meat is no longer pink when sliced.

HEARTLAND GRILLING

James E. Calhoun, an explorer, wrote about a barbecue party in 1823: "We made our supper of the spoils of the hunt, which we had brought fastened to our saddles. We cooked the meat in our usual way by inclining to the fire the sharpened stick thrust through it and stuck into the ground."

Today grilling is more popular than ever in the Northern Heartland— even in winter.

SEASONED FLANK STEAK
FOR SUMMER AND WINTER

SERVES 4 TO 6

*I*n this simple recipe the steak is first rubbed with mustard and seasonings, then broiled or grilled, depending on the weather. In winter serve the steak thinly sliced on a bed of Wild Rice Pilaf with Dried Cherries and Walnuts (page 279) and topped with Sweet Corn Relish (page 290) or Cranberry-Sage Butter (page 196). In summer serve the steak thinly sliced on a salad of seasonal vegetables, tossed in a Creamy Mustard-Herb Dressing (page 256).

> *4 tablespoons olive oil*
> *1 tablespoon Dijon mustard*
> *Salt and freshly ground pepper*
> *1 flank steak (about 1½ pounds)*

*M*ix together the olive oil, mustard, salt and freshly ground pepper, and rub over the entire steak.

SUMMER

> *2 cups mixed greens (spinach, beet greens, mustard greens, watercress)*
> *2 cups mixed vegetables (baby bok choy, radishes, baby carrots, sugar snap peas, broccoli flowerets), cut into fork-size pieces*
> *½ cup Creamy Mustard-Herb Dressing (page 256)*

*G*rill the steak about 3 to 5 minutes per side for medium-rare. Remove the steak from the grill and allow to stand about 3 minutes. If using broccoli, sugar snap peas, and carrots, cut them into bite-size pieces and quickly blanch by dipping them in boiling water for about 2 minutes, until the color is bright; then rinse in cold water and drain. Cut thin slices of steak and lay them on a bed of greens and surround with the assorted vegetables. Drizzle all with the Creamy Mustard-Herb Dressing and pass additional dressing alongside.

WINTER

Wild Rice Pilaf (page 279)
½ cup Sweet Corn Relish (page 290) or 4 tablespoons
    Cranberry-Sage Butter (page 196)

*P*repare the Wild Rice Pilaf according to directions on page 279. Preheat the broiler and broil the steak about 5 to 6 minutes per side for medium-rare. Remove the steak from the broiler and allow to rest about 3 minutes. Cut the slices and lay them on ½-cup servings of the pilaf. Top with equal portions of either the Sweet Corn Relish or the Cranberry-Sage Butter and serve immediately.

4-H Clubs (Head, Heart, Hands, and Health) were founded in the early 1900s to give farm youngsters the hands-on learning that schools could not provide. This young man proudly leads his prizewinning bull at the Minnesota State Fair, 1920.

AMANA COLONIES

In 1859 the followers of a German religious movement known as the Community of True Inspiration established the Amana Colonies in eastern Iowa. All property was held in common, and church and secular affairs were governed by the same leaders. The cluster of seven villages revolved around two hubs: church and kitchen. Sixteen communal kitchens catered to about 2,000 residents. In 1930, the Amanas, hit by the Great Depression, voted to separate church and state and emerged from isolation.

In 1950 Elsie Oehler, granddaughter of a community "kitchen boss," established the Ronnenberg restaurant in the same building where she learned to bake, can, and cook over half a century ago. She recalls: "We went to school year-round, with breaks at harvest and planting time. Some of the children helped in the fields, harvesting apples, plowing vegetable patches, picking potato bugs off the vine. I carried baskets of food to the elderly and took sandwiches and cakes to the field-workers for their morning and afternoon coffee breaks.

"We made everything in that community kitchen: sauerkraut, rye bread, coffee cakes, cottage cheese, elderberry wine. The weekly menu always included favorites like sauerbraten with red cabbage. We wasted nothing. Back then, even pine trees in the yard were considered frivolous; only fruit-bearing trees were permitted."

Amana women sorting the small, flavorful "Ebenezer" onions, which they sell.

HEARTLAND BRISKET

SERVES 6 TO 8

*T*his simple braised dish tastes even better warmed in its sauce the next day, or shredded and served on a crusty bun. Serve the brisket with steamed new potatoes and a crisp salad in a lively Shallot Vinaigrette (page 252). If you have any left, it's especially good in the Casserole of Caramelized Onions and Leftover Meat (page 182).

1 brisket (about 3 pounds), rolled and tied
2 tablespoons bacon fat or butter
6 onions, peeled and thinly sliced
4 cloves garlic, peeled and minced
2 cups homemade Dark Stock (page 142) or low-salt
*   canned broth*
¼ cup tomato paste
1 bottle beer (12 ounces)
2 bay leaves
2 teaspoons dried thyme
1 tablespoon caraway seeds
1 tablespoon cracked pepper

*I*n a large, flameproof casserole or roasting pan, brown the meat on all sides in the bacon fat. Remove the meat and set aside. Sauté the onions and garlic until very soft and light brown. Add the stock and stir, making sure to scrape up any of the brown bits on the bottom. Add the remaining ingredients *except the caraway seeds and pepper,* and stir. Put the meat back into the pan, cover, and place in a preheated 350°F oven for about 2½ to 2¾ hours, basting the meat occasionally with the sauce and spreading some of the onions on top. About 30 minutes before the meat is done, sprinkle the top with caraway seeds and pepper. To serve, slice the meat and spoon the sauce on the top.

SWEDISH MEATBALLS

SERVES 8

On Christmas Eve in Swedish homes throughout the Midwest, Swedish meatballs take a prominent place on the traditional smörgåsbord table. "Swedish meatballs were there for the children and anyone else who did not like lutefisk," says Mrs. Wendell Johnson of Ames, Iowa.

There are as many different meatball recipes in the Northern Heartland as there are Swedes. Some recipes call for bread, others for mashed potatoes; some favor an all-beef mixture, while others combine ground pork with beef. Seasonings of allspice, nutmeg, cardamom, and ginger give the Swedish meatball its unique flavor.

The meatballs are traditionally served with a thick gravy made from the pan drippings, boiled new potatoes, lefse, and drawn butter.

1 pound pork sausage
½ pound ground beef
½ pound ground veal
2 slices white bread
¼ cup milk
2 eggs
½ teaspoon ground cardamom
¼ teaspoon ground nutmeg
½ teaspoon ground allspice
¼ teaspoon ground ginger
Salt and freshly ground pepper to taste
Butter or vegetable oil for frying meatballs

GRAVY

2 tablespoons butter
2 tablespoons unbleached all-purpose flour
1 teaspoon Dijon mustard
2 cups homemade Dark Stock (page 142) or low-salt canned broth

*I*n a large bowl, mix together all the ingredients except the butter. (It's best to use your hands to do the mixing.) Shape into small meatballs. Then heat the butter in a large skillet set over medium-high heat and gently brown the meatballs on all sides. Place them on a heated platter in the oven to keep warm.

To make the gravy, blot the grease from the skillet. Add the butter and melt over low heat. Stir in the flour and cook about 1 to 2 minutes, or until brown and bubbly. Stir in the mustard. Slowly stir in the stock and cook until the gravy is thickened and does not taste "floury." Put the meatballs back into the skillet, cover, and cook over very low heat for about 10 minutes.

Substitute ground pork for the sausage, increase the amount of ground beef to 1 pound, and omit the ground veal.

Substitute ¼ cup mashed potatoes or ¼ cup cooked white rice for the bread.

To make a Swedish Meat Loaf, follow the original recipe and pack the mixture into a 9-inch loaf pan. Bake in a 350°F oven about 50 minutes.

SMÖRGÅSBORD

Quality, not quantity, distinguishes a true smörgåsbord. Garnishes are very important: dill, parsley, greens, rinds of citrus fruits. Food and presentation should represent the sun, sea, and earth—the three key elements in Swedish life: the sun in the cheeses, eggs, omelets, and floral arrangements; the sea in the fish, in the blue colors of china and the ribbons; and the earth in the potatoes, vegetables, and greens.

"We always have our smörgåsbord on Christmas Eve, after the late church service, with three settings," says Irene F. Carlson of Minneapolis. "Guests take a clean plate for each table, beginning with the fish table: gravlax, pickled herring, anchovies, and fish salads. It's considered polite to take small portions and return often. No one loads down his plate.

"The second table is the cold table, with several cheeses, deviled eggs, *rulle polse,* liver pâté, beet salad, among other selections. Finally, the guests round the hot table of Swedish meatballs, spareribs, Swedish brown beans, ham, Jansson's Temptation (scalloped potatoes with cream and anchovies), and parslied whole potatoes, to name a few. We conclude our feast with a simple rice pudding and hot, strong coffee."

SAUERBRATEN WITH THREE-GINGER GRAVY

SERVES 6 TO 8

Sauerbraten is a tangy-sweet German pot roast, worth the time it takes to marinate. The longer the meat sits in its vinegar-and-spice blend, the stronger its flavor will be. We recommend leaving it the full five days, though you may wish to shorten the time to a few days or even just overnight.

The gravy for sauerbraten is usually made with crushed gingersnaps; here we combine fresh ginger, dried ginger, and crystallized ginger for extra zip. While this looks like a lot of meat, it shrinks almost by half during the long, slow cooking time.

1 round rump roast or beef pot roast (about 4–5 pounds),
*   rolled and tied*

MARINADE

2 cups red wine vinegar or cider vinegar for a sharper taste
¼ cup brown sugar, light or dark
1 onion, peeled and sliced
2 cloves garlic, peeled and crushed
20 peppercorns
10 whole cloves
1 tablespoon whole cardamom
4 bay leaves
2 tablespoons grated fresh gingerroot
2 tablespoons grated orange rind
1 tablespoon vegetable oil for browning meat

SAUCE

1 tablespoon butter
1 tablespoon unbleached all-purpose flour
½ teaspoon dried ginger
¼ cup chopped crystallized ginger
2 tablespoons brown sugar, light or dark

*R*inse and pat the meat dry and place in a nonaluminum dish or pan.

In a small saucepan, combine all of the ingredients for the marinade and bring to a simmer over low heat. Chill the marinade until cool. Pour the marinade over the meat, cover, and refrigerate 4 days, turning the meat once a day. On the fifth day, remove the meat from the marinade and dry it with a paper towel.

In a stewpot or ovenproof casserole, heat the oil and brown the meat on all sides. Drain off the oil and add the marinade. Cover the pot tightly and simmer slowly for about 3 hours. When the meat is tender, place it on a platter and cover with an aluminum foil tent to keep warm.

To make the sauce, strain the cooking liquid and reserve it. Melt the butter in the pot and add the flour, stirring constantly and cooking until the mixture turns golden brown, about 30 seconds. Add the strained liquid and stir; then add the remaining ingredients and simmer gently until the sauce is thick. Slice the meat and pour the sauce over it. Sauerbraten is usually served with dumplings and braised red cabbage.

Singing societies such as the Wausau choral society of Wisconsin, 1913, provided entertainment and fostered good fellowship in German biergartens (beer gardens) throughout the state.

VEAL POT ROAST
WITH MAPLE-MUSTARD GLAZE

SERVES 6 TO 8

*T*his traditional Yankee pot roast recipe originally called for molasses, and was modified by a Wisconsin cook who substituted local maple syrup. We've chosen a tender cut of veal and added mustard to the glaze for snap.

Veal is extremely lean and needs a little extra fat to keep it from becoming dry. It's best cooked in a low oven; high heat makes it tough.

> *1 round veal roast (about 3 pounds)*
> *¼ cup maple syrup*
> *2 tablespoons Dijon mustard*
> *½ pound bacon*
> *4 cups homemade Dark Stock (page 142), or low-salt*
> *   canned broth, or water*
> *1 cup white wine*
> *2 cups heavy cream*
> *Salt and freshly ground pepper to taste*

*P*rick the roast gently 4 or 5 times with a fork. Mix together the maple syrup and mustard, and smear it completely over the meat.

Lay the strips of bacon over the veal roast in a lattice pattern. Put the veal in a roasting pan and add about *2 cups* of the stock to just cover the bottom of the pan. Roast the veal in a preheated 325°F oven for about 1 hour and add the remaining 2 cups of stock. Continue roasting for another 15 to 30 minutes, or until the juices run clear. (The internal temperature should be about 140° to 150°F.)

Remove the roast from the pan. Add the wine. Place one quarter of the pan over a high flame, bring the juices to a simmer, and cook until the liquid is reduced by half. Add the cream and reduce again by half. Add salt and pepper to taste. Serve this sliced, with the sauce drizzled over.

VEAL CHOP WITH
SHIITAKE MUSHROOMS AND PEARS

SERVES 4

*T*he shiitake mushroom, from Japan and Korea, is now cultivated in northern Minnesota and Wisconsin, and is called the "golden oak". Its dark brown cap can grow as large as ten inches across, and its thick flesh has an almost meaty flavor. Fresh shiitakes are harvested in the fall, as are the tiny golden sweet pears of northern Wisconsin. In this recipe mellow pears blend with the dark, musky mushrooms in a light, fragrant sauce. The dish makes a lovely autumn supper when served with parsley-buttered noodles or wild rice. (If ripe pears are unavailable, apples can be substituted.)

> *4 thick premium veal chops (10 ounces each)*
> *Salt and freshly ground pepper*
> *2 tablespoons olive oil*
>
> *SAUCE*
>
> *2 tablespoons butter*
> *1 shallot, chopped*
> *1 cup sliced shiitake mushrooms**
> *2 tablespoons Madeira, or red wine or sherry*
> *1 cup homemade Dark Stock (page 142) or low-salt*
>   *canned broth*
> *1 ripe pear, thinly sliced*
> *Chopped chives for garnish*
>
> ** Shiitake mushrooms are available in the gourmet sections of most*
> *grocery stores and food co-ops. Any mushroom may be substituted,*
> *but the wild ones taste best with the pears.*

*S*eason the chops with salt and freshly ground pepper. In a medium skillet set over medium-high heat, sear the chops in the oil, about 6 minutes per side. Set the chops in a roasting pan and place in a preheated 350°F oven while

Veal Chop with Shitake Mushrooms and Pears (continued)

you make the sauce. The chops should be cooked to medium-rare (about 6 minutes more in the oven), or until the juices run clear.

To make the sauce, blot the oil from the skillet used for the chops and melt *1 tablespoon* of the butter over medium heat. Sauté the chopped shallot and the mushrooms, cooking until golden brown. Add the Madeira and the stock, scraping the bottom of the pan to release the flavorful bits, and cook until the sauce is reduced and slightly thick. Add the sliced pear and cook 2 minutes more, then swirl in the remaining *tablespoon* of butter. To serve, pour the sauce over each chop and garnish with chopped chives.

BRAISED LAMB SHANKS
WITH WINTER VEGETABLES

SERVES 4 TO 6

*B*ack on the farms of central Minnesota, lamb was raised for its wool, then slaughtered as old mutton. The meat was tough but flavorful, and it would be braised, stewed, or boiled for long periods of time.

Cook meaty lamb shanks over low, slow heat to impart a wonderful, rich flavor and make a delicious, warming winter meal. This dish tastes even better the next day. Serve in a big bowl over rice with crusty Potato Bread (page 21) and a dollop of horseradish sauce.

> *Olive oil*
> *4 lamb shanks*
> *2 cloves garlic, chopped*
> *1 bay leaf*
> *1 tablespoon chopped fresh thyme*
> *1 tablespoon chopped fresh rosemary*
> *½ teaspoon freshly ground pepper*

1 teaspoon salt
1 onion, peeled and chopped
1 cup high-quality red wine
About 6 cups homemade Chicken or Dark Stock
  (pages 141 and 142) or low-salt canned broth
1 small turnip, cut into chunks
2 carrots, cut into chunks
½ rutabaga, cut into chunks
6 shallots, peeled
1 potato, cut into chunks
1 small parsnip or celery root, peeled and cut into chunks
Fresh parsley and horseradish for garnish

*I*n a large, deep skillet or stewpot, heat enough olive oil to cover the bottom of the pan and sear the lamb shanks. Remove all but 2 tablespoons of the fat. Add the garlic, bay leaf, thyme, rosemary, pepper, salt, and onion, and stir. Immediately add the wine to the pot and enough stock to barely cover the meat, stirring to scrape the bottom and release all the flavorful scraps. Simmer about 1½ hours, uncovered, turning the shanks occasionally and skimming any fat or scum that rises to the surface. Then add all the vegetables and simmer, uncovered, for another 45 minutes.

Serve the shanks, vegetables, and broth over rice. Sprinkle with fresh parsley and serve with a dollop of horseradish.

SPRING LEG OF LAMB
WITH OLD-FASHIONED MINT SAUCE

SERVES 6 TO 8

*D*aisy Samuelson of Oxlip, Minnesota, remembers that her father used to hang a leg of lamb in the smokehouse along with the hams. Called *spekeke-jott,* it was eaten in thin slices as a snack meat, like beef jerky.

This old-fashioned roast is timeless. Make the sauce with fresh garden mint and serve with roasted new potatoes.

> *1 leg of lamb (about 6½ pounds), boned out, not tied*
> *3 shallots, peeled and chopped, or 3 scallions, chopped*
> *1 teaspoon coarsely ground pepper*
> *2 tablespoons olive oil*
> *3 tablespoons whole fresh mint leaves*

> ### OLD-FASHIONED MINT SAUCE
>
> *1 cup water*
> *¾ cup confectioners' sugar*
> *¾ cup high-quality champagne vinegar, or white wine*
> *   vinegar*
> *1 cup finely chopped fresh mint leaves, packed*
> *Pinch of salt to taste*

*R*ub the leg of lamb all over, inside and out, with the shallots, pepper, and olive oil. Stuff the whole mint leaves inside the leg cavity. Put the lamb in a roasting pan and place in a preheated 350°F oven. Roast for 1½ hours for medium-rare. Pull the lamb from the oven and allow it to sit about 15 minutes before carving. While it is "resting," make the sauce.

Bring the water, confectioners' sugar, and vinegar to a boil. Boil about 15 minutes, or until the liquid is reduced and slightly thick. Remove the sauce from the heat and add the mint leaves and a pinch of salt. Carve the lamb and serve with the sauce.

SAVORY SAUSAGE PATTIES

**MAKES ABOUT 4½ POUNDS (ENOUGH
TO SERVE 10 TO 12 FOR BREAKFAST)**

*E*very fall, Rose Block of Minneapolis returns to her family's farm in Pierz, Minnesota, to help with sausage making. "When I was little, my job was to snip off the links after they were tied. Now I stuff the casings—tricky work. If packed too full, they split; but if there is too much air, the meat will shrink down too far when they're cooked. We hang them in the smokehouse for about a week. Work done, we make a dinner of sausage patties and home-made bread topped with cream and sugar."

It's easy to bring the north country smell of sizzling homemade sausage to an urban kitchen; sausage patties are as simple as hamburgers to make. Serve them with fried eggs (sunny side up) or with toasted Old-fashioned Milk Bread (page 6) spread with Maple-Almond-Pecan or Spicy-Nut Butter (page 95).

This recipe makes a large amount, but the sausage freezes well. The recipe can easily be cut in half.

> *3½ pounds ground veal, pork, or beef*
> *1 pound bacon, finely chopped or ground**
> *1½ cups peeled, chopped onions*
> *¼ cup finely chopped fresh parsley*
> *1 tablespoon grated lemon zest*
> *¼ teaspoon salt*
> *⅛ teaspoon freshly ground pepper*
> *2 teaspoons vinegar*
> *2 teaspoons fennel seeds*
>
> **For ease of handling, put the bacon in the freezer before chopping so it will be firm. A food processor fitted with a steel blade works well.*

*M*ix all of the ingredients together in a medium bowl. Shape into patties and sauté over medium heat on a griddle or in a skillet until the inside is no longer pink.

SAUSAGE BASICS

*T*he best ways to cook sausage are the simplest: grilled, braised, or just boiled and served on a hard crusty roll or with buttered steamed potatoes, sauerkraut, coarse mustard, and plenty of beer.

GRILLED SAUSAGE

*W*hether using a charcoal or gas grill, keep the flames low. Prick the sausages lightly with a fork and place on the grill. Turn the sausages frequently so they brown evenly, and be careful not to overcook them.

Raw, fresh sausages such as fresh bratwurst will take about 12 to 15 minutes to cook. Cooked or smoked sausages such as kielbasa take about 7 to 10 minutes to become hot all the way through.

The sausages should be evenly browned and juicy when done and served on a crusty roll.

SAUSAGE BRAISED IN BEER

*B*ratwurst and knockwurst are the types of German sausage most often braised in German beer. The process is simple. Put the sausages in a deep pan with enough beer to cover them halfway. Bring the beer to a low boil and cook until it has evaporated; then brown the sausages in the pan or put them on the grill.

BOILED SAUSAGE

*B*oiled sausages and potatoes make a hearty country dinner served with Braised Red Cabbage with Apples and Bacon (page 271). Simply place scrubbed new potatoes and sausage (Polish or Swedish potato sausage) in a pot with enough water just to cover. You might add a clove or two and a bay leaf. Bring the water to a simmer and cook until the potatoes are tender, about 20 minutes. Drain. Serve the potatoes and sausage together, with a side of sauerkraut or braised cabbage and lots of mustard.

LEFTOVER SAUSAGE

*L*eftover cooked sausages (if you're lucky enough to have them) make flavorful additions to soup, spaghetti, and casseroles. Here are a few ways to spice things up:

- Add cooked sausage to Yellow Split Pea Soup (page 150).
- Stuff mushroom caps with cooked sausage, top with shredded cheese, and bake until the caps are tender.
- Toss cooked, sliced sausage links with pasta, pesto, and chopped green peppers.
- Toss cooked, sliced sausage links with cooked white beans, blanched broccoli, and Rosemary-Balsamic Vinaigrette (page 251), and serve on greens.
- Peel sweet onions, core out the centers, and stuff with cooked, crumbled sausage; then bake until the onions are tender.
- Garnish the Wisconsin Cheddar Cheese and Vegetable Soup (page 144) with crumbled, cooked sausage.
- Add crumbled, cooked sausage to the Tourtière (page 178).
- Tossed cooked, sliced sausage with cooked black beans and toss with Cilantro-Lime Vinaigrette (page 255).

GREAT BEAST OF THE PLAINS

"Prepare for me a pasture for the buffalo bull, his wife and young, at some distance so that by means of them I and my people may keep alive. Among them I shall survive."

—SIOUX BUFFALO SONG

"One hundred thousand [buffalo] thundered the plains in herds that took five days to pass—twenty miles wide and fifty miles long. The Indians lived from this beast as we now live from the cow, using every part for food, clothing and shelter. Of buffalo skins they made robes, lodges, saddles, war bonnets, gloves—all their clothing. Out of the thick neck of the skin they made glue. From the tuft on the forehead, ropes and lariats were made, and from the tendons, thread and bowstrings. From the shoulders, axes, knives and arrows. From the hair, pillows. The trachea they used for a paint sack and the papillae of the tongue made brushes. The tail made knives, rattles; the dried udder, dishes; the ribs, small dog sleds. The gall became an intoxicating liquor. The paunch was a remedy for disease and the intestines were dried in the sun and eaten; buffalo chips were burned as fuel."

—MERIDEL LE SUEUR, *NORTH STAR COUNTRY*

Today's North American buffalo, known as bison, are raised for their flavorful, nutritious meat, which is lower in fat and cholesterol than even chicken or turkey, and high in thiamin, iron, and protein. According to Ed Eichten, who raises the semidomesticated bison, "The meat tastes the way beef used to taste when cattle roamed the grasslands—not gamy or wild, clean-tasting, almost sweet."

Substitute bison in any recipe calling for beef with the following adjustments:

🐃 Cut back on the cooking time; it cooks faster than beef and dries out easily.

🐃 Roast at 275°F (not 325°F) and plan on the same cooking time as for beef.

🐃 Make ground bison patties thick. They cook through quickly, especially on the grill.

BISON STEAKS
WITH CHUTNEY GLAZE

SERVES 4

*T*his simple recipe is also delicious with sirloin steak. Bison cooks more quickly than beef, so watch that it doesn't overcook.

> *4 bison steaks (about 6 ounces each)*
> *4 tablespoons Dijon mustard*
> *1 tablespoon cracked pepper*
> *6 tablespoons Rhubarb Chutney (page 292) or prepared*
>   *chutney*

*R*ub the steaks with the mustard and pepper and refrigerate, covered with plastic wrap, for several hours. Prepare the grill for medium-low grilling. Grill or broil the steaks for a minute on each side, then spoon the chutney over each steak. Cover the grill and cook for about 10 to 15 minutes, or until it's done to your liking. Serve immediately with additional chutney passed on the side.

Chicken Stock

Dark Stock

Cabbage, Ham Hock, and Leek Soup

Wisconsin Cheddar Cheese and Vegetable Soup

Beef, Wild Rice, and Winter Vegetable Soup

Creamy Chicken and Barley Soup

Sausage and White Bean Soup

Yellow Split Pea Soup

Hmong Market Soup

Spring Borscht

Sweet Corn Chowder

Pumpkin Soup

Fall Lentil and Fresh Tomato Soup

Iced Cream of Lettuce and Pea Soup

Cherry Riesling Soup

SEASONAL KETTLE

HOT AND COLD SOUPS

The same hearty soups that bubbled away over an open hearth in a pioneer kitchen have stoked up farmers, miners, lumbermen, railroad workers, fishermen, and cross-country skiers through several generations. Everyone loves soup, especially the cook. Nutritious soups can be made with whatever is on hand, turning leftovers into warming meals for subzero nights.

Soups have long been credited with psychological and physical healing properties. The Ojibway Indians make a thin gruel of wild rice for stomach disorders; the Germans believe cream soup—*Rahm*—cures any number of ailments from the common cold to a broken heart; an Alsatian chicken-and-egg-drop soup called *Weinsuppe* is the remedy for arthritis and other bone ailments; and the traditional Scandinavian gift for new mothers is fruit soup, to give strength while nursing.

As versatile as they are seasonal, soups may be the main dish or first course in either an elegant or an informal meal. Several of the same vegetable and cream soups that steam kitchen windows on a frosty night may also be served cold in the dense heat of August.

Our Northern Heartland soups are deliciously varied with ethnic flavors. There are meat-based clear soups, chowders, cream soups, soups of legumes and vegetables, and wine and fruit soups. Certain dishes like borscht are firmly identified with the Old World; others like Wisconsin Cheese and Cauliflower Soup blend rich, tangy Cheddar cheese into a hearty potage. Hmong Market Soup, made with coconut milk seasoned with lemongrass and cilantro, reflects the sweet-and-sour flavors typical of Cambodian food. When making soup, we rely on *Buckeye Cookery*'s nineteenth-century advice: "The good soup-maker must be a skillful taster."

STOCKING UP

The thrifty pioneer cook saved bones, scraps of meat, and the odds and ends of vegetables, as well as the water that vegetables had been cooked in (especially potato water), for the stockpot that simmered away throughout the day. The liquid would be strained and saved, often frozen outside, then used as the base for soups and stews.

It is very easy to make a delicious stock from the bones of a roast chicken, standing rib roast, turkey, or pork roast. Simply put the bones in a large pot, along with any vegetable scraps, vegetable water, and a few herbs. Add enough water just to cover the bones, partially cover the pot, and simmer the stock for several hours, skimming off any scum that rises to the top.

The two recipes that follow are a little more demanding and call for more ingredients than most stock recipes, but they yield rich, flavorful stocks that, with the addition of noodles or rice, make lovely soups. Both recipes freeze beautifully.

CHICKEN STOCK

MAKES ABOUT 1 QUART

Bones from 2 chickens or 1 whole chicken,* or approximately
  5–6 pounds chicken necks and backbones (reserved from
  cutting up chickens)
2 carrots (scrubbed, not peeled), cut into chunks
4 stalks celery, cut into chunks
1 onion, peeled and studded with 4 cloves
2 bay leaves
2 sprigs fresh parsley
1 small bunch fresh thyme or 1 teaspoon dried
4 black peppercorns
1 square inch of gingerroot, peeled (optional)
1 tablespoon fresh lemon juice (optional)

* If cooking a whole chicken, remove the chicken, reserve the meat
for Chicken Salad with Apples, Walnuts, and Maple-Mustard
Vinaigrette (page 74) or Chicken (or Turkey) Pot Pie with Bis-
cuit Crust (page 170), and use the broth for the sauce.

*P*lace the bones or whole chicken, along with the remaining ingredients, into a large stockpot. Cover with about 4 quarts of cold water. Bring the liquid to a boil and skim (see page 149). Reduce the heat and simmer 2 to 2½ hours. Strain the stock, chill, and remove the fat.

DARK STOCK

MAKES ABOUT 1 QUART

*T*his recipe, though somewhat fussy, yields a wonderful rich dark stock and is worth the extra time and effort. It is delicious served alone for a light first course. Add noodles or rice to make a flavorful soup. Veal or beef bones are available from local butchers and supermarket meat departments—many meat departments will give them away. You may also use turkey, chicken, or duck bones for a flavorful poultry stock. (If using poultry bones, don't cook them quite as long.)

> *6 pounds of bones*
> *2 carrots (scrubbed, not peeled), cut into chunks*
> *1 onion, peeled and cut into chunks*
> *2 stalks celery, cut into chunks*
> *1 head garlic, peeled and cut into chunks*
> *¼ cup tomato paste*
> *½ bottle red wine (optional)*
> *2 bay leaves*
> *1 small bunch fresh thyme or 1 teaspoon dried*
> *2 sprigs fresh parsley*
> *5 peppercorns*
> *Water to cover bones*

*S*pread the bones on a roasting pan and bake in a preheated 400°F oven, turning occasionally, about 45 minutes to 1 hour, or until golden brown. Watch that they don't burn.

Drain off most of the fat (reserving about 3 tablespoons) and toss in the vegetables. Continue baking another 35 to 45 minutes, or until the vegetables are nicely browned. Remove from the oven, and if desired, add wine, stirring to scrape up flavorful browned bits. Turn into a stockpot, along with the remaining ingredients and enough cold water to cover the bones. Bring the liquid to a boil, skim (see page 149), and then reduce the heat and simmer about 4 hours. Strain the broth, chill, and remove the thick layer of fat before using.

To make a double-rich stock, reduce the liquid by half or more over moderate-high heat. Then cool, skim, and freeze in ice-cube trays.

CABBAGE, HAM HOCK, AND LEEK SOUP

SERVES 8 TO 10

"*I* always add a touch of vinegar to my cabbage soup," notes Elsie Kohler of White Bear Lake, Minnesota. "My German mother swore it added oomph."

We serve this hearty soup topped with big croutons (see page 18), thick slices of rye bread toasted with Swiss cheese, and mugs of beer.

> 3 tablespoons butter or bacon fat
> 4 cups shredded cabbage
> 1 big leek, cleaned under running water, cut horizontally,
>   and diced (about 2 cups)
> 2 cups diced carrots
> 2 cups diced celery
> 2 cloves garlic, minced
> ½ pound ham hocks or a leftover ham bone with meat
> 1 tablespoon chopped fresh thyme or 2 teaspoons dried
> 2 bay leaves
> 2 tablespoons cider vinegar
> About 6 cups water

*H*eat the butter or bacon fat, add the vegetables, and stir to coat. Cover the pot and cook about 5 minutes. Add the remaining ingredients and enough water just to cover. Bring the liquid to a boil, skim (see page 149), cover, and reduce the heat. Simmer, partially covered, about 2 hours. Pull out the hocks, remove the meat, and cut or shred it into bite-size pieces; then return the meat to the soup and simmer another 5 minutes and serve.

WISCONSIN CHEDDAR CHEESE AND VEGETABLE SOUP

SERVES 6 TO 8

*C*heese soup has always been a staple among the settlers who came from European dairy cultures. The Alsatians have a version made with Gruyère cheese and onions. Italians make theirs with Parmesan cheese and pepperoni and the Swiss with cheese and bourbon.

This cheese soup combines the region's fine, sharp Cheddar cheese with local cauliflower. It makes a hearty supper served with rye bread, a salad of bitter greens, and dark beer.

> 3 tablespoons butter
> ½ cup peeled, chopped onions
> ½ cup chopped celery
> 1 cup chopped cauliflower
> 2 large russet potatoes, peeled and chopped
> 2 cups homemade Chicken Stock (page 141) or
>   low-salt canned broth
> 1 quart milk
> ⅛ teaspoon nutmeg
> ⅛ teaspoon freshly ground pepper
> 2 cups shredded Cheddar cheese (use orange for color)
> ¼ cup sherry
> 1 tablespoon Dijon mustard
> Tabasco sauce for seasoning
> Worcestershire sauce for seasoning
> Croutons (page 18) for garnish
> Shredded cheese for garnish

*I*n a large soup pot, melt the butter and sauté the vegetables over low heat until soft. Add the stock, milk, nutmeg, and pepper, and simmer the soup until the vegetables are tender, about 5 minutes. Purée the soup in batches in a blender, return to the pot, and bring to a boil. Turn off the heat. Gradually add the Cheddar cheese in batches, stirring after each batch before adding more. (Be careful. If the soup is too hot and the cheese is added all at once, it may "break" and become stringy and gloppy.) Gradually reheat the soup, stirring, being careful not to boil, and add the sherry, mustard, and Tabasco and Worcestershire sauces to taste. Garnish with croutons and more shredded cheese. Serve at once.

Amana communal kitchen

BEEF, WILD RICE, AND WINTER VEGETABLE SOUP

SERVES 8 TO 10

*T*his recipe is based on an older version called Root Cellar Soup that used whatever roots and tubers the cook had stored in bins in the cellar at the time.

> *2 tablespoons bacon fat or butter*
> *1 cup peeled, diced winter squash*
> *1 cup peeled, diced turnips*
> *1 cup peeled, diced parsnips or salsify*
> *1 cup peeled, diced rutabaga*
> *1 onion, peeled and diced*
> *1 clove garlic, diced*
> *1 teaspoon dried thyme*
> *1 bay leaf*
> *½ cup wild rice*
> *½ cup red wine (optional)*
> *8–10 cups homemade Dark Stock (page 142) or*
>   *low-salt canned broth*
> *2 tablespoons tomato paste*
> *1 cup cooked, cubed beef*
> *Salt and freshly ground pepper to taste*
> *Chopped fresh parsley for garnish*

*I*n a large saucepan, heat the bacon fat or butter and sauté the vegetables, including the diced garlic, until the onion is soft. Add the thyme, bay leaf, wild rice, wine, and stock, along with the tomato paste. Bring to a boil, reduce the heat, cover, and simmer about 1 hour, or until the wild rice is soft and the kernels have popped open. More stock can be added, if desired. Add the cooked beef, heat through, then season with salt and pepper to taste and serve garnished with fresh parsley.

CREAMY CHICKEN
AND BARLEY SOUP

SERVES 8 TO 10

Given the many dairy farms clustered throughout Wisconsin, Minnesota, and Iowa, it's not surprising that many of our Northern Heartland soups are made rich with cream and butter. Cream of chicken soup is an old-fashioned favorite that appears in many of the early cookbooks as a way to use up old hens. *Buckeye Cookery* advises, "An old chicken for soup is much the best."

> *2 tablespoons butter*
> *2 cups peeled, diced onions*
> *2 cups diced carrots*
> *3 cups diced celery*
> *2 cloves garlic, peeled and diced*
> *1½ cups peeled, diced russet potatoes*
> *½ cup barley*
> *8 cups homemade Chicken Stock (page 141) or*
> *   low-salt canned broth**
> *2 bay leaves*
> *1 tablespoon fresh thyme or 1 teaspoon dried*
> *½ cup white wine*
> *½ cup heavy cream*
> *2 cups cooked chicken or turkey meat**
> *Salt and freshly ground pepper to taste*
> *Fresh parsley for garnish*
>
> ** If making your own Chicken Stock (page 141), use the reserved chicken to make this soup.*

In a large stockpot, melt the butter and sauté the onions, carrots, celery, and garlic until soft. Add the potatoes, barley, stock, bay leaves, and thyme. Cook, partially covered, for 1 hour (adding more stock as desired), and then add the wine, cream, chicken, and salt and pepper to taste. Serve garnished with chopped fresh parsley.

SAUSAGE AND WHITE BEAN SOUP

SERVES 8 TO 10

*U*se just about any sausage in this satisfying winter soup.

> *1 cup white beans, soaked overnight in water to cover**
> *3 tablespoons bacon fat or butter*
> *1 medium onion, peeled and cut into chunks*
> *2 stalks celery, cut into chunks*
> *1 medium carrot, cut into chunks*
> *½ green and ½ red bell pepper, cored, deveined, seeded,*
>   *and cut into chunks*
> *2 cloves garlic, peeled and chopped*
> *8 cups homemade Chicken Stock (page 141) or low-salt*
>   *canned broth*
> *2 cups chopped tomatoes, canned or fresh*
> *1 tablespoon tomato paste*
> *2 teaspoons dried thyme*
> *1 bay leaf*
> *½ cup red wine*
> *¾–1 pound link sausages (Ukrainian, Italian, or Polish)*
> *Salt and freshly ground pepper to taste*

** If you haven't time to soak the beans overnight, simply put them
in a large saucepan, cover with water, and bring to a boil. Reduce
the heat and simmer the beans about 5 minutes. Then remove
from the heat and allow the beans to stand about 1 hour. Drain
and rinse, then proceed with the recipe.*

*D*rain the beans, rinse again, and set aside. In a large stockpot, heat the bacon fat or butter and sauté the onion, celery, carrot, green and red peppers, and garlic until soft. Add the stock, tomatoes, tomato paste, thyme, bay leaf, and beans and ¼ *cup* of the red wine, and bring to a simmer.

While the soup simmers, cook the sausages. Place the sausages in a cold skillet, then cover and cook on medium-high heat for about 6 minutes, turning often. Pour off the fat. Add *the remaining ¼ cup* red wine, cover, and cook over low heat for another 15 minutes. Cut the sausages into rings and put them, along with any liquid in the skillet, into the soup. Continue simmering the soup for about 1 hour, uncovered, then add salt and pepper to taste.

SKIMMING

Skimming the top of a soup or stew is an easy, time-saving means of clarifying the stock by discarding the fat and scum that interfere with flavor. While some cooks allow the soup to cool so the fat becomes a pliable layer that can be lifted off, we sometimes can't wait. Skimming accomplishes the same results.

To skim, place one quarter of the pot on a high flame so that some of the liquid continues to boil and the rest is still. The fat and scum will travel to the cooler area of the pot, where they may be spooned off.

Hot and hearty soups were a mainstay in logging camps. When men worked too far away from the cook shack, their noon dinner was brought out to them on a horse-drawn cart or sled.

YELLOW SPLIT PEA SOUP

SERVES 10 TO 12

*T*he Swedish custom of eating pea soup and pancakes on Thursdays had its beginning before the Reformation, when Sweden was a Catholic country. Eating meat was forbidden on Fridays, so Swedish citizens filled themselves up on pea soup and pork on Thursday to fortify themselves against the next day's meager fare. While the Catholic Church has long since lifted its Friday ban on meat, and the majority of American Swedes are Lutheran, the tradition of Thursday pea soup and pancakes with lingonberries or jam continues in some homes today. It's a simple supper and plain good.

We serve this golden, silky smooth soup garnished with cracked black pepper.

2 tablespoons bacon fat or butter
1 onion, peeled and diced
2 stalks celery, diced
3 carrots, diced
1/2 teaspoon turmeric
1/2 cup sherry (optional)
4 cups yellow or green dried peas
10 cups water, or homemade Chicken Stock (page 141), or
*   low-salt canned broth*
1 meaty ham bone or 2 ham hocks (optional)
Salt and freshly ground pepper to taste
Freshly cracked black pepper for garnish

*I*n a large stockpot, heat the bacon fat or butter and sauté the onion, celery, and carrots until the onion is soft. Add the turmeric, sherry, peas, water, and ham bone, and cook, covered, about 1 hour. Remove the ham bone; remove the meat and reserve. Purée the soup in batches in a food processor fitted with a steel blade or in a blender, then add salt and pepper to taste. Return the meat to the soup (if you are using the ham bone or ham hocks). Serve garnished with cracked black pepper.

HMONG MARKET SOUP

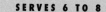

SERVES 6 TO 8

Whether you eat or not, at least hold a spoon. Whether you
laugh or not, at least force a smile

—HMONG PROVERB

*T*his soup is a delicious combination of the sweet, sour, and hot flavors characteristic of Hmong cuisine.

Hmong Market Soup (continued)

> ½ onion, peeled and chopped
> 1 carrot, cut into thin matchstick-size pieces
> 2 tablespoons dark sesame oil
> 1 clove garlic, peeled and crushed
> 1 tablespoon shredded fresh gingerroot
> 1 stalk lemongrass or 1 tablespoon fresh lemon juice
> 2 cups homemade Chicken Stock (page 141) or low-salt
>   canned broth
> 3 cups coconut milk*
> 2 tablespoons peanut butter
> 1 cup shredded cooked chicken meat
> Salt and freshly ground pepper to taste
> ½ teaspoon turmeric
> ½ teaspoon red pepper flakes
> ¼ cup chopped fresh cilantro for garnish
>
> *To make coconut milk, combine ¾ cup packaged coconut with
> 2 cups milk in a large saucepan. Bring to a low simmer for a few
> minutes. Then pour it into a blender or food processor and purée.
> It can also be bought in cans.

In a large saucepan, cook the onion and carrot pieces in the sesame oil over medium heat until just tender-crisp. In a blender or food processor fitted with a steel blade, purée the garlic, ginger, lemongrass stalk, stock, and coconut milk. Pour this into a large pot, add the sautéed vegetables, and bring to a simmer.

In a small cup, mix the peanut butter with about ¼ cup of the hot soup so that the mixture is liquid, then pour this back into the pot. Add the cooked chicken, salt and pepper to taste, turmeric, and red pepper flakes. Serve immediately, garnished with lots of fresh cilantro.

SPRING BORSCHT

SERVES 4 TO 6

*B*orscht, a traditional Eastern European soup, comes in endless varieties. This version is typical of farm country soup, blending garden vegetables and dill.

Salt the beets first, to set their wonderful magenta color, then toss them with a handful of vegetables and serve this light, fresh-tasting soup cold with a dollop of sour cream or Thickened Cream (page 87).

> *3–4 cups thinly sliced (julienned) beets (from about 2*
> *   medium or 4 small beets)*
> *2 tablespoons salt*
> *1 tablespoon butter*
> *½ cup peeled, diced potatoes*
> *½ cup diced carrots*
> *½ cup peeled, diced onions*
> *1 clove garlic, crushed*
> *1 tablespoon lemon juice*
> *½ cup cut string beans*
> *¼ cup peas*
> *¼ cup sliced green onions*
> *2 tablespoons chopped fresh dill*
> *2 tablespoons chopped fresh parsley*
> *Sour cream for garnish*

*T*oss the beets with salt and set aside. This sets the color; do not rinse them. In a large, deep saucepan, melt the butter and sauté the beets, potatoes, carrots, onions, and garlic for about 1 minute. Add the lemon juice and enough water to just cover the vegetables, and simmer until soft. Add the string beans, peas, and green onions, and simmer until just tender. Chill the soup. Add the herbs and serve garnished with sour cream. Delicious hot or cold.

SWEET CORN CHOWDER

SERVES 8 TO 10

*W*e make this creamy chowder when the corn is so fresh and sweet that the farmers at market give away samples to eat just off the cob. It really doesn't need to be cooked.

If using fresh corn on the cob, scrape off and reserve the kernels, then add the cobs to the stock. Just before serving, remove the cobs and add the corn kernels. Garnish with bits of bacon and freshly chopped parsley.

4 ounces bacon
1 large onion, chopped
1 stalk celery, chopped
¼ cup unbleached all-purpose flour
2 medium potatoes, peeled and diced
1 pint homemade Chicken Stock (page 141) or low-salt canned broth
1 bay leaf
1 pint whole milk
½ red and ½ green pepper, cored, deveined, seeded, and chopped
4–5 ears fresh sweet corn, shucked, with corn kernels cut from the cob (about 3 cups kernels)—save the cobs to enrich the stock
Salt and freshly ground pepper to taste
Chopped fresh parsley for garnish

*I*n a large saucepan, sauté the bacon until crisp, but be careful not to burn it. Remove, drain on paper towels, and chop. Add the onion and celery to the pan and sauté in the bacon fat until soft. Sprinkle with flour and cook, stirring, for about 3 to 4 minutes. Add the potatoes, chicken stock, and bay leaf (and corn cobs if you are using them), and bring the mixture to a boil; then reduce the heat and simmer until the potatoes are soft, about 20 minutes. Remove the corn cobs, add the milk, and be careful not to let the soup boil again, since it might

Pumpkins were planted with corn because they helped keep the corn's roots cool in the hot summer sun.

separate. Stir in the chopped red and green peppers, corn kernels, and salt and pepper to taste. Simmer for 2 to 3 minutes. Serve garnished with the bacon and chopped fresh parsley.

PUMPKIN SOUP

SERVES 6 TO 8

*P*umpkins add bright color to the gray October landscape. Many of the pick-your-own apple farms feature pumpkins, too. This soup blends apples, pumpkins, and cider—the flavors of fall.

Try serving this soup in small scooped-out pumpkins or winter squash, garnished with Spicy Nuts (page 296) and a hunk of Corn Bread (page 19) alongside.

You may substitute any of the winter squashes for pumpkin in this soup. Delicata (sweet potato) squash is especially good.

Pumpkin Soup (continued)

> About 3–4 pounds pumpkin
> ½ stick (4 tablespoons) butter
> 2–4 tablespoons brown sugar, light or dark
> 1 teaspoon ground cinnamon
> ¼ teaspoon ground cloves
> Salt and freshly ground pepper to taste
> 1 onion, peeled and finely diced
> 1 apple, peeled, cored, and finely diced
> 1 cup apple cider
> 1–2 cups milk
> Freshly ground nutmeg to taste
> Chopped Spicy Nuts (page 296) or toasted chopped pecans
>   for garnish

Cut the unpeeled pumpkin into large chunks and place on a baking sheet. Dot with butter and sprinkle lightly with brown sugar, cinnamon, cloves, salt and pepper, then cover with aluminum foil. Bake in a 350°F oven for about 1 to 1½ hours, or until tender. After you remove it from the oven, keep it covered with the aluminum foil so that the pumpkin will steam and become very soft.

Scoop out the flesh of the pumpkin—you should have about 6 cups—and put it into a large pot. Add the onion, diced apple, apple cider, and enough milk just to cover. Bring the mixture to a low simmer and cook about 30 minutes. Put the soup into a blender or food processor fitted with a steel blade and blend, in batches, adding milk to bring it to the consistency you like. Season with nutmeg and more salt and pepper to taste. Serve garnished with Spicy Nuts or toasted chopped pecans.

To serve this as a baked soup, cut 4 additional squashes in half, cover with foil, put in a roasting pan with 1 inch water, and bake in a preheated 350°F oven until not quite tender, about 20 to 30 minutes. Scoop out about half—not all—of the flesh. Fill the halves with the prepared soup, place on a large pan, and bake another 30 minutes, or until the squash shell is tender. The soup will be very thick.

FALL LENTIL AND FRESH TOMATO SOUP

SERVES 6 TO 8

*T*his is an easy, fresh-tasting late-summer-into-fall soup, delicious hot or cold. It's seasoned with orange, fresh thyme, and rosemary, and it is a fitting tribute to the short but splendid tomato-and-herb season.

> *2 tablespoons butter or olive oil*
> *2 cups peeled, chopped onions*
> *2 tablespoons peeled, chopped garlic*
> *1 cup each, seeded, chopped red and green bell peppers*
> *1 tablespoon chopped fresh thyme or 1 teaspoon dried*
> *½ cup red wine*
> *1 cup lentils*
> *Salt and freshly ground pepper to taste*
> *About 2 cups homemade Chicken Stock (page 141) or low-*
>   *salt canned broth*
> *2 cups diced fresh tomatoes*
> *2 tablespoons chopped fresh rosemary or 1 teaspoon dried*
> *1 tablespoon grated orange zest*
> *1 tablespoon undiluted frozen orange juice concentrate*
> *Orange zest and chopped fresh basil for garnish*

*I*n a large soup pot, heat the butter or oil and sauté the onions, garlic, and red and green pepper until soft. Add the thyme, red wine, lentils, salt and pepper, and enough chicken stock to cover. Bring the soup to a boil, then reduce the heat and simmer about 30 to 45 minutes, or until the lentils are tender. Add the tomatoes, rosemary, orange zest, and concentrated orange juice. Season with salt and pepper to taste and serve garnished with more orange zest and chopped fresh basil.

ICED CREAM OF LETTUCE
AND PEA SOUP

SERVES 4 TO 6

*I*n January the seed catalogs begin to arrive, and farmers and backyard green thumbs start to daydream about tender lettuces and sweet peas. While snow swirls up against the windows, we're filling out order forms and writing away with visions of a full summer garden.

In late June, when the shell peas are at their peak, we make this soup with a broth of the stewed shells and climbing vines that we buy by the case from the Hmong, refugees from northern Laos and Cambodia (page 248), at the farmers' market. The fresh-tasting soup is worth the tedious effort of all that shucking.

2 cups peas, fresh or frozen
2 medium russet potatoes, peeled and sliced
1 small onion, peeled and sliced
4 cups homemade Chicken Stock (page 141), or low-salt
  canned broth, or shell pea stock*
4 cups lightly chopped fresh garden greens† (tender
  young spinach, romaine, Bibb, or looseleaf lettuce)
2 tablespoons chopped fresh chives, plus a little more
  for garnish
1 cup heavy cream
Juice of ½ lemon
Salt and freshly ground pepper to taste
Thinly sliced mint leaves for garnish

*Make a shell pea stock by simmering the vines and shells from the shucked peas in just enough water to cover, for about 30 minutes. (You should have about 4 cups.) Substitute the fresh shell pea stock for the chicken stock, and continue following the recipe accordingly. This soup is especially good garnished with fresh mint.

†For a peppery bite, add a few sprigs of arugula or watercress.

*P*ut the peas, potatoes, onion, and stock into a saucepan, bring to a boil, reduce the heat, and simmer about 15 minutes, or until the potatoes are just tender. Remove from the heat and stir in the greens and 2 tablespoons of the chives. With a food processor fitted with a steel blade or a blender, purée the soup in batches, adding the cream as you blend until smooth. Season with the lemon juice, and add salt and pepper to taste. Chill and serve garnished with chopped chives or thinly sliced mint leaves.

Substitute all fresh shell peas for the lettuce in the recipe.

CREAM OR MILK SOUP

Years ago, when butter and cream were thought to strengthen bones and contribute to overall health and well-being, cream soups were considered catch-all cures. Elsie Oehler of Amana, Iowa, remembers: "Young or old, anyone suffering from any ailment, be it childbirth, broken bones, or the common cold, was administered a bowl of cream soup. Even today in many homes you will find a patient being tucked in with a warm, comforting dose of what we Germans call *Rahm* soup."

Here's Elsie's recipe: "Take a few pieces of bread and cut them into cubes. Brown them in a little butter, then add milk and bring just to a boil, then reduce the heat to a simmer and add some cream and salt and pepper to taste. We like this soup with big soda crackers."

CHERRY RIESLING SOUP

SERVES 6

*T*he Germans, Swedes, and Norwegians all serve variations of fruit soup, sometimes warm at the beginning of a special meal, or cool as a snack or dessert, with a dollop of sour or whipped cream. The Scandinavians often bring fruit soup to the home of a new mother because it is light, easy to digest, and thought to give strength.

Riesling wine adds depth to this traditionally sweet recipe. The soup makes a nice choice for a light first course on a hot summer night. You may want to adjust the amount of sugar in this recipe according to the sweetness of your wine. Try it with blueberries.

2 pounds cherries, stemmed and pitted, to equal 4 cups
2 cups water
2 cups Riesling wine (medium dry)*
¼ cup sugar (depending on taste)
1 tablespoon plus 1 teaspoon cornstarch
1 teaspoon grated orange zest
2 tablespoons orange juice
1 teaspoon lemon juice
Sour cream for garnish
Ground cardamom for garnish

* It's important to use a high-quality wine in this soup. Taste the wine and adjust the amount of sugar when making the soup. Sometimes we omit the sugar in the recipe and add a little brown sugar to the sour cream garnish.

*P*ut half of the cherries in a pan with the water and wine. Simmer over low heat about 15 minutes, or until the cherries are soft. Turn the mixture into a blender and purée. Stir together the sugar with the cornstarch, add 3 tablespoons of the cherry juice, and blend into a paste. Turn the puréed cherries in their liquid back into the saucepan, along with the paste, and heat until the mixture becomes thick. Add the orange zest, orange juice, and lemon juice, and the remaining cherries. Chill. Garnish with sour cream and sprinkle with ground cardamom.

Jansson's Temptation (Potato Casserole)

Roasted Vegetable Strudel

Wild Mushroom Stroganoff

Chicken (or Turkey) Pot Pie with Biscuit Crust

Thresher's Beef Stew (with Onions, Beer, and Blue Cheese)

Sarma (Stuffed Cabbage Rolls)

Tourtière (French Meat Pie)

Ellen Ostman's Pasty

Casserole of Caramelized Onions and Leftover Meat

Sausage, Beans, and Pepper Stew

THE COMMUNAL POT

ONE-DISH MEALS

C asseroles, stews, covered suppers, and one-dish meals have long been an expression of a cook's creativity and thrift. In the Northern Heartland "hot dishes" are toted to church dinners, town picnics, holiday parties, and potluck suppers. Reliable and generous, appealing to young and old, this warm, easy fare is always welcome when there are large gatherings of family and friends.

"We farm women got together and we 'neighbored,'" said Evelyn Birkby, author of *Cooking with the KMA Radio Homemakers.* "It was lonely in the countryside. Women would go all day with no company save the small children, and endless housework. We formed 'country clubs' and met once a month for a potluck lunch at each other's houses. This was how we stayed in touch."

Many traditional Northern Heartland recipes for one-dish meals were created originally to please big outdoor appetites. The no-fuss preparation freed a busy cook for other tasks and made nourishing use of kitchen odds and ends. The pasty (a savory meat-filled pie) was nicknamed "boarding-house meal under a crust."

163

Today casseroles are often ridiculed by those who remember dinners bound in canned cream soup and topped with potato chips. But there are delicious ways of combining leftovers from a memorable dinner or holiday meal into one easy-to-make, satisfying dish. And there is nothing like a flavorful one-dish supper that can be easily popped into the oven to be reheated on a hectic night. For this chapter we've gathered classic recipes such as French-Canadian *Tourtière,* a fragrant meat and onion pie. And we've created a hearty Wild Mushroom Stroganoff that calls forth the flavors of the soft woods. Don't let the term scare you. When made with fresh, wholesome ingredients, a "hot dish" is delicious.

The Krengel family breaks for noon dinner in the field, 1911

J A N S S O N ' S   T E M P T A T I O N

SERVES 4 (RECIPE IS EASILY DOUBLED.)

*N*o one is quite sure of the origins of this popular holiday dish, traditionally served during the second phase of the smörgåsbord dinner. Some claim that it was named for Erik Jansson, a religious leader who left Sweden to found the Bishop Hill community in Illinois.

The recipe calls for Swedish anchovy fillets, less salty than the more popular Portuguese variety. If you'd like to substitute Portuguese anchovies, rinse them well and add a little extra cream. This sturdy dish may be made ahead.

> *2 medium yellow onions, peeled and thinly sliced*
> *½ stick (4 tablespoons) butter*
> *5 medium potatoes, peeled and thinly sliced*
> *1 can (3½ ounces) Swedish anchovy fillets**
> *Freshly ground white pepper*
> *1 cup whipping cream*
> *Chopped fresh parsley for garnish*
>
> **If using Portuguese anchovies, rinse them well and add an extra*
> *¼ cup whipping cream.*

*S*auté the onions in *1 tablespoon* of the butter until soft. Butter a medium baking dish and layer the potatoes, onions, and anchovies, finishing with a layer of potatoes. Dot the casserole with the remaining butter and sprinkle with a few grinds of white pepper. Bake in a preheated 400°F oven. After the first 10 minutes, add half of the cream and continue baking another 10 minutes. Add the remainder of the cream and bake 30 minutes. Reduce the heat to 300°F and bake 30 minutes more. The dish is ready when the potatoes are soft and the top is golden brown. Serve immediately, garnished with chopped fresh parsley.

ROASTED VEGETABLE STRUDEL

SERVES 6 TO 8

*S*trudel is a type of pastry made up of many layers of very thin dough, spread with filling and rolled, then baked until crispy brown. While it is usually associated with German apple strudel, all manner of fillings, savory and sweet, are popular among those who settled here from Germany and Eastern Europe.

Homemade strudel dough is very tricky to handle, requiring patience and experience. But you can easily substitute paper-thin phyllo, which is similar to strudel dough and is available frozen. We serve this strudel with Red Pepper Purée (page 220).

You may vary the vegetables you choose according to the season.

> *1 red onion, peeled and diced in ½-inch pieces*
> *1 carrot, peeled and diced in ½-inch pieces*
> *1 small eggplant, peeled and diced in ½-inch pieces*
>   *(to make 2 cups)*
> *1 small turnip, peeled and thinly sliced*
> *2 zucchini, sliced*
> *2 cloves garlic, chopped*
> *¼ cup olive oil*
> *1 teaspoon salt*
> *1 teaspoon freshly ground pepper*
> *1 tomato, peeled, seeded, and diced*
> *Zest and juice of 1 orange*
> *¼ cup chopped fresh parsley*
> *2 tablespoons chopped fresh rosemary*
> *1 cup crumbled feta cheese*
> *Salt and freshly ground pepper to taste*
> *6 sheets phyllo dough*
> *½ stick (4 tablespoons) butter, melted (approximately)*

*T*oss the onion, carrot, eggplant, turnip, zucchini, and garlic with the olive oil, salt and pepper, then spread on a roasting pan and bake in a preheated 400°F

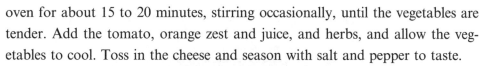

oven for about 15 to 20 minutes, stirring occasionally, until the vegetables are tender. Add the tomato, orange zest and juice, and herbs, and allow the vegetables to cool. Toss in the cheese and season with salt and pepper to taste.

Follow the directions for filling and rolling the strudel given on page 348. Bake the strudel in a preheated 350°F oven about 45 minutes, until golden brown and flaky. Slice and serve with Red Pepper Purée (page 220).

To bake this in a dish, turn the roasted vegetables into a casserole and dot with the feta cheese. Cover with 2 sheets of phyllo dough, brush these liberally with butter, and layer 6 more sheets, brushing each one liberally with butter as you go. Bake in a 350°F oven for 45 minutes, or until the top is crusty brown.

ROASTED ONIONS:
"AN EXCELLENT ARTICLE OF FOOD"

Today's interest in roasting vegetables is really not so new. Nicholas Perrot, an early explorer, described in his journal how wild onions were roasted by the Indians of the Upper Great Lakes in the late 1600s.

"They first place the onions, covering them with a thick layer of grass; and by means of the heat which the fire communicates to them, the acrid quality leaves them, nor are they damaged by the flame. They become an excellent article of food."

The simple process of roasting vegetables given in the above recipe keeps the vegetables moist and flavorful, and requires little attention from the busy cook. Roasted vegetables are delicious when served on pasta or rice and sprinkled with cheese for a main course, or they may be served as a side dish. Roasted vegetables also make a great filling for sandwiches and an interesting topping for pizza.

WILD MUSHROOM STROGANOFF

SERVES 6 TO 8

*M*ushroom hunting has always been popular throughout the Northern Heartland, where puffball, chanterelle, and wood ear mushrooms grow abundantly, even in the front yards of homes on busy streets. Today's interest in wild foods has "mushroomed," and many hunters are taking mushrooming classes offered at local colleges and cooking schools throughout the region.

Most stroganoff recipes call for beef tenderloin or top loin. This version uses meaty shiitake and dark oyster mushrooms, cultivated on farms in central Wisconsin and Minnesota.

This casserole is wonderful to tote to potluck suppers and reheats nicely.

> *3 pounds mixed wild mushrooms (oyster, shiitake,*
> *   wood ear, and button)**
> *2 tablespoons butter*
> *1 cup peeled minced onions and shallots*
> *1 tablespoon salt, plus more to taste*
> *½ teaspoon freshly ground pepper, plus more to taste*
> *2 tablespoons unbleached all-purpose flour*
> *1 cup homemade Chicken or Dark Stock (pages 141*
> *   and 142) or low-salt canned broth*
> *1 cup heavy cream*
> *¼ cup tomato paste*
> *½ cup dry sherry*
> *1 tablespoon chopped fresh thyme or 1 teaspoon dried*
> *1 pound wide noodles*
> *Chopped fresh parsley for garnish*
> *¼ cup toasted, buttered bread crumbs*
>
> **You may also substitute a mixture of button mushrooms and*
> *dried wild mushrooms. Use 2 pounds of button mushrooms and 1*
> *ounce of dried mushrooms reconstituted in 1 cup hot chicken broth.*

*C*lean and roughly chop the mushrooms. Melt the butter in a large skillet and sauté the onions and shallots until soft; then add the mushrooms, 1 tablespoon salt, and ½ teaspoon pepper, and cover and cook about 10 minutes to release the juices, stirring occasionally. Sprinkle the vegetables with flour and stir, cooking about 3 to 4 minutes. Add the stock, cream, tomato paste, sherry, and thyme, and cook on low, stirring occasionally, until the mixture is thick, about 30 minutes.

While the stroganoff is cooking, bring a large pot of water to a boil and cook the noodles for 10 to 12 minutes until done. Drain well. Toss the stroganoff with the noodles, add salt and pepper to taste, and turn into a lightly buttered oven-proof casserole and top with the parsley and bread crumbs. To reheat, cover with aluminum foil and place in a 300°F oven until bubbly and hot.

WILD MUSHROOMS

"I learned to hunt mushrooms from my Czech grandmother. We went after puffballs that she called *pepienki,* out in the pasture, around oak trees and old stumps. You can't be too careful. Sometimes if you have a whole family of mushrooms and there is one off a ways, you pick it, too, and that's the one that gets you sick.

"We'd eat a lot of mushrooms. Those we didn't eat fresh, she'd dry. She'd slice them so that the air could get to them quicker, about half an inch thick. She'd string them with a needle and thread. You need to do this when they're wet because if the mushroom gets too dry, you can't get the needle through it. Then she'd hang them in the attic like a valance. They looked like Hawaiian leis. When she wanted them for soup or stews, she'd pull them off and put them in a dishpan with water and they'd puff back up. She'd then have them ready for those Slovak dishes that call for mushrooms."

—JIM KWITCHAK OF ANOKA, MINNESOTA

CHICKEN (OR TURKEY) POT PIE
WITH BISCUIT CRUST

SERVES 6 TO 8

*P*ot pies are popular at church socials, Grange suppers, and neighborhood potlucks, where everyone who comes contributes to the dinner. This one-dish meal is easy to tote, and the crust top gets crisper in the oven when it is reheated before serving.

We add thyme and nutmeg to the chicken filling and grate sharp Cheddar cheese into our buttermilk biscuit crust. Making a pot pie is a good way to use leftover chicken and turkey.

For variety, try adding ham or mushrooms to the filling.

FILLING

3 cups homemade Chicken Stock (page 141) or low-salt
  canned broth
1 pound chicken or turkey breast or 2½ cups diced cooked
  chicken or turkey meat
3 carrots, diced
2 medium potatoes, peeled and diced
2 stalks celery, diced
½ stick (4 tablespoons) butter
1 cup peeled, chopped onions
4 tablespoons unbleached all-purpose flour
½ cup whole milk
½ teaspoon dried thyme
¼ teaspoon ground nutmeg
¼ cup peas
¼ cup corn kernels (fresh or frozen)
Salt and freshly ground pepper to taste

CRUST

1½ cups unbleached all-purpose flour
½ teaspoon baking powder
½ teaspoon baking soda
¾ teaspoon salt
½ stick (4 tablespoons) butter, cut into bits
⅓ cup grated sharp Cheddar cheese
1 egg
½ cup buttermilk
*Egg wash (1 egg yolk combined with 1 tablespoon milk to
    brush over top of crust)*

To make the filling, bring the stock to a low simmer in a large stockpot. Add the chicken or turkey breast and poach the meat on low (never allowing the water to boil) for about 20 to 30 minutes, or until the meat is no longer pink when cut. Remove the meat from the pot and set aside. Add the carrots, potatoes, and celery, and simmer until the vegetables are soft, about 5 minutes. Dice the meat. Drain and reserve the stock and set the vegetables aside.

Melt the butter in a deep skillet and cook the chopped onions, stirring over medium heat until they are soft, then sprinkle in the flour and cook some more, stirring, about 3 to 5 minutes. Add the milk and *2 cups* of the chicken stock in a stream, stirring, and bring to a boil. Add the thyme and nutmeg, and cook about 5 minutes—the mixture should be thick. Add the peas and corn, taste, and adjust the seasoning. Add the diced chicken and the cooked carrots, potatoes, and celery to the pot and stir to combine. Turn the mixture into a casserole dish or deep pie tin* and make the crust.

To make the crust, sift together the flour, baking powder, baking soda, and salt. Cut in the butter until the dough resembles coarse meal, then toss in the grated cheese. Whisk the egg with the buttermilk. Add to the flour mixture and gently stir to make a soft dough. Turn the dough out onto a lightly floured board and pat it into a large round. Cut the dough into 2½-inch circles.

Place the biscuits on top of the chicken filling and brush with the egg wash. Bake in a preheated 425°F oven for 20 to 25 minutes, or until the crust is golden brown.

**This dish may also be made in individual pies. Use single serving
ramekins and shorten the cooking time to 15 minutes.*

Threshers near Grafton, North Dakota, 1900
Threshers worked from sunup to sundown to "make hay while the sun shines."

THRESHING SEASON
(FEEDING THE CREW)

Among the many farming activities, such as barn raising and hog butchering, threshing was the most tumultuous of the year. Late in August, while the crew worked in the field getting the oats, wheat, barley, or rye into the threshing machine, the women gathered to cook the threshing dinners.

One family owned the threshing machine, and neighbors would work together in crews to bring everyone's harvest in. The day was long—beginning at sunrise and ending well after sunset—for it was critical to get the crop in when it was ready and before the weather turned.

Elinor Watson, Lucia's aunt, remembers: "How hard my mother worked at threshing time! She never left the kitchen. Coffee was ready by four o'clock in the morning. After she finished her milking chores, she served breakfast to my father and the farmhands. Neighbors joined to work in the fields by six o'clock. We served 'lunch' at ten—sandwiches and doughnuts and coffee that we'd drive out to the fields on the tractor.

"For noon 'dinner' we'd set up long tables outside the house. The men would feast on beef stew or a roast with potatoes, heaps of fresh tomatoes, and coleslaw. Cake, pie, coffee, for dessert. They'd stretch out under the big black walnut trees that shaded our backyard, put their hats over their eyes, and rest until it was time to go back out. At four o'clock we'd drive out another 'lunch' with more sandwiches, leftover cake or pie, cookies, and vinegar lemonade [see recipe below].

"Neighbor women came in and out of the kitchen all day long, peeling potatoes, gathering vegetables from the garden, delivering pies, cakes, and cookies. They'd help serve and clean up. Competition was pretty stiff all around. At the table the men boasted about how much they had threshed and how quickly they worked compared with crews on nearby farms. The women got into it, too. My mother tried to serve the best food and plenty of it (most men took third helpings). She always used her china and silver.

VINEGAR LEMONADE

½ cup apple cider vinegar
1 gallon water
1 cup sugar

Mix all the ingredients together and serve cold. Makes 1 gallon. (Recipe is easily doubled.)

THRESHER'S BEEF STEW (WITH ONIONS, BEER, AND BLUE CHEESE)

SERVES 6 TO 8

*F*or this rich stew, the onions are cooked over low heat until golden brown; their sweet flavor is complemented by the sharp blue cheese and full-bodied beer. Serve with Limpa Rye (page 23), a salad of bitter greens with Shallot Vinaigrette (page 252), and glasses of the same beer used in the stew. This recipe is easily expanded to feed a crowd.

2 strips good-quality bacon (optional)
3 tablespoons unsalted butter
2–3 onions, peeled and thinly sliced
Pinch of salt and a pinch of sugar
2 pounds lean, boneless stew meat, cut into 1½-inch cubes
Vegetable oil for sautéing
1½ tablespoons unbleached all-purpose flour
1 bottle strong dark beer (12 ounces)
½ teaspoon salt
3 grinds fresh pepper
2 bay leaves
1 whole sprig thyme
2 sprigs parsley
1 quart homemade Dark Stock (page 142) or low-salt canned broth (enough to cover the meat)
2 tablespoons good-quality red wine vinegar
1 cup crumbled blue cheese for garnish

*I*n a heavy skillet, cook the bacon over medium-high heat to render the fat. Remove the bacon and add the butter to the pan and melt; then add the sliced onions and a pinch of salt and sugar. Cook over very low heat, stirring occasionally, until the onions become a rich caramel color, about 30 minutes.

In a separate stewing pot, sear the meat in a little oil to a nice brown color. Sprinkle with the flour and stir. Then add the beer and scrape up any brown bits from the bottom of the pot. Add the onions to the meat, and be sure to scrape the skillet for every last bit of flavoring. Season with the salt and pepper. Tie the bay leaves, thyme, and parsley into a square of cheesecloth to make a pouch (bouquet garni) and add to the pot. Cover it all with stock, reduce the heat, and simmer about 1½ hours, stirring occasionally. Remove the bouquet garni and add the vinegar. Serve the stew in bowls with the blue cheese sprinkled on top.

GRANGE POTLUCK

In 1867 Iowa farmers banded together and founded the Grange to fight the railroad. "They were gouging the farmers on their shipping prices so badly it was tough for anyone trying to make a little money on their crops," says Adolph Altemeir of Grinnell, Iowa, an active Granger since 1925.

The Grange, which has continued to lobby for the rights and interests of farmers, has become a national organization with over 500,000 members across the country. Grange women are tireless community boosters, raising money for local charities throughout the rural Midwest. They sponsor annual sewing contests, make stuffed toys to sell at craft shows, and hold cakewalks (the lucky "walker" who lands on the winning number at the end of a tune wins a homemade cake) and box-supper auctions.

Grange potluck suppers traditionally end most Grange meetings. A buffet of local specialties, the potluck might include chicken pot pie, turkey salad, corn relish, rice pudding, brownies, fresh zucchini bread, beef stew, and homemade rolls. It's a showcase for proud cooks, a chance to try new recipes and exchange ideas.

SARMA
(STUFFED CABBAGE ROLLS)

SERVES 8 TO 10 (FREEZES WELL.)

*A*lso known as "pigs in the blanket," *sarmas* are a mainstay in miners' homes across the Iron Range. Cooks of Croatian origin add ground ham to the filling of ground beef, pork (and sometimes veal), and rice. Polish cooks use only ground beef and add pork short ribs to the kettle for flavoring.

Years ago, when families made their own supply of sauerkraut, they also put up whole heads of sour cabbage and used the leaves to roll up *sarmas*. Today canned or jarred sauerkraut, added to the pan with the cabbage rolls, gives a similar flavor.

The cabbage leaves must first be softened (usually blanched) before they can be rolled around the filling. Helen Drazenovich Berklich of Eveleth, Minnesota, suggests: "Take your large head of cabbage and put it in your freezer a few days and take out the night before making *sarma*. This wilts your cabbage perfectly. You need not parboil your cabbage."

Sarmas are made by rolling the cabbage leaves up twice—first vertically, then horizontally—so they resemble small fists.

1 large head cabbage
¼ pound pork sausage
¾ pound lean ground beef
½ cup uncooked rice
½ cup minced onions
1 clove garlic, crushed
1 egg
½ teaspoon ground nutmeg
1 tablespoon fennel seed
1 tablespoon Worcestershire sauce
1 tablespoon dried oregano
½ teaspoon each, salt and freshly ground pepper
1 quart sauerkraut, drained
1 large onion, peeled and sliced
1 fresh fennel bulb, chopped (optional)
2 tablespoons caraway seeds
1 quart puréed tomatoes with their juice
½ cup white wine (optional)
Chopped fresh fennel for garnish (optional)

*B*lanch the cabbage head by immersing it in a large pot of rapidly boiling water for about 5 minutes, or until the leaves are soft and pliable. Or, follow Mrs. Berklich's advice (above). (You may need to do this again as you peel off the leaves. Sometimes the interior leaves do not soften with the first blanching.) Set the cabbage head aside to cool.

In a large bowl, mix together the sausage, beef, rice, minced onions, garlic, egg, nutmeg, fennel seed, Worcestershire sauce, oregano, salt, and pepper.

Make oblong balls of the meat mixture (as though to fit a clenched fist), then set each ball on the bottom of a cabbage leaf. Roll the leaf vertically first, then horizontally. Place the sauerkraut, sliced onion, and chopped fennel bulb on the bottom of a large, deep saucepan. Place the cabbage rolls on top. Scatter the caraway seeds over that. Add the tomatoes and wine. Cover the saucepan, bring to a simmer, and cook over low heat for about 35 to 45 minutes, or until the cabbage is soft and, when you slice into a roll, the meat is no longer pink. Serve garnished with chopped fresh fennel, if desired.

TOURTIÈRE
(FRENCH MEAT PIE)

SERVES 8 TO 10

*T*he French who settled along the shores of the Great Lakes would prepare this simple meat pie for Christmas Eve supper. Years ago the pie was baked in a pottery casserole called a *tourte,* hence the name *tourtière.*

Adele Bierke of Bayfield, Wisconsin, remembers: "Mother made this a day ahead so she wouldn't have to fuss when we returned from midnight mass. She set a splendid table with lots of breads, cakes, and fruit, plus home-made chokecherry wine and plenty of hot chocolate for the children."

PASTRY

1½ cups unbleached all-purpose flour
½ teaspoon salt
½ cup lard or vegetable shortening
6–8 tablespoons ice water

FILLING

2 tablespoons butter
½ cup peeled, chopped onions
1 clove garlic, peeled and chopped
1½ pounds ground veal/pork/beef (meat loaf) mix
¼ cup homemade Dark Stock (page 142) or low-salt
  canned broth
1 teaspoon salt
½ teaspoon freshly ground pepper
½ teaspoon ground nutmeg
½ teaspoon ground cinnamon
¼ teaspoon dried thyme
1 medium boiling potato
Salt and freshly ground pepper to taste

*T*o make the pastry, sift the dry ingredients into a large bowl. Cut in the lard with a pastry cutter, two knives, or your fingertips until the flour and lard form small peas. Add 6 tablespoons ice water and stir the dough until it forms a ball, adding more water if it seems too dry. Cover with plastic wrap and refrigerate at least 30 minutes (or overnight) before rolling out.

To make the filling, sauté the onions and garlic in *1 tablespoon* of the butter until soft. Add the meat and sauté until it is no longer pink. Add the stock and seasonings, reduce the heat to low, and simmer, uncovered, for about 10 minutes, or until about 2 tablespoons liquid remain. In a separate pot, boil the potato, then skin and mash it.

Add the potato to the meat, then add salt and pepper to taste. Cool the mixture.

Place the filling in a deep dish, an 8-inch pie tin, or a casserole. Dot the top of the casserole with the remaining *1 tablespoon* butter. Roll out the dough on a floured board and place it on top of the filling. Cut decorative slashes into the top of the dough. Bake it in a 425°F oven for 15 minutes, then lower the temperature to 375°F and bake 25 minutes, or until golden brown.

Summer picnics and winter potlucks brought congregations together with lots of homemade food.

PASTY

The Cornish who came to work on the Iron Ranges of Michigan's Upper Peninsula and northern Minnesota in the late 1800s introduced the pasty (pronounced *pass*-tee), a meat-and-potato-filled pastry turnover, to their Finn, Czech, Irish, Italian, and Yugoslavian co-workers, who made it their standard noon meal. A miner's lunch pail held hot coffee or soup in the bottom to warm the pasty in the top compartment. Early pasty makers would bake a whole meal into the crust, filling one end with meat and the other with apples or cherries. Made with a firm, lard dough that would not crumble, a good pasty was supposed to hold up if dropped down the mine shaft.

Today the homey pasty is a popular staple in northern Minnesota, northern Wisconsin, and the Upper Peninsula of Michigan, and the subject of much debate. Eleanor Ostman of Hibbing, Minnesota, remembers: "We ate them with ketchup, not gravy and mashed potatoes—that's Michigan. Whether to cook the meat first (my mother never did) and whether to add 'bagas [rutabagas] was always an issue." Three vent slashes cut on top of the pasty means made with 'bagas, and two slashes without. Michigan cooks choose turnips over 'bagas. Purists add suet before closing up the crust; we favor butter, plus garlic and herbs.

Regardless of geography, all pasty lovers agree that a pasty is properly made "when the juice runs off your elbow as you eat it."

ELLEN OSTMAN'S PASTY

**MAKES 2 LARGE PASTIES (ENOUGH FOR
2 OR 4 PEOPLE, DEPENDING ON APPETITE)***

*E*leanor Ostman, who grew up in Hibbing, Minnesota, says that there are several schools of thought regarding the assembly of a pasty. "Some schools insist that the vegetables and meat be layered. My mother, Ellen, liked them tossed together so they were colorful. She always used a good cut of meat—diced round steak—something not too fatty and not too dry. She never cooked the meat first, but cut it up into small pieces, as she did the vegetables. She was a great believer in butter. Others added suet."

1 recipe Rich Tart Crust (page 353), but omit the sugar
1 cup peeled, finely diced potatoes
1 cup finely diced carrots
1 cup peeled, finely diced onions
1 cup finely diced rutabaga or turnips
1 cup finely diced meat (round steak)
1 teaspoon salt
½ teaspoon freshly ground pepper or to taste†
2 cloves garlic, peeled and minced (optional)
1 tablespoon dried thyme (optional)
⅛ teaspoon ground nutmeg (optional)
2 tablespoons butter

*Some folks like to make them into finger food for the cocktail tray.
*†Some like their pasties made with lots of pepper. Double or
triple the quantity in this recipe to taste.*

*R*oll out the two crusts to the size of dinner plates. Toss together the vegetables, meat, and seasonings. Divide the mixture, mound it onto the piecrusts, and then dot with butter. Fold each crust in half and put the pasties into a large, lightly greased, round cake tin or on a lightly greased baking sheet. Bake in a preheated 375°F oven for 50 minutes to 1 hour, or until the crust is nicely browned.

Michigan Variation: Reduce the amount of beef to ½ cup and add ½ cup pork. Substitute turnips for rutabaga.

CASSEROLE
OF CARAMELIZED ONIONS
AND LEFTOVER MEAT

SERVES 4 TO 6

*U*se any kind of leftover meat in this easy, rich casserole. Try it with leftover Heartland Brisket (page 123), Veal Pot Roast with Maple-Mustard Glaze (page 128), Pork Loin with Apples and Cider Sauce (page 110), or Holiday Roast Wild Turkey (page 190). Serve it with a tossed green salad and Cottage Cheese Dill Bread (page 20).

About 1 pound leftover roast
2 tablespoons butter plus 1 teaspoon or more for top of
*   casserole*
2 onions, peeled and thinly sliced
1 clove garlic, crushed
1 cup sliced mushrooms
2 tablespoons cognac or red wine (optional)
2 cups homemade Dark Stock (page 142) or low-salt
*   canned broth*
2 sprigs parsley
2 sprigs fresh thyme or 2 teaspoons dried
1 bay leaf
Salt and freshly ground pepper to taste
½ cup bread crumbs
½ cup grated sharp cheese (Parmesan, Asiago, or sharp
*   Cheddar)*
Butter

*S*lice the meat thin and set aside. In a large saucepan, melt the butter over low heat and sauté the onions until they are soft and have turned a caramel color (allow about 1 hour). Add the garlic and mushrooms and cook a few minutes more, until the mushrooms are soft. Stir in the cognac and stock. Tie the parsley, thyme, and bay leaf in a square of cheesecloth to form a bouquet garni. Add to stock. Cook over low heat, stirring occasionally, for about 10 to 15 minutes. Add salt and pepper to taste.

Pour a layer of the mushroom-onion sauce into a casserole dish, then cover with a layer of meat, top with the sauce, add more meat, and continue layering until all of the meat is in the dish; then top with the remaining sauce. Sprinkle the casserole with bread crumbs and grated cheese and dot it with butter. Bake the dish in a preheated 350°F oven until it is hot and crusty.

HOT DISH

Garrison Keillor once observed that when Lutheran women reach heaven, they think they are in church and immediately look for the basement stairs to find the kitchen. And they are carrying a "hot dish."

Hot dish is pronounced as though it was one word—hottish—almost like Scottish. In the Northern Heartland the term is often used interchangeably with casserole. For some, it describes a type of casserole made with macaroni, ground meat, assorted cooked vegetables (usually corn or peas), maybe tomatoes, bound together with cream-of-anything soup and topped with shredded cheese and bread crumbs, cracker crumbs, potato chips, canned fried onion rings, or cereal flakes.

While the variations are endless, the theme is universal. The hot dish is a simple, satisfying, fix-ahead meal that generally appeals to both grown-ups and kids, makes use of leftovers, and can be made in quantity to serve a crowd. It is often brought to informal gatherings, for it reheats nicely and holds through the long serving time.

SAUSAGE, BEANS, AND PEPPER STEW

SERVES 8 TO 10

*T*his easy supper can be made in a Crockpot and tastes even better the next day. Try serving over noodles with a crisp salad of bitter greens and Rosemary-Balsamic Vinaigrette (page 251) and a loaf of Potato Bread (page 21).

1 cup dry navy or kidney beans
3 pounds sausage links (a mixture of sweet and hot is best)
Vegetable oil for sautéing
1 large onion, peeled and chopped
3 cloves garlic, minced
1 medium eggplant, peeled and cut into 2-inch cubes
1 zucchini, cut into 2-inch cubes
½ cup chopped parsley
1 quart plum tomatoes (fresh or canned)
2 cups homemade Dark Stock (page 142) or low-salt
    canned broth
1 cup red wine
1 tablespoon dried oregano
2 green peppers, deveined and coarsely chopped
1 red pepper, deveined and coarsely chopped
1 yellow pepper, deveined and coarsely chopped
¼ cup grated Parmesan cheese for garnish
2–3 tablespoons chopped fresh parsley for garnish

*R*inse and sort the beans, put them in a pot, and cover with water to soak overnight.*

Cut the sausage into bite-size pieces and sauté in a large kettle until brown. (You may need to do this in batches.) Remove the sausage and set it aside. Add a little oil, if necessary, and sauté the vegetables (except the peppers) in batches until soft. Return the meat to the pot and add the parsley, tomatoes, stock, wine, and oregano. Drain the beans and add to the pot. Partially cover, bring the kettle to a simmer, and cook for about 2 hours, or until the beans are soft. Remove the lid and simmer until the stew is as thick as you like. Add the peppers and cook another 10 to 15 minutes. Top with grated Parmesan cheese and chopped parsley.

> *If you haven't time to soak the beans overnight, simply put them in a large saucepan, cover with water, and bring to a boil. Reduce the heat and simmer the beans about 5 minutes. Then remove from heat and allow to stand about 1 hour. Drain, rinse, and proceed with the recipe.*

Breast of Pheasant with Shallot-Wine Sauce

Holiday Roast Wild Turkey

Roast Duck with Berry Purée

Duck, Wild Rice, and Hazelnut Salad

Grouse with Cranberry-Sage Butter

Squab Braised with Tomatoes and Rosemary

Woodcock with Wild Mushrooms

Quail with Sorrel-Ricotta Stuffing

Rabbit with Rosemary, Garlic, and Sweet Peppers

Grilled Venison Steaks with Dried Cherry-Tarragon Sauce

Uncle Byron's Game Sausage

Mincemeat

North Woods
and Prairies

Large and Small Game

Early explorers rejoiced in the abundant game that stalked the woods, swam the lakes, and flew low over the open prairies. Venison, bear, wild turkey, grouse, partridge, and the ubiquitous wild pigeon (mourning dove) saved many a struggling pioneer family from starvation. Even the poorest shot could bag a pigeon or, when the birds were roosting, knock one from a tree with a stick. In the fall, ducks fed on wild rice and became so fat and slow that hunters simply whacked them with paddles and pulled them into their canoes.

The native Ojibway tribes and the French explorers shared the spoils of their hunt in great mutual feasts. The Ojibway taught the explorers to pound dried venison with dried berries and fat and shape it into cakes known as pemmican—survival food for the long winter. The natives taught them to roast game on spits over an open fire. The explorers gave the natives metal skewers to conduct the heat through the roasting meat and they introduced salt for seasoning and preserving. To this day, Ojibway elders shun salt, preferring the traditional maple syrup and dried berries to flavor roasts and stews.

Game provided more than food in pioneer life. The settlers wore the fur and stuffed the feathers into quilts and pillows. They used the fat for softening leather, greasing axles, and oiling squeaky hinges, and made it into hand lotion, soap, and medicinal rubs for chests and joints.

Fall hunting remains a strong tradition throughout the Northern Heartland. When the leaves begin turning and the air becomes crisp, sportsmen and -women take to the wilds in hopes of bagging their limit. For many families, the spoils of the weekend hunt stock the freezer with duck, venison, and game birds.

Our recipes blend the classic rich flavor of game with fresh, local herbs, vegetables, and berries. Many of these dishes call for special herbs and aromatics that go with game, such as juniper, dried fruits, wines, and liqueurs. Too often, game is just thrown on the grill or cooked without much attention to enhancing its wonderful flavor. Here we offer recipes such as Grilled Venison Steaks with Dried Cherry-Tarragon Sauce and Roast Duck with Berry Purée. Domesticated game may be substituted for wild game in many of these recipes; in others, it's best to stay wild.

AUTUMN

Autumn is a fine season with the blaze of swamp maple, the hills afire moving up the sky, the stooped back in the field gleaming, the fat quiet ripeness hanging under the sniff of smoke, the rising mists, the sudden frosts, the Indian summer haze hanging under the hills—grapes and chrysanthemums, shocks of corn, and the white hoar frost in the morning. At night there is the high wedge and honk of birds flying south...

—MERIDEL LE SUEUR, *North Star Country*

BREAST OF PHEASANT
WITH SHALLOT-WINE SAUCE

SERVES 4

*T*his simple recipe works well with the breast of any small game bird—grouse, woodcock, pheasant, pigeon, even a small duck. Serve with wild rice. It's very important to use a good-quality wine when making the sauce.

> *2 pheasants, breasts boned out**
> *Salt and freshly ground pepper*
> *2 tablespoons of half butter and half vegetable oil*
> *3 tablespoons peeled, minced shallot*
> *1½ cups good-quality red wine*
> *1 cup homemade Chicken Stock (page 141) or low-salt*
>   *canned broth*
> *2 tablespoons chopped fresh thyme*
> *1 tablespoon cold butter*
>
> **Use the carcasses to enrich the homemade Chicken Stock or*
> *canned broth.*

*P*ound the breasts flat, then season with salt and pepper. Heat the butter and oil in a large skillet and sauté the breasts about 10 minutes per side, or until the juices run clear. Remove from the pan and blot up any excess grease with a paper towel. Add the minced shallot and sauté 1 minute. Stir in the wine and then the stock. Simmer the mixture until it is reduced by more than half and is thick and shiny. Stir in the thyme and swirl in the cold butter.

Serve the breasts over wild rice, drizzle the sauce over them, and garnish with any remaining thyme.

HOLIDAY ROAST WILD TURKEY

SERVES 10 TO 14

*W*ild turkeys feed on acorns and as a result they have an exceptionally rich flavor that is not at all gamy. Ranging in size from 8 to 30 pounds, wild turkeys are leaner than their domestic counterparts and require frequent basting during roasting.

Try stuffing the turkey with Corn Bread Stuffing (page 69). Just before pulling the turkey from the oven, baste it with Maple-Almond-Pecan or Spicy-Nut Butter (page 95), and serve it with Cranberry Leek Compote (page 287) and Perfect Mashed Potatoes (page 272) with plenty of Pan Gravy (below).

1 wild (or domestic*) turkey, about 8–12 pounds
1 stick (8 tablespoons) soft butter
Salt and freshly ground pepper
1 recipe Corn Bread Stuffing (page 69), or 2 cups of your
  favorite stuffing
3 tablespoons Maple-Almond-Pecan or Spicy-Nut Butter
  (page 95), or regular butter

*Domestic turkeys have more fat and may be rubbed with half the specified amount of butter and basted less frequently.

PAN GRAVY

2 tablespoons unbleached all-purpose flour
2 cups homemade Turkey or Chicken Stock (page 141) or
  low-salt canned broth
Salt and pepper to taste
Brandy or applejack as desired

*R*inse the turkey inside and out and pat it dry. Rub it all over with plenty of butter, then sprinkle generously with salt and pepper. Fill the cavity loosely with stuffing. Truss the turkey by tying its legs together over the body cavity with kitchen string. To prevent the wings from drying out, tuck the tips under the turkey's back. Place the turkey on a roasting rack and roast in a preheated 350°F oven approximately 2½ to 3 hours, basting frequently (adding more butter if necessary), or until the internal temperature is 180°F and the juices run clear when the meat is pricked with a fork. About 5 minutes before pulling the turkey from the oven, brush it all over with the Maple Butter or melted butter. Allow the turkey to rest about 20 minutes before carving.

To make the gravy: Drain off and save the roasting juices, then remove and discard all but ¼ cup of fat and return to the roasting pan. Set the roasting pan over low heat, add the flour to the pan and blend thoroughly, scraping to loosen the bits of dark drippings. Cook over low heat about 2 minutes, stirring constantly, until smooth. Gradually stir in the pan juices and enough stock to make 2 cups and cook, stirring constantly, until the mixture thickens, about 5 minutes. Salt and pepper to taste, and add a splash of brandy or apple-jack, if desired.

WILD TURKEY

With its thirty-inch fan, the wild turkey is America's most spectacular game bird. Hunters who have been outwitted by one often assign the turkey a high level of intelligence. But its remarkable ability to elude hunters probably owes more to its extraordinary hearing and eyesight. The turkey can spot trouble from a distance of more than five hundred yards away. When it senses danger, the bird reacts instantly and will hit the ground running at twenty miles per hour (as fast as a deer) or burst into flight, reaching upwards of fifty miles per hour in seconds.

Wild turkeys roost in trees at night, and sometimes a whole flock of one dozen will fill the thick branches of an old oak. Successful turkey hunters become skillful turkey callers, luring a lusty gobbler with mouth diaphragms, tubes, bellows, and hooters that imitate a hen in heat.

ROAST DUCK
WITH BERRY PURÉE

SERVES 6

*W*ild duck is far leaner and sometimes tougher than its domestic counterpart. To keep it moist when roasting, it should be covered with bacon or basted frequently with butter.

Domestic duck must be pricked continuously while roasting, just enough to pierce the skin and release the fat and juices to baste the meat, imparting flavor and keeping in moisture.

Cooking time depends on the size of the duck. Larger ducks such as mallards, canvasbacks, black ducks, and redheads will serve two people each. Gadwalls, widgeons, wood ducks, pintails, ringnecks, scaups, and goldeneyes are smaller: three ducks will serve four. Allow one teal per person. (Supermarkets most commonly sell the larger ducks.)

Our sweet, tart berry sauce is delicious with the dark flavor of duck. We serve this with Roasted Sweet Potato Purée (page 273) and sautéed mustard greens.

> *3 large ducks (wild or domestic)*
> *Salt and freshly ground pepper*
> *3 to 4 strips bacon (for wild duck)*
>
> *BERRY PURÉE*
>
> *3 cups fresh or frozen berries (raspberries, blackberries,*
>   *strawberries—alone or in combination)*
> *2 tablespoons sugar (to taste, depending on how sweet the*
>   *berries are)*
> *1 cup high-quality red wine*
> *6 whole cloves*
> *3 bay leaves*
> *3 tablespoons Grand Marnier*
> *½ stick (4 tablespoons) butter*

*R*inse the ducks and pat dry. Sprinkle with salt and pepper and prick lightly all over with a fork. If cooking wild duck, drape the breasts with bacon to keep moist. Place the ducks on racks and roast in a preheated 300°F oven for about 1 hour (for rare) to 1½ hours (well done). If cooking domestic duck, prick it periodically throughout the cooking to release the fat and juices, until the ducks are golden brown.

While the ducks are roasting, prepare the sauce. Purée the berries with the sugar in a food processor fitted with a steel blade or in a blender. Strain out the seeds and reserve the purée. In a small saucepan, simmer the wine, cloves, and bay leaves until the liquid is reduced by half. Strain the wine. Return the berries and wine to the saucepan and add the Grand Marnier, bring to a boil, and swirl in the butter. Carve the ducks and serve with some sauce drizzled over each serving and the rest passed on the side.

DUCK, WILD RICE,
AND HAZELNUT SALAD

SERVES 8

*D*uck, wild rice, and hazelnuts are tossed with a bit of jalapeño for kick, and a light, sweet dressing laced with Frangelico (hazelnut liqueur), though you may opt for a dash of orange juice instead. This makes a delicious main course or hearty first course, blending the flavors of autumn in a colorful, simple salad, served slightly warm or at room temperature.

*1 cooked duck (page 192), brushed with Frangelico several
    times the last ½ hour of cooking*
3 cups cooked wild rice (page 275)
2 oranges, peeled and cut into sections
½ cup sliced radishes
½ cup fresh spring peas (or frozen)
1 small jalapeño pepper, deveined, seeded, and diced
¼ cup chopped scallions
1 stalk celery, chopped
¼ cup white wine vinegar
1 shallot, peeled and chopped
1 tablespoon mustard
¼ cup hazelnut oil (or olive oil)
¼ cup peanut (or vegetable) oil)
1 tablespoon Frangelico (or frozen orange juice concentrate)
Salt and freshly ground pepper to taste
Salad greens
½ cup toasted, chopped hazelnuts (page 216) for garnish

Skin the duck, remove all of the meat, then cut into 1-inch pieces. In a large bowl, toss together the duck meat, wild rice, oranges, radishes, peas, jalapeño, scallions, and celery. In a medium-sized jar with a lid, shake together the vinegar, shallot, and mustard until combined. Add the two oils and Frangelico, then shake until the mixture is emulsified. Taste and adjust the seasoning. Pour the dressing over the wild rice and duck mixture and toss to combine. Serve the salad over greens, garnished with the chopped hazelnuts.

HAZELNUTS

The Ojibway of Fond du Lac in northern Minnesota would pick hazelnuts, store them in birch-bark bags, and leave them to dry until winter. During the long, cold season, tribe members would gather around the cook fire inside the tepee to listen to the storyteller and shuck the nuts of their prickly hulls.

GROUSE WITH
CRANBERRY-SAGE BUTTER

SERVES 4

*G*rouse, also known as partridge, feed on wild berries, nuts, and seeds. Lucia remembers bagging grouse near a wild cranberry bog in southern Wisconsin. The wild berries had turned the birds' flesh a bright, beautiful pink and the meat was light and succulent.

In this recipe, we drape the grouse with bacon, then baste it with a compound butter of cranberries and fragrant sage. This recipe will work equally well with pheasant or small Cornish game hen.

> *2 dressed grouse (about 1 pound each)**
> *Salt and freshly ground pepper*
> *1 tart apple*
> *8 sprigs fresh sage*
> *¼ cup cranberries*
> *2 tablespoons water*
> *1 stick (8 tablespoons) butter*
> *1 tablespoon chopped fresh sage*
> *1 shallot, peeled and minced*
> *4 pieces good-quality bacon*
> *Dark Stock (see page 142), or low-salt canned broth, or*
> *   wine or water to cover bottom of roasting pan*
> *Sage leaf for garnish*
>
> **Most hunters skin the grouse when they clean them. If using domestic game hens, leave the skin on, rub the butter under the skin, and omit the bacon.*

*R*inse the birds and pat dry. Sprinkle inside and out with salt and freshly ground pepper. Core the apple and cut into quarters. Place 2 quarters of apple and 4 sprigs of sage in each of the bird's cavities.

In a small saucepan, cook the cranberries in the water just until they pop. Let cool. Pour the berries along with the butter, sage, and shallot into a food processor fitted with a steel blade and process until combined. Rub the birds with half of the mixture; drape 2 slices of bacon evenly over each of the birds, and place on a roasting rack, set over a roasting pan. Put about 2 inches of stock, water, or wine into the bottom of the pan; tent the birds with aluminum foil, then place the pan in a preheated 350°F oven.

Roast the birds about 40 minutes. Remove the foil, baste with a little more of the butter if necessary, and continue roasting another 5 to 10 minutes, or until they are nicely browned. Carve the grouse into quarters and serve with little pats of the compound butter melting over each piece, and garnish with sage leaf.

SQUAB BRAISED WITH TOMATOES AND ROSEMARY

SERVES 4

*S*quab, perhaps the most common game bird, is now raised commercially for retail markets and restaurants. Squab has a dark meat that is rich-tasting, but it can be tough. We like to braise squab with a full-bodied red wine, rosemary, and tomato, allowing all the flavors to blend through long, slow cooking.

> *4 squab or 4 large duck breasts*
> *Salt and freshly ground pepper*
> *3 tablespoons olive oil*
> *1 tablespoon minced garlic*
> *1 medium red onion, peeled and coarsely chopped*
> *1 cup high-quality red wine*
> *2 cups homemade Chicken Stock or Dark Stock (pages*
> *   141 and 142) or low-salt canned broth*
> *2 sprigs fresh rosemary or 1 teaspoon dried*
> *2 fresh tomatoes, cut into 2-inch pieces*
> *2 tablespoons cold butter*

*R*inse the squab and pat them dry, then sprinkle salt and freshly ground pepper into each body cavity and over each bird. In a large, heatproof casserole or Dutch oven, heat the oil and brown the squab on all sides. Add the garlic and onion and sauté for about 1 minute. Add the wine and the remaining ingredients *except the butter,* cover the pot, and braise the birds in a preheated 350°F oven for about 45 to 50 minutes, or until the thigh juices run clear when pierced with a fork. Remove the rosemary sprigs. Remove the squab and place on individual plates or a serving platter and tent them with aluminum foil to keep warm. Place the casserole or Dutch oven on top of the stove and bring the braising liquid to a boil. Reduce the liquid by half, about 10 to 15 minutes. Turn off the heat and whisk in the cold butter to make a rich sauce. Serve the squab drizzled with the sauce.

WOODCOCK
WITH WILD MUSHROOMS

SERVES 2

*T*he woodcock, or "timberdoodle," with its mottled brown-and-black-speckled feathers, often escapes hunters simply by staying perfectly still. It also has such keen hearing that it can locate worms by listening to them underground.

The tiny breast of the woodcock is dark and has a strong flavor, not unlike liver. It's delicious with wild mushrooms and shallots.

> *8 woodcock breasts or 4 duck breasts*
> *½ stick (4 tablespoons) butter*
> *4 shallots, peeled and chopped*
> *1 cup mushrooms (use wild if you can, or good-quality*
>   *button)*
> *2–4 tablespoons balsamic vinegar or fresh lemon juice*
> *2 tablespoons water*
> *¼ cup chopped fresh parsley*
> *Fresh sprigs parsley for garnish*

*L*ightly pound the breasts flat. In a large skillet, melt the butter over medium-high heat and sauté the breasts, about 4 to 5 minutes per side. (Duck breasts will need about 8 minutes per side.) Remove and place on a heated plate. Add the shallots and mushrooms to the skillet and cook until limp. Add the vinegar and water to deglaze the pan, then add the chopped parsley. Return the breasts to the skillet and toss to coat. Serve with wild rice, garnished with fresh parsley.

QUAIL WITH
SORREL-RICOTTA STUFFING

SERVES 4

*Q*uail, often erroneously called partridge, are small nonmigratory birds that nest on the ground and prefer walking to flying. They are very sociable and travel in small groups known as coveys. Many Northern Heartland game farms raise quail, which are sold frozen in the meat departments of grocery stores.

Quail meat is white and delicate. In this recipe we blend ricotta cheese and tangy sorrel (a sour grass used for centuries by Europeans in cooking) into a delicious stuffing. We fill the body cavity and press the stuffing under the skin; then we roast the birds until they are plump and golden brown. If fresh sorrel is unavailable, you may substitute fresh spinach. This stuffing is also delicious in grouse, game hen, and chicken. Serve with Gratin of Pumpkin and Leeks (page 266).

4 quail
Salt and freshly ground pepper
1 small onion, peeled and chopped
½ stick (4 tablespoons) butter, softened, plus a little more
    for basting
1 cup ricotta cheese
¼ cup grated Parmesan cheese
1 cup thinly sliced sorrel or fresh spinach
1 egg
⅛ teaspoon ground nutmeg

*R*inse the quail and sprinkle each body cavity and the outside of the birds with salt and freshly ground pepper.

In a small skillet, sauté the onion in *1 tablespoon* of the butter. Combine the cooked onion, remaining butter, ricotta cheese, grated Parmesan, sorrel, egg, and nutmeg. Add salt and pepper to taste. Using your fingers, gently lift the skin and stuff the mixture around the breast, being careful not to tear the skin, then fill the cavities with the remaining stuffing. Rub the quail with the extra softened butter and roast, basting occasionally, in a preheated 350°F oven for about 45 to 50 minutes, or until the thigh juices run clear when pierced with a fork.

WILD PIGEONS

When the Northern Heartland was first settled, wild pigeons (now called mourning doves and known to cooks as squab) were especially abundant and unbelievably easy to come by, even for the poorest shot. At sunset huge flocks would settle in the oaks to roost; so numerous were they that often they piled up on top of one another until their weight would break the branches.

Many settlers adopted the Indian method of cooking a pigeon. They covered the pigeon with clay, poked the clay with a few holes to release the steam, then baked it in the fire. When the bird was fully cooked, the clay was broken off, removing with it the feathers and skin, leaving the succulent, moist flesh.

This method of cooking squab and other lean, small game birds over low heat in a tightly covered pot keeps the meat moist in much the same way as the Indian method, and it is still the most reliable way to prepare the birds today.

RABBIT WITH ROSEMARY, GARLIC, AND SWEET PEPPERS

SERVES 6

*R*abbit, both wild and domestic, is a favorite dish among the Eastern Europeans who settled Wisconsin and Minnesota. This recipe works quite well with cut-up chicken if you can't find rabbit. Serve this dish with *Spaetzle* (page 101). Don't hesitate to use an abundance of fresh rosemary in this recipe.

> *3 rabbits*
> *Unbleached all-purpose flour seasoned with salt and freshly*
>   *ground pepper*
> *4 tablespoons olive oil*
> *1 tablespoon minced garlic*
> *2 cups high-quality red wine*
> *Two 3-inch sprigs fresh rosemary or 1 teaspoon dried*
> *1 bay leaf*
> *2 juniper berries*
> *6 cups homemade Dark Stock (page 142) or low-salt*
>   *canned broth*
> *Salt and freshly ground pepper to taste*
> *1 each, yellow, green, and red bell peppers, deveined,*
>   *seeded, and cut into strips*
> *Fresh sprigs rosemary for garnish*

*T*rim the fat from the rabbits, rinse, pat dry, and cut into saddle, leg, and loin sections. Dredge the rabbit in seasoned flour. Heat the oil in a large, deep skillet or Dutch oven and sauté the rabbit quarters until browned, then set them aside on a heated plate.

Add the garlic to the skillet and toss; then add the wine, rosemary, bay leaf, and juniper berries and bring the mixture to a boil. Reduce the heat and add the browned rabbit with enough stock to cover; then cover the pan and braise in a preheated 350°F oven for about 2 hours.

Remove the rabbit pieces and set them aside on a heated plate. Strain the liquid. Simmer on low to reduce the sauce by one third, add salt and freshly ground pepper to taste, then return the rabbit to the skillet, along with the peppers. To serve, place one saddle, one leg, and one rib section on each plate; then spoon a generous amount of sauce and peppers over the rabbit on each plate. Garnish the plates with tiny sprigs of rosemary.

ALEXIS BAILLY WINES...
"WHERE THE GRAPES SUFFER"

Alexis Bailly Winery, in the St. Croix River Valley, produces eight distinctly dry red table wines from hardy hybrid, native grapes. The winery's slogan is apt: The grapes suffer extreme temperatures—from the bitter cold of −40°F to scorching summers of 100°F. For protection in the winter, the vines are laid on the ground and buried with 6 to 10 inches of soil; the snow adds another blanket of insulation. These extreme temperature swings lend an unusual and very pleasing crispness and flavor to the wines. Alexis Bailly produces only 3,000 to 5,000 gallons of wine per year.

Founded by Nan and David Bailly and named for Nan's great-great-grandfather, an early French pioneer and settler, the Alexis Bailly Winery does not sell to retail customers nationally, but their bottles are often on the wine lists at fine restaurants in California, Chicago, and New York City.

GRILLED VENISON STEAKS WITH DRIED CHERRY-TARRAGON SAUCE

SERVES 4

Years ago butcher shops throughout the Northern Heartland sold cuts of venison, along with their beef and pork, to city folk who didn't care to bag their own. Today only a few specialty shops carry venison, and those of us who love this lean, flavorful meat must either learn to hunt or know someone who does.

If you can't find venison steaks, bison (see page 137) or a good lean cut of lamb or beef will do nicely. This sauce is equally delicious over grilled chicken (substitute Chicken Stock for the Dark Stock in the recipe).

4 venison steaks (about ¾ inch thick and 6 ounces each)
   or lamb or beef
Salt and freshly ground pepper to taste
1 cup orange juice
½ cup dried cherries or diced dried apricots
1 cup homemade Dark Stock (page 142) or low-salt
   canned broth
1½ teaspoons crushed juniper berries
1 tablespoon fresh tarragon or 1 teaspoon dried
2 oranges, peeled and thinly sliced
1 tablespoon peppercorns
½ stick (4 tablespoons) unsalted butter
Chopped fresh chives for garnish

Lightly sprinkle the venison steaks with salt and freshly ground pepper and set aside.

In a medium-sized saucepan, heat the orange juice to a boil and add the dried cherries. Simmer 1 minute, remove from the heat, and allow to stand about 30 minutes, or until the cherries are plump. Remove half of the cherries and reserve for garnish.

Add the remaining ingredients to the pan, *except the unsalted butter,* and simmer, uncovered, until the liquid is reduced to ½ cup, about 1 hour. Strain the sauce and keep it warm while grilling the steaks.

Grill the steaks over medium-high heat for about 5 minutes per side, or until they reach an internal temperature of 130°F. Just before serving the steaks, whisk the butter into the sauce. Serve the steaks drizzled with the sauce and garnished with the reserved plumped cherries and chopped fresh chives.

A couple with deer head in Morrison County, 1900

"FOOT-TRODDEN MEAT"

Like many a lucky hunter today, the Ojibway, who lived inland from the Great Lakes, enjoyed an overabundance of deer meat. They boiled venison with wild rice or sliced it, roasted it, and pounded it out on a flat stone. They stored these tenderized steaks in birch-bark boxes called "makuks" and sewed the covers down with split spruce root. They dried deer meat by hanging it over a fire; then they packed it in hide and ate it throughout the long, cold winter.

Sometimes they cut the venison into small pieces, spread them out on birch bark, and stamped the pieces until they were soft and pliable. The men were honored to do this work because it was difficult and required strength. The meat was literally called "foot-trodden meat."

Women and children made the pemmican (concentrated, dried venison) by pounding dried meat and berries with a stone and mixing it with fat or marrow, then packing it into hide sacks and sealing it with melted fat. Thus preserved, pemmican would keep as long as three years.

Today's deer hunter is equally creative with venison—grilling, roasting, and stewing this lean, flavorful meat. Fresh and smoked venison sausage, venison mincemeat, and venison jerky are often gifts hunters make (or have their butchers make) of the kill.

UNCLE BYRON'S GAME SAUSAGE

MAKES ABOUT 4 POUNDS (RECIPE IS EASILY CUT IN HALF.)

*T*his easy recipe for uncased sausage requires no fancy equipment, just a food processor or meat grinder. It was created by Uncle Byron, a better storyteller than he was a marksman, and an excellent cook.

You can use just about any kind of game to make sausage: venison, duck, pheasant. We add one part bacon to three parts trimmed meat for a juicy, flavorful sausage. For easier grinding, keep the fat and meat very cold.

We often make this sausage meat in big batches, freezing patties for later use. It's delicious on top of pizza, in hearty soups, or grilled and served between layers of chewy Potato Bread (page 21) with roasted red peppers.

> *3 pounds venison or any other game meat*
> *1 pound bacon*
> *2 cups peeled, finely chopped onions*
> *1 red bell pepper, seeded, deveined, and finely chopped*
> *1 cup finely chopped fresh parsley*
> *2 tablespoons finely chopped garlic*
> *2 tablespoons seeded, finely chopped fresh hot chili peppers*
> *2 teaspoons crushed, dried hot red pepper*
> *2 teaspoons freshly ground black pepper*
> *2 teaspoons dried thyme*
> *¼ cup fennel seed*
> *½ teaspoon ground allspice*
> *1 tablespoon salt*

*I*n a food processor fitted with a steel blade, or in a meat grinder, coarsely grind the meat and bacon with the onions. Turn the ground meat into a bowl and mix together all of the remaining ingredients, using your hands if necessary, until the seasonings and flavors are evenly distributed.

To cook the sausage, shape into individual patties and sauté or grill until the inside is no longer pink. Or crumble a large portion of the sausage meat into a large skillet and cook until it is no longer pink.

MINCEMEAT

MAKES 4 QUARTS OR 8 PINT JARS

Mincemeat, that rich, spicy preserve, used to be prepared as a means of preserving the fall harvest of game. Mincemeat is surprisingly easy to make. Simmering on the back of the stove, it will fill the house with a spicy, sweet holiday smell. It is traditionally used as a filling for Thanksgiving and Christmas pies, and is delicious served with whipped cream cheese and crackers for a party appetizer and alongside Chicken Liver Pâté (page 80).

This generous recipe will leave you enough to can in pretty jars for hostess gifts and holiday presents. If venison is not available, substitute lean beef or bison.

Mincemeat may be stored in the refrigerator for three days or frozen in containers up to a year. It may also be canned in pint jars and kept up to a year.

2 pounds lean ground venison or beef
¼ pound beef suet, ground medium-fine
5 cups golden raisins
4 cups chopped tart apple
3 cups apple cider
2 cups currants
2½ cups brown sugar, packed, light or dark
1 cup white sugar
¾ cup cider vinegar
1 cup coarsely chopped almonds
Grated zest of 4 medium oranges
2 teaspoons salt
3 teaspoons ground cinnamon
2 teaspoons ground nutmeg
1 teaspoon ground cloves
1 teaspoon ground allspice
½ teaspoon ground ginger
¼ cup brandy or applejack

*C*ombine all of the ingredients in a large stockpot, except the brandy, and mix well. Bring the mixture to a boil, stirring frequently. Reduce the heat, cover, and simmer for about 2 hours, stirring occasionally. Cool the mincemeat and then stir in the brandy.

DEEP LAKES AND SWIFT STREAMS

FRESHWATER FISH

Indian, voyageur, settler, commercial and sport fisherman—all have shared the bounty of our deep cold lakes and swift streams. Since the earliest days that man lived in this area, sweet, firm freshwater fish have sizzled in fry pans across the region. The native Ojibway Indians taught settlers to smoke and dry their catch and to freeze and bury it in snowbanks. They showed them how to weave gill nets, later used by commercial fishermen. Even in the toughest winters, when no other food was available, fish could be hooked, speared, or netted through the ice.

In the mid- to late 1800s fur trappers and voyageurs settled along the northern shores of Lake Superior to work in the then burgeoning fishing industry, netting huge schools of whitefish and herring. The smoking and pickling of fish for East Coast markets left the scent of herring on every gale.

Sport fishing, a big business since the early 1900s, draws anglers nationwide with the promise of a trophy trout, walleye, or bass. Fishing legally begins with "The Opener," the second weekend in May. With new licenses in hand, fishermen head to northern lakes for the traditional weekend of

211

(mostly) male camaraderie, late nights of beer drinking and storytelling. Not that all the women are left out. The Minnesota state legislature decreed that on the second Sunday in May (Mother's Day) mothers fish for free!

Thanks to a growing number of quality fish farms across the Northern Heartland, fresh trout and salmon are available year-round. We've created recipes like Grilled Baby Coho Salmon with Lemon-Ginger Marinade and Pan-Fried Trout with Smoky Bacon, Hazelnuts, and Lemon-Sage Butter that recall the flavors of outdoor cooking in the north woods. Fresh fish, from the cold waters of the Northern Heartland, is most delicious when cooked most simply.

The result of 1 ½ hours of fishing at Leech Lake in 1898

BAKED WALLEYE WITH ASPARAGUS AND FIDDLEHEAD FERNS

SERVES 4

*F*iddleheads, those pale green ferns shaped like the scroll of a violin, and wild asparagus push their heads up through the damp spring forest floor just around the "Fishing Opener" that often falls on Mother's Day in Minnesota. At Lucia's Restaurant we serve this light and pretty entrée for Mother's Day brunch, along with parslied new potatoes.

> *½ stick (4 tablespoons) butter, softened*
> *4 walleye fillets (about 4–6 ounces each)*
> *8 asparagus spears*
> *8 fiddlehead ferns or sugar snap peas*
> *¼ cup snipped fresh chives*
> *1 lemon, cut into quarters*
> *Salt and freshly ground pepper*

*C*ut four 1-foot-square sheets of aluminum foil. Liberally butter each sheet. On each sheet place 1 walleye fillet, 2 asparagus spears, cut into 1-inch pieces, and 2 fiddlehead ferns. Sprinkle the snipped fresh chives equally over each portion, squeeze the juice of a lemon quarter over each fillet, and then sprinkle with salt and freshly ground pepper. Fold the aluminum foil to cover the fish and bake in a preheated 350°F oven for about 12 minutes.

WALLEYE

Among north woods anglers, fresh walleye is generally preferred over the noble, sportier trout. Walleye meat is snowy white, fine-flaked, sweet, and tender. It is often called the "sole of freshwater fish" because it's so versatile. Walleye fillet greatly improves any recipe calling for sole. Sometimes referred to as walleyed pike, the fish is not a pike at all, but a member of the perch family, and it is closely related to the sweet yellow perch.

Walleyes are fished commercially in the Great Lakes, usually in the winter, with gill nets set under the ice. On the Wolf River in Wisconsin, they migrate a hundred miles upstream from Lake Winnebago. To thousands of walleye fanciers, this run is the first harbinger of spring.

NORTH SHORE LUNCH

SERVES 6

*I*n the summer on Madeline Island, Lake Superior, Wisconsin, we set out in a skiff before dawn to fish, and by eleven o'clock we are ready to head to the beach for lunch. We build a campfire on the sand, clean the fish, and cook it in a big cast-iron skillet over a small fire. While we stretch and warm up in the high sun, the smell of sizzling fish mingles with the cool scent of the piney woods. The fish cooks up crisp outside, tender and flaky inside. We eat it off tin plates with Homemade Tartar Sauce (see page 215), Overnight Coleslaw (page 264), and plenty of beer from the cooler—a classic shore lunch.

> 6 whole walleye, trout, or any small, whole fish
>   (about ½ pound each)
> ¼ cup unbleached all-purpose flour
> ½ cup cornmeal

Salt and freshly ground pepper to taste
¼ teaspoon each, onion powder and garlic powder
¼ teaspoon paprika
6 tablespoons bacon fat or equal parts butter and oil

Clean, wash, and pat the fish dry. Combine the flour, cornmeal, and seasonings. Roll the fish in the seasoned flour and tap off the excess.

Heat the bacon fat in a skillet large enough to hold at least one of the fish, and fry the fish, 5 minutes per side, or until the flesh begins to separate from the backbone, is firm to the touch, and nicely browned. Serve right away

HOMEMADE TARTAR SAUCE

MAKES ABOUT 1¾ CUPS

1½ cups Basic Mayonnaise (page 259) or good-quality
prepared mayonnaise
1 dill pickle, minced
2 shallots, peeled and minced, or 2 tablespoons chopped
scallions
1 tablespoon chopped capers
1 tablespoon chopped fresh parsley
1 tablespoon chopped fresh chives
1 tablespoon Dijon mustard
1 teaspoon lemon juice
Salt and freshly ground pepper to taste

Whisk all of the ingredients together.

PAN-FRIED TROUT WITH SMOKY BACON, HAZELNUTS, AND LEMON-SAGE BUTTER

SERVES 4

*T*his combination of smoky bacon and fresh brook trout is a north woods classic. Serious fishermen favor bacon over butter for its flavor and because it keeps better. Lucky is the angler who finds a few wild hazelnuts to toss into the pan.

This recipe is reminiscent of summer canoe trips through the Boundary Waters that join Canada and northern Minnesota, when freshly caught trout are tossed right off the hook into a fry pan set over a campfire. Serve with Basic Wild Rice (page 275).

> *1 cup whole hazelnuts*
> *6 slices smoked country bacon*
> *4 trout (about 8 ounces each), cleaned, with heads left on*
> *Salt and freshly ground pepper*
> *8 scallions, washed and trimmed to the length of the fish*
> *Unbleached all-purpose flour seasoned with salt and freshly*
> *   ground pepper*
> *1 stick (8 tablespoons) butter*
> *Juice of 1 lemon*
> *12 large fresh sage leaves or 1 teaspoon dried*

*S*pread the hazelnuts on a baking sheet and toast in a preheated 350°F oven about 15 minutes, or until the skins have split. Put them in a dish and cover with plastic wrap until they've cooled a bit; then rub them with a towel to remove as much skin as possible. Chop the nuts.

Cook the bacon in a large skillet until crisp and reserve the drippings in the skillet. Drain the bacon on paper towels, crumble it, and set aside. Add salt and pepper to the cavity of each trout and then place 2 trimmed scallions in each as well. Dredge the trout in seasoned flour. Heat the bacon drippings in the skillet and fry the trout, about 6 minutes per side.

In a small saucepan, heat together the butter and lemon juice and add the sage leaves. Spoon the lemon-sage butter over the trout and sprinkle with the hazelnuts and crumbled bacon.

FISH FARMS

Fresh brook trout and young coho salmon, once limited to the kitchens of accomplished anglers, are now as available as fresh pheasant and bison in supermarkets and restaurants. The fast-running streams and clear spring-fed lakes cultivated by fish farmers throughout Minnesota, Wisconsin, and northern Iowa are producing vast numbers of rainbow trout and coho salmon in neat, fry-pan sizes—convenient and deliciously fresh.

Trout spawn in multiple seasons, and salmon but once a year. Both types adapt to fresh or salt water. Freshwater fish tend to be more tender and finely flaked, says Mac Graham of Star Prairie Trout Farm, Star Prairie, Wisconsin. "The skin of saltwater fish is tougher, and the scales are firmer. Some people say saltwater salmon are to freshwater salmon what beef is to veal. Freshwater fish is lighter and has a milder flavor."

TROUT HEMINGWAY

SERVES 4

*T*his recipe is named for that august angler Ernest Hemingway. It is a regional favorite on the Upper Peninsula, the setting for his short story "Up in Michigan." Equally good on the stove or over a campfire, the trout is done when the sesame seeds turn golden brown. We serve this with a side of Sweet Corn Relish (page 290).

> *4 whole trout (about 8–10 ounces each), cleaned, with*
> *   heads left on*
> *Salt and freshly ground pepper*
> *½ cup freshly squeezed lemon juice*
> *½ cup each, cornmeal and unbleached all-purpose*
> *   flour seasoned with salt, freshly ground pepper, and*
> *   a dash of cayenne*
> *½ cup sesame seeds*
> *4 tablespoons equal parts butter and oil*
> *Chopped fresh parsley and lemon wedges for garnish*

*R*inse the trout and pat them dry. Slit the trout open along the belly, starting just under the gills and ending just short of the tail. Rinse out the guts. Run a knife along the top of the rib cage to separate the bones from the flesh on both sides. Then work the knife under the spine. Break the spine at the tail and head. Using the knife, work out the spine and ribs, leaving the flesh exposed like an open book. Season liberally with salt and freshly ground pepper. Dip the flesh side of the trout in the lemon juice, dust lightly with the seasoned cornmeal flour, dip again in the lemon juice, then coat the flesh with the sesame seeds.

Heat the butter and oil in a heavy skillet over medium heat, add the trout, skin side up first, and pan-fry for about 3 minutes. Gently flip the fish and fry the coated flesh for another 3 minutes, until the seeds are golden brown. Serve immediately with chopped fresh parsley and lemon wedges.

GRILLED BABY COHO SALMON WITH LEMON-GINGER MARINADE

SERVES 4

*T*his light, tangy marinade is also delicious on trout, whitefish, or sturgeon. Use caution when marinating fish. If the mixture is too acidic or if it is left on the fish too long, a marinade will quickly turn the fish flesh to mush. Trout, salmon, and sturgeon—because they are denser and oilier than whitefish and walleye—will stand up to stronger marinades for longer periods of time.

LEMON-GINGER MARINADE

½ cup lemon juice
2 medium cloves garlic, peeled and minced
1 tablespoon minced fresh gingerroot
¼ cup olive oil
¼ cup vegetable oil

4 coho salmon (about 8–10 inches each), cleaned, with heads on
Salt and freshly ground pepper
8 sprigs fresh thyme
4 scallions, trimmed
Vegetable oil for the grill
Chopped fresh parsley and lemon wedges for garnish

*M*ix together the marinade ingredients. Rinse the salmon and pat them dry. Generously salt and pepper the cavity of each fish and place 2 thyme sprigs and 1 scallion (cut lengthwise) into each cavity. Place the salmon in a large dish, pour the marinade over them, and allow to stand about 1 hour.

Generously brush a preheated, medium-high grill with lots of vegetable oil. Remove the salmon from the marinade and place on the grill. Cook about 4 to 5 minutes per side, gently turning the fish and brushing liberally with the marinade, until it is opaque and flakes lightly. Serve each fish garnished with chopped fresh parsley and lemon wedges.

CHILLED POACHED SALMON WITH RED PEPPER PURÉE

SERVES 4

*P*oaching is a gentle way to cook fish, and the Fish Broth (page 221) infuses a subtle flavor. In August's blasting heat we serve chilled poached salmon with a sauce of red bell peppers, sweet and fresh from the garden.

> *4 salmon steaks (about 6 ounces each)*
> *Fish Broth*
> *Red Pepper Purée (see below)*

*P*our about 1 quart of Fish Broth into a wide saucepan and bring to a simmer. Drop the fish steaks into the liquid and cook about 6 to 8 minutes, then gently remove and chill. Gently peel off the skin and serve drizzled with Red Pepper Purée.

RED PEPPER PURÉE

> *2 red bell peppers, deveined, seeded, and chopped*
> *2 tablespoons butter*
> *½ cup water*
> *1 tablespoon balsamic vinegar*
> *Salt and freshly ground pepper*

*I*n a skillet, sauté the peppers in butter for 2 minutes, add the water, cover, and cook until soft, about 8 to 10 minutes. The liquid will reduce by half. Turn the mixture into a blender or a food processor fitted with a steel blade and purée. Then strain the sauce and add the vinegar. Season with salt and pepper to taste. Serve at room temperature or chilled.

FISH BROTH

MAKES 1 GALLON

*W*e use this light broth of vegetables, herbs, and wine to poach or steam fish like salmon, whitefish, and trout. It is simple to make and will keep about a week in the refrigerator, or about four months in the freezer.

> *1 gallon water*
> *1 sprig each, fresh thyme and parsley*
> *1 bay leaf*
> *1 medium onion*
> *1 stalk celery*
> *1 leek, trimmed and washed*
> *2 cups white wine or vermouth*

*P*ut all of the ingredients, *except the wine,* into a large stockpot. Simmer, uncovered, about 20 minutes. Add the wine and simmer 20 minutes more. Strain the liquid and refrigerate.

WISCONSIN FISH BOIL

Up along the northern shore of Wisconsin's Lake Superior, signs for "Fish Boils" signal the beginning of the summer season, enticing locals and tourists to lodges, restaurants, fraternal organizations, and churches. Continuing a tradition begun with the Scandinavian fishermen back in the late 1880s, fish boils are a reason to gather the community together around a big caldron for an outdoor feast.

Greunke's Inn, in Bayfield, Wisconsin, offers a Saturday night fish boil that is considered to be one of the region's best. Fish boils were extremely popular at the turn of the century, when Wisconsin's fishing industry was at its peak. Fishermen and their families would gather in the shipyard for beer and lots to eat.

The traditional fish boil is a showy, all-you-can-eat outdoor affair. A huge stainless-steel pot is filled with water and set so that it is slightly tipped on its side on a stand over a wood fire. Salt is added to the water to make impurities float to the surface, but that does not affect the flavor of the fish or vegetables.

Once the water boils, a stainless-steel basket, like a huge colander, filled with red boiling potatoes and onions, is lowered into the pot and boiled for about thirty minutes. Then thick pieces of unskinned, unboned whitefish steaks are lowered in another colander, for about seven minutes.

Just before the fish and vegetables are lifted from the pot, a bucket of kerosene is thrown on the fire. Flames leap, and the pot boils over on its tipped side, and the impurities and froth run off.

Cooked this way, the fish tastes light, fresh, and sweet—almost lobsterlike. It's served with the potatoes and onions and lots of drawn butter, plus homemade rolls, coleslaw, and tart cherry crisp, all spread out on checkered tablecloths.

The experience of a fish boil is nearly impossible to duplicate at home. Without the drama, camaraderie, the soft lake breeze, and the experienced "boil master" to explain all the steps and tell stories of the lake, the meal itself just doesn't taste the same.

SUNDAY MORNING FISH HASH
WITH PEPPERS AND TOMATOES

SERVES 6

*W*hether as a hearty breakfast for hungry fishermen or a leisurely Sunday brunch, this easy, fresh-tasting hash is delicious served with fried or poached eggs.

> *3 tablespoons butter*
> *8 new potatoes, thinly sliced*
> *1 red bell pepper, seeded, deveined, and chopped*
> *1 green bell pepper, seeded, deveined, and chopped*
> *1 red onion, peeled and diced*
> *1 teaspoon chopped garlic*
> *4 walleye or any white fish fillets, cut into 1-inch cubes*
> *2 fresh tomatoes, peeled, seeded, and diced*
> *Dash of nutmeg*
> *Dash of balsamic vinegar or lemon juice*
> *Salt and freshly ground pepper to taste*
> *1 tablespoon each, chopped fresh parsley and thyme*

*I*n a heavy skillet, melt the butter over medium heat until it foams. Add the potatoes and sauté until they become tender and start to brown. Add the peppers, onion, and garlic, and sauté for about 5 minutes, stirring occasionally. Add the walleye and cook for 5 minutes more. Then add the tomatoes, nutmeg, vinegar, salt and pepper to taste, and cook about 1 minute longer, just to warm, and toss in the herbs. Serve with fried or poached eggs.

STURGEON

This prehistoric fish can grow to 1,500 pounds and has inspired countless legends and tall tales along the coast of Lake Superior. The fearsome-looking sturgeon is boneless, and its big, hard scales act as an outside skeleton. Its long slim body and pointed snout have earned it the nickname "nail file fish." A mild, tender, yet extremely firm-fleshed fish, sturgeon is quite versatile.

The roe from sturgeon and its even stranger-looking cousin, the flat-nosed paddlefish, is made into caviar. Russian caviar masters dismiss Great Lakes sturgeon roe, claiming it is inferior to that of the Russian sturgeon, which swim in the salty Baltic Sea.

Fresh sturgeon is delicious grilled because of its dense texture and high oil content. It is also good baked, braised, broiled, and sautéed. When smoked, it tastes very similar to smoked breast of turkey. Sturgeon will keep several days longer in the refrigerator than other fresh fish. (It actually tastes better as it ages.) Shark, marlin, and swordfish, though a bit leaner, make good substitutes for sturgeon.

STURGEON BAKED IN A FRESH HERB CRUST

SERVES 6

*T*his easy recipe makes a splendid presentation for any meaty fresh fish steak, such as salmon, tuna, swordfish, or marlin. Serve with steamed tiny new potatoes tossed in lemon-and-parsley butter.

6 sturgeon steaks (about 1 inch thick)
White wine or water for bottom of roasting pan
½ cup peeled, chopped onions
1 cup chopped fresh herbs (use a combination, such as parsley, thyme, tarragon, chervil)

½ cup bread crumbs
1 stick (8 tablespoons) butter, softened
¼ cup fresh lemon juice
Salt and freshly ground pepper to taste

*R*inse the sturgeon steaks and pat them dry. Lay the steaks on a buttered rack set over a deep dish or casserole and fill the bottom of the pan with about 1 inch of white wine or water. In a food processor fitted with a steel blade, whirl together the remaining ingredients. Pat equal amounts of crust on top of each steak and place on the rack. Bake the fish in a preheated 350°F oven for about 12 to 15 minutes, or until the flesh flakes.

A 95-pound, 6-foot 3-inch sturgeon, about 1900. It was tangled in the net and captured by William Maloney, who rode it in 4 feet of water for 15 minutes before finally landing it.

RAINY LAKE FISH CAKES
WITH LEMON-DILL MAYONNAISE

SERVES 4 TO 6

*S*wedes, Finns, and Norwegians who settled the northern lake region of Minnesota and Wisconsin substituted local freshwater fish, like walleye or whitefish, for Atlantic cod in their homey fish cake recipes. We've added a few new seasonings to this traditional mix. Serve with Lemon-Dill Mayonnaise or Red Pepper Purée (page 220) as a first course or for dinner.

> *1 pound white fish (walleye, whitefish, or cod)*
> *¼ cup (or more) heavy cream*
> *1 cup Perfect Mashed Potatoes (page 272)*
> *1 tablespoon lemon juice*
> *⅛ teaspoon cayenne pepper*
> *¼ teaspoon salt, plus more to taste*
> *⅛ teaspoon freshly ground pepper, plus more to taste*
> *1 teaspoon Worcestershire sauce*
> *¼ cup chopped scallions*
> *Equal parts butter and oil or vegetable oil for sautéing*
> *Unbleached all-purpose flour seasoned with salt and freshly*
>   *ground pepper*

*T*rim the fish of all gristle, silver skin, and bones. In a food processor fitted with a steel blade, purée the fish in small batches, adding just enough cream to keep the mixture loose and moving. (It tends to ball up in the middle, so you will need to spread it out frequently with a spatula.)

Turn the fish mixture into a large bowl and add the potatoes (they should be warm or at least at room temperature), lemon juice, cayenne pepper, salt, pepper, Worcestershire sauce, and the scallions. Mix well and if the mixture seems too thick, add more cream until it becomes the consistency of hamburger. Make a small patty and sauté it in the equal parts butter and oil, taste it, then adjust the seasoning to taste.

We use an ice-cream scoop to spoon out the fish mixture into 8 to 12 cakes. Flatten the cakes slightly with your palms, then lightly dust them with the flour. The cakes may be prepared ahead and kept refrigerated overnight.

Heat the butter and oil or the vegetable oil in a large frying pan over medium heat and cook the cakes in batches, about 4 minutes per side, until they are golden and fluffy-looking.

LEMON-DILL MAYONNAISE

1 cup Basic Mayonnaise (page 259) or good-quality
   prepared mayonnaise
¼ cup fresh lemon juice
1 teaspoon grated lemon rind
2 tablespoons chopped fresh dill, plus a little more for
   garnish
1 teaspoon capers

*W*hisk together all the ingredients. Serve garnished with fresh dill.

BASS

Every good angler has a story or two about the huge bass that swallowed the fly and got away. These game fish are real fighters, the ultimate challenge to fly fishermen.

Freshwater bass—largemouth and smallmouth—are not related to black or striped sea bass, and recipes for one will seldom work for the other. Freshwater bass are actually members of the sunfish family, and they are not sold in commercial markets.

If the lucky angler brings home bass for dinner, it will make a very good meal, the subtle flavor lending itself to many different ways of cooking. Freshwater bass may be deep-fried, baked, broiled, and pan-fried. It is easily substituted in recipes calling for walleye, flounder, or sole.

"ICE FISHING OPENER"

On January 1, fishermen and -women in Minnesota and Wisconsin forgo New Year's Day celebrations in favor of the "Ice Fishing Opener." They drive their cars onto the frozen lakes, set up ice huts, drill holes in the ice, drop their lines, and wait. On large open lakes, like Mille Lacs in northern Minnesota, entire ice-fishing communities are erected, with named streets as well as garbage collection and delivery services. Some huts have color TVs, refrigerators, heating units, and running water.

Those who wish to get away from civilization head to remote lakes deep in the north woods. Doug Stange, editor of *In-Fisherman* Magazine, fishes Roland Lake in northern Minnesota. "There are no roads in, so we take snowmobiles, carrying enough wood and supplies for several days. We fish outside all day. The only danger is having the fish we've caught freeze before we're finished fishing; so we dig a sort of trench in the ice with a small hole that fills it with water and keep the fish there. We cook the fish on our cabin's wood stove."

SPRING CRAPPIES
WITH MOREL MUSHROOMS

SERVES 4

*O*nce the ice has melted, small, round crappies (as well as sunfish) swim to the flat surface of deep ponds and lakes at about the same time that the morels are starting to peep up from the forest floor. So we have combined them here. Crappies will bite at just about anything (including bare toes) and are caught as easily with a handmade bamboo pole as with any fancy rig.

The crappies' sweet flesh makes great eating for those patient enough to fillet at least four to six tiny fish per small serving. When pan-fried with a few morels, they make a fine spring feast.

> *16–24 crappie fillets*
> *Unbleached all-purpose flour seasoned with salt and freshly*
> *   ground pepper*
> *¼ cup equal parts butter and oil*
> *8–12 fresh morel mushrooms, sliced*

*D*ust the fillets with seasoned flour. Heat the butter and oil in a large skillet and sauté the mushrooms until limp. Put the mushrooms on a warm plate and quickly cook the fillets, just a few seconds per side. Serve the fillets topped with the mushrooms.

LUTEFISK

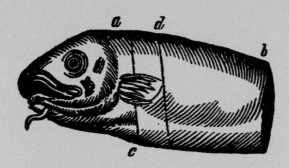

Norwegian-Americans believe their ancestors brought lutefisk with them on the ships when they emigrated and that it was all they had to eat at first on the frontier. A boardlike, salt-preserved codfish treated with lye, repeatedly rinsed, then boiled, lutefisk seems to polarize those who discuss it. One either loves it or detests it. It is a dish that Norwegians who visit this country know little or nothing about. In Norway it is treated as "fisherfolk" food, and few people prepare it because of the smell that lingers in the kitchen. Today the fish is linked symbolically with hardship and courage, and it is included in ethnic and religious celebrations.

Florence Peterson of St. Paul remembers: "About a month before Christmas Eve we purchased the lutefisk, which was in a dry state and had been standing outside the butcher shop in the cold weather like cords of wood. Because of exposure to the elements, it was 'well flavored' by the time it was purchased. Mother had been saving maple ashes, which were a product of our wood-burning stove. The dried lutefisk was brought to the cellar along with the maple ashes and put in a washtub of water to soak for a period of time. Each of us took turns changing the water on the fish, and this procedure was followed until the fish, in its dried state, softened so that on Christmas Eve it could be boiled in a huge kettle. The odor could be overwhelming to a guest."

Here are two recipes for lutefisk from the *Norske-American Cookbook*, Minneapolis, 1925.

LUTEFISK NO. 1

9 lbs. dried fish
2 lbs. slaked lime
1 and one-third lbs. washing soda
Water

Saw the fish into convenient pieces if necessary. Place in a wooden receptacle and cover with cold water. Let it lie for a week, changing water every day. Make a solution of the slaked lime, soda, and fifteeen quarts of water. Place the fish in this solution under weights to keep the pieces in position as they swell. Add more water if necessary to keep the pieces covered. In about a week, or when properly softened through, take out, rinse thoroughly, and place in cold water for eight days, changing water twice daily during the first few days. Cut in pieces the size you wish to serve, skin, and wash. Tie in a cloth and place in boiling water to cook for ten or fifteen minutes until tender. Serve with drawn butter.

LUTEFISK NO. 2

Dry Codfish
Water
Lewis Lye

To prepare "lutefisk" requires at least two weeks' time. Place the fish in clean cold water, and let it remain for one week, changing water every morning. To each four or five pounds of fish use about one teaspoon of lye in enough clean soft water to cover well. If the "lut" is too strong the fish will soften too rapidly. The fish must stand in this solution in a cold place for three or four days. Pour off the solution and pour clear water over the fish. Keep the fish in clear water for three or four days, changing the water each morning. Keep in a cold place. It is now ready for cooking. Place the fish in boiling salted water and let it boil slowly a very short time. Serve with melted butter.

Note: It is now possible to procure prepared "lutefisk"—ready for boiling—at the markets.

BAYFIELD BEER-BATTER-FRIED FISH

SERVES 4

*J*ust about any firm white fish may be used in this recipe. Cut the fish into fingers of equal size so they will fry evenly. Use peanut oil or corn oil (with a little dark sesame seed oil for a nutty flavor), and be sure it's plenty hot, between 360 and 380 degrees Fahrenheit. Fry the fish a few fingers at a time and allow the oil to return to its hot temperature between batches. Be sure you use a deep pan so that the fish can be submerged without the oil being too close to the surface of the pot. When camping in the woods, a coffee can suspended over a campfire works perfectly.

The batter is best when it's ice-cold, and the fish pieces should be patted dry before being submerged. After frying, drain the fish on paper towels. We serve the fried fish with fat wedges of lemon or malt vinegar, Homemade Tartar Sauce (page 215), and freshly sliced tomatoes. It's great with a full-bodied Wisconsin brew.

1½ pounds perch, walleye, whitefish, or any firm, white fish
*   fillets*

¾ cup unbleached all-purpose flour
1 teaspoon each, salt and freshly ground pepper
Dash of cayenne pepper
¼ teaspoon baking soda
1 cup milk
1 egg
2 tablespoons beer

Vegetable oil for frying (about 6 cups), plus 2 tablespoons
*   dark sesame oil (optional)*
Flour for dusting

*R*inse the fillets and pat them dry; then cut them into "fingers" about 3 inches long and 1 inch wide, and keep them in the refrigerator until ready to fry. Mix together all of the ingredients for the batter until smooth, then allow it to rest for about 15 minutes.

Heat both the vegetable oil and the sesame oil in a deep-fat fryer or a large, heavy-bottomed saucepan to 360° to 380°F. Lightly dust the fish in flour, then submerge each fillet in the batter. Shake each piece quickly and drop it into the hot oil in batches. Fry until golden, turning occasionally so that the pieces don't stick. Remove the fish after about 3 to 4 minutes and drain on paper towels. Let the oil heat up before doing the next batch. Serve right away or, to keep the fish warm, spread the pieces in a single layer on a baking sheet in a low oven. Don't hold it too long, or it will become soggy.

FRIDAY NIGHT FISH FRY

The Friday night fish fry is a legacy of French-Canadian fur trappers turned fishermen; it's their way of observing the Catholic Church's Friday ban on meat. The Friday night fish fry still funds many a church auxiliary, but it also draws tourists to inns, lodges, and lakeside diners throughout Wisconsin. Years ago the fish fry centered around yellow perch from Lake Superior. This sweet, firm fish has, unfortunately, been fished out, so at the reputable establishments fresh walleye or whitefish is used. (Some restaurants try to sneak by with frozen pollock from Alaska.)

The fried fish is served with golden home fries, coleslaw, tartar sauce, and applesauce, followed by fresh strawberry-rhubarb or blueberry pie with a big scoop of vanilla ice cream.

SMOKED TROUT
AND WATERCRESS SALAD

SERVES 4

*I*n March watercress grows along the banks of icy streams through melting snow, where trout begin their up-current swim to spawn. In this recipe smoked trout and spicy cress are paired in a light creamy dressing.

> *2 smoked trout*
> *2 cups rinsed, dried watercress*
> *1 tart apple, cored and cut into ½-inch chunks*

*R*emove the skin from the trout and pick the flesh off the bones. Arrange the watercress on a large platter or individual plates, then arrange the trout over the watercress and distribute the apple chunks evenly over the trout. Serve with the following dressing alongside.

CIDER-THICKENED CREAM DRESSING

> *½ cup Basic Mayonnaise (page 259) or good-quality*
> *prepared mayonnaise*
> *2 tablespoons frozen apple juice concentrate or 2 cups*
> *apple cider boiled until reduced to 2 tablespoons*
> *½ cup Thickened Cream (page 87), or sour cream, or*
> *yogurt*

*W*hisk all ingredients together.

The Ojibway, who lived along the coast of Lake Superior in Minnesota and Wisconsin, taught trappers and voyageurs to weave the gill nets, which are still used by the fishing industry today.

GRAVLAX

SERVES 10 TO 12 FOR APPETIZERS

Gravlax, the traditional salt-and-sugar-cured salmon, was the preferred breakfast of Norwegian kings and princes before a day of angling, and a rare holiday treat for Scandinavians who settled in the Northern Heartland.

Gravlax is always featured on the cold table of a traditional smörgåsbord. It makes a wonderful appetizer on dark pumpernickel, with mustard, sliced eggs, chopped dill, and thinly sliced cucumbers. Serve it with chilled aquavit or a light ale, such as Summit from St. Paul.

Gravlax (continued)

> 2 pounds dressed Atlantic, sockeye, coho, or chinook salmon
> ¼ cup coarse salt
> ½ cup sugar
> 1 tablespoon crushed white peppercorns
> 2 bunches fresh dill

*R*inse the salmon and make a center cut, removing the head just below the gills and the tail just below the small bottom fin. Cut the fish into 2 lengthwise pieces along the line of the backbone; pull out the pin bones and wipe dry. Combine the salt and sugar and sprinkle one third of it on the bottom of a large earthenware dish. Place a fillet, skin side down, on top of the salt and sugar, then sprinkle another third of the salt and sugar over the fillet, along with the crushed white peppercorns, and lay half of the dill on top of the fillet. Place the remaining fillet, skin side up, on the first fillet (as though reconstructing the fish), sprinkle this with the remaining salt-and-sugar mixture, and top with the remaining dill.

Cover the fish with a sheet of aluminum foil and a light weight, such as a chopping board, and place in the refrigerator. The fish will leach out fluid. After about 4 to 5 hours, drain off any liquid. Keep the gravlax refrigerated about 48 hours, turning the fish at least twice. It may be stored for a week.

To serve gravlax, cut the skin from as much fish as you plan to serve, then thinly slice the fillets.

WHITEFISH

*F*ound primarily in the cold waters of the Great Lakes to Hudson Bay, whitefish has a delicate, almost sweet flavor and snow-white meat that has large flakes. Most whitefish sold at market comes from Canada, though a few small commercial fisheries in northern Wisconsin are still active.

Whitefish livers are a delicacy in restaurants along the north shore, served lightly sautéed in bacon fat or batter-fried. Whitefish roe is as prized as fine caviar, and smoked whitefish is often served for breakfast with scrambled eggs or as a snack late in the day with beer.

SMOKED WHITEFISH MOUSSE

SERVES 10 TO 12

*T*he firm texture and delicate flavor of whitefish make it an excellent candidate for smoking. Many of the small fish houses along the northern shore of Lake Superior sell smoked whitefish as well as fresh walleye, lake trout, and whitefish. It is delicious in this easy mousse for a quick appetizer. You may substitute any smoked fish for the whitefish in this recipe.

> *3 ounces smoked whitefish*
> *1 cup cream cheese*
> *1 tablespoon lemon juice*
> *1 teaspoon grated onion*
> *½ teaspoon salt*
> *¼ teaspoon white pepper*
> *Dash of Tabasco sauce*
> *Half-and-half or whole milk, as needed*
> *1 tablespoon snipped fresh chives*

*P*ick any bones from the fish. Put all of the ingredients *except the chives* into a food processor fitted with a steel blade. Process until the mixture is really smooth. You may need to thin this with a little half-and-half or whole milk. Fold in the chives. Turn into a serving bowl and serve with crackers or croutons.

Spring Sauté

Hungarian New Potato Salad

German Potato Salad

Morels, Asparagus, and Sunchokes in Brown Butter with
Toasted Hazelnuts

Fresh Spinach Custard

Greens in Basic Vinaigrette

Rosemary-Balsamic Vinaigrette

Shallot Vinaigrette

Maple-Mustard Vinaigrette (and Basting Sauce)

Walnut Oil Vinaigrette

Cilantro-Lime Vinaigrette

Creamy Mustard-Herb Dressing

Lemon, Thyme, and Mint Vinaigrette

Blue Cheese Dressing

Basic Mayonnaise

Fresh Succotash Salad with Wilted Greens

Radish and Cucumber Salad in Yogurt Dressing

Fresh Corn Pudding

Overnight Coleslaw

Summer Tomato, Potato, and Eggplant Bake

Gratin of Pumpkin and Leeks

Country Sauerkraut

Brussels Sprouts with Toasted Almonds

Braised Red Cabbage with Apples and Bacon

Perfect Mashed Potatoes

Roasted Sweet Potato Purée

Basic Wild Rice

Wild Rice, Cranberry, Walnut, and Vegetable Salad

Wild Rice Pilaf with Dried Cherries and Walnuts

BACKYARD GARDENS AND SACRED PADDIES

VEGETABLES AND WILD RICE

In spring, lilac trees—purple, white, and mauve—edge the quiltlike fields, and gardens sprout neat rows of tender vegetables. The abundance seems like a reward for all the patience and thrift practiced throughout the harsh winter.

Our growing season is splendid, if short, and offers a great variety of cultivated and wild vegetables: asparagus, watercress, morel mushrooms, broccoli, new potatoes, cauliflower, carrots, tomatoes, countless lettuces and herbs. At the turn of the century Italian and Mexican immigrants introduced purple eggplants, plum tomatoes, and multicolored bell peppers to our farmers' markets. Today's newcomers—the Hmong (from northern Laos) and the Vietnamese—bring gnarled squash, fiery peppers, daikon, cilantro, lemongrass, and roots, herbs, and bulbs of no English name.

The Ojibway Indians marked the beginning of the new year with the harvest of the corn and wild rice. Every tribe held elaborate feasts thanking the spirits of the forest, lake, and field. Today Native Americans continue to reap rice by hand, poling their canoes quietly through remote northern paddies.

Throughout the Northern Heartland "corn roasts" (feasts of unhusked cobs grilled over open fires) celebrate this swift, rich season. Iowa and Minnesota state fairs both claim to host the "World's Biggest." Corporate farms, supplying General Mills, Pillsbury, and Faribault Foods, harvest over 85 percent of the nation's corn.

Once relegated to small, shallow bowls (hence the term "side dish"), now vegetables take center plate. Those who used to boil a vegetable "until there was no more fight in it" would be surprised at how today's cooks fix greens, roots, and tubers. No more swampy broccoli or limp beans. Asparagus is served tender-crisp, and watercress is splashed with vinaigrette.

We've organized this chapter by season, with a selection of recipes, old-fashioned and new. Perfect Mashed Potatoes, made rich with cream and a pat of butter melting down the side, are still as delicious as our childhood memory of them. We've taken succotash, a regional favorite, and lightened it up in a Fresh Succotash Salad on Wilted Greens, and there are light vinaigrettes and simple, fresh sautés inspired by our backyard gardens and the woods.

SPRING SAUTÉ

SERVES 2 TO 4

*T*he tender young greens of spring are a gentle promise of warmer days and softer nights. We like to quickly sauté spring things so they stay bright and crisp, using a little butter or nutty oil and a splash of lemon juice, vinegar, or wine.

The only trick here is to cut the vegetables to a uniform size and be careful not to overcook.

> *2 cups mixed spring vegetables (baby bok choy, mustard*
> *greens, chard, mushrooms, green onions, ramps or leeks,*
> *sugar snap peas, pearl onions,* peeled sunchokes)*
> *2 tablespoons butter or oil (try hazelnut or walnut oil for*
> *flavor)*
> *2 tablespoons fresh lemon juice, balsamic vinegar, or dry*
> *white wine*
> *Salt and freshly ground pepper to taste*
> *Chopped fresh chives for garnish (use chive flowers, too)*
>
> **Pearl onions will need to be peeled and blanched in rapidly boil-*
> *ing water for about 5 minutes, then drained before sautéeing.*

*R*inse the vegetables, pat them dry, and cut into uniform size (about 1-inch pieces). Heat the butter or oil in a medium skillet over medium-high heat and quickly sauté the vegetables for about 30 seconds to 1 minute. Squirt with lemon juice, vinegar, or wine. Cover and continue cooking another 30 seconds to 1 or 2 minutes, or until the vegetables are tender-crisp. Add salt and pepper to taste and serve garnished with chopped fresh chives or chive flowers.

HUNGARIAN NEW POTATO SALAD

SERVES 6 TO 8 (RECIPE IS EASILY DOUBLED.)

*I*n mid-June avid backyard gardeners dig up baby potatoes the size of marbles. They are thin-skinned, delicate, and absolutely delicious when steamed with a touch of butter.

To make this simple salad, let the warm cooked potatoes marinate in a light vinaigrette. New potatoes don't need to be peeled; mature red or white boiling potatoes do. This salad holds nicely and can easily be toted to spring picnics and potlucks.

> *2½ pounds new potatoes*
> *½ cup peeled, chopped red onions*
> *½ seeded, chopped green peppers*
> *2–3 tablespoons chopped fresh dill*
> *2 teaspoons Hungarian paprika*
> *¼–½ cup Basic Vinaigrette (page 249)*
> *½ cup sour cream*
> *Salt and freshly ground pepper to taste*
> *1 hard-boiled egg, coarsely chopped*
> *Fresh dill for garnish*
> *½ red bell pepper, seeded and cut into strips for garnish*

*I*n a large saucepan, cover the potatoes with water and bring to a boil. Reduce the heat and gently boil the potatoes, partially covered, until tender (about 12 to 15 minutes for 3-inch new potatoes; cooking time for larger potatoes will vary according to their size). Drain the potatoes.

While the potatoes are hot, cut them in half and toss with the onions, green peppers, dill, paprika, and vinaigrette, using just enough dressing to coat the potatoes well. Let the mixture stand for 30 minutes so that the dressing seeps in.

Gently mix in the sour cream, salt and pepper to taste, and fold in the hard-boiled egg. Serve the salad at room temperature or lightly chilled, garnished with more fresh dill and strips of red pepper.

GERMAN POTATO SALAD

SERVES 6 TO 8

Serve with grilled "brats and kraut" and plenty of ice-cold beer for a back-yard party on a hot summer afternoon.

2½ pounds boiling potatoes
4 strips bacon
1 cup peeled, sliced red onions
3 tablespoons cider vinegar
2 tablespoons chopped fresh parsley
Salt and freshly ground pepper to taste

Cook the potatoes according to the directions on page 242. Meanwhile, fry the bacon in a large skillet until crisp. Remove the bacon to drain on paper towels, then crumble it. Reserve the fat in the skillet. Sauté the onions in the fat until golden. Add the vinegar and the potatoes to the skillet and toss to coat. Turn into a large bowl and toss in the parsley and crumbled bacon; then add salt and freshly ground pepper to taste. Serve warm or at room temperature.

MOREL FEVER

When the lilacs are as big as a mouse's ear, morel fever strikes. Craving those dark, spongelike, cone-shaped fungi, we set off to secret places deep in the backwoods. Some of us are very territorial about morel hunting grounds and insist guests be blindfolded for the trip.

We creep quietly through the moist forest, searching under stumps of old trees and through the velvety dead leaves, using intuition and a gentle hand to uncover these glorious woodland treasures. We fill our cloth sacks, then steal back to the meeting place like robbers giddy with their stash. We build a hasty fire, cook the morels with plenty of butter in a cast-iron skillet, and feast on mushrooms, crusty bread, mild cheese, and cold beer.

SIMPLE TIPS FOR PREPARING MORELS

In the woods, the bit of grit and earth inside the morel's stem is of little concern. In the kitchen, however, we wash them thoroughly and check for forest pests.

To clean morels, split the stem down the middle vertically and rinse thoroughly in running water. If you see ants or other insects, soak the morels in a little salted water for a few minutes, then rinse them under running water. Dry the mushrooms, laying them on paper towels and gently patting the moisture off, before using.

A prizewinning umbrella-like mushroom, 1926

MORELS, ASPARAGUS, AND SUNCHOKES IN BROWN BUTTER WITH TOASTED HAZELNUTS

SERVES 4 TO 6

Sunchokes (Jerusalem artichokes) were an Indian staple that was introduced to the French-Canadian trappers in the Upper Midwest and adopted by the early settlers, who called them "Canadian potatoes."

This simple recipe combines the flavors of a wild spring harvest with butter that has been browned until nutty tasting. The dish is best served with a wedge of lemon.

> *⅓ cup hazelnuts*
> *2–3 tablespoons butter*
> *⅓ pound sunchokes, peeled and sliced into 1-inch sticks*
>   *(about 1 cup)*
> *⅓ pound asparagus, rinsed, hard stems snapped off, cut*
>   *into 1-inch pieces*
> *½ cup morel mushrooms (if large, cut in half horizontally),*
>   *rinsed in salt water; or good-quality button mushrooms*
> *Juice of ½ lemon*
> *Lemon wedges for garnish*

Put the nuts on a small baking sheet in a preheated 400°F oven and roast about 10 to 15 minutes, until the skins begin to turn dark and crack. Remove, roll them in a clean dish towel, and rub the skins off. Chop coarsely and set aside.

In a large skillet, heat the butter over medium-low heat until it becomes foamy. Just as it begins to brown and smell nutty, add all of the vegetables and cook, stirring often, about 1 to 2 minutes. Squirt with the lemon juice and cover the pan for another 1 or 2 minutes or so, until the vegetables are tender-crisp. Sprinkle the vegetables with the toasted hazelnuts and serve with a wedge of lemon on the side.

FRESH SPINACH CUSTARD

SERVES 4 TO 6

*I*n our version of this old-fashioned recipe, the spinach becomes a brilliant green and is baked into individual custards that we unmold to serve garnished with bright Red Pepper Purée (page 220) or freshly sliced tomatoes. This is wonderful alongside a simple entrée of grilled fish or poultry, or as a first course.

> *3 shallots, peeled and chopped*
> *1 tablespoon butter*
> *2¼ pounds raw spinach, rinsed (about 2 cups cooked)*
> *¾ cup heavy cream, warmed to "baby bottle" temperature*
>   *(105° to 115°F)*
> *3 eggs*
> *¼ teaspoon freshly ground nutmeg*
> *Salt and freshly ground pepper to taste*

*S*auté the shallots in the butter over medium heat until they are soft. Steam the spinach in a colander or steaming basket over rapidly boiling water until it is limp, about 3 to 5 minutes, then squeeze it dry. While warm, turn the spinach and shallots into a blender or food processor fitted with a steel blade. Process, adding the cream in a slow, steady stream until the mixture is smooth.

In a large bowl, beat the eggs with the nutmeg. Stir in the spinach purée and add salt and pepper to taste. Butter 6 to 8 individual baking dishes, and if you are planning to unmold the timbales to serve, line the bottom of each with a round of buttered waxed paper or parchment paper. Pour the spinach mixture into the prepared dishes and set them in a large, high-sided baking pan. Pour boiling water into the pan to come two-thirds up the sides of the spinach-filled dishes.

Bake in a preheated 350°F oven for 45 minutes. (The custards are ready when a skewer plunged into the center of a dish comes up clean.) Turn the oven off and let the timbales rest about 5 minutes in the oven with the door ajar. To unmold the timbales, run a knife around the edge of each dish, invert onto a plate, and tap lightly on the bottom. (Peel off the paper if it is stuck to the timbale.)

SPRING IN THE NORTHERN HEARTLAND

"Nowhere in the world can spring burst out of the iron bough as in the Northwest. When the plains swell with heat, and the delicate glow and silence of the melting moisture fills the pure space with delicate winds and the promise of flowers, we all came, like the crocus, out of the winter dark, out of the captive village....The people warmed, came together in quilting bees, Ladies' Aid meetings, house raisings. The plowing and the planting began as soon as the thaw let the farmers into the fields. Neighbors helped each other. As soon as the seed was in, the churches had picnics and baptizings. The ladies donned their calico dresses and spread a great board of food, while the children ran potato races and one-legged races and the men played horseshoes and baseball."

—MERIDEL LE SUEUR, *ANCIENT PEOPLE AND THE NEWLY COME*

FARMERS' MARKETS

Come mid-May, farmers throughout the Northern Heartland literally take to the streets, turning city alleys, empty lots, and pedestrian malls into gardens of earthly delights. Throughout the summer, even the most brown-thumbed city dweller can feast on tomatoes and corn picked that morning for dinner.

Farmers' markets have always been the seedbeds for new influences and ethnic diversity. Once the domain of sturdy Norwegian potato farmers, the markets have helped bring the exotic flavors of far-flung homelands to this hungry new world. In the 1890s St. Paul's Mexican and Italian immigrants planted peppers, tomatoes, and squash not sold in grocery stores, and were soon selling to other immigrants—and curious Swedes, Poles, and Germans.

More recently the Hmong and Vietnamese immigrants have brought with them seeds for peppers and herbs, and a passion for hot, sour, and bitter flavors. They offer such Asian exotica as lemongrass, cilantro, bitter melon, lotus root, all manner of peppers (big, tiny, fat and slim, red and green), and vegetables whose names have never been translated.

Following the Vietnam War, 12,000 Hmong left their mountain village homes in northern Laos and Cambodia and traveled to neighboring Thai refugee camps and then on to the Twin Cities. There a group of churches sponsored the new immigrants' resettlement and drew them into language-retraining programs. Soon many of them were farming areas of industrial wasteland—burned-out plots and unbuildable tracts along the railroad tracks and highways—donated by the cities of Minneapolis and St. Paul.

At market, Hmong teenage boys and girls, dressed in the latest-style blue jeans, handle the money and explain to customers how to make a simple soup or stir-fry. Occasionally they'll speak in Hmong to a mother or an aunt, who sits behind the stall, nursing a baby or stitching a bright tapestry with scenes telling of their former homeland—farming, fighting, and escape.

The markets have always provided an arena for small producers of unique foods, many of them just starting out. Today business is thriving for regional entrepreneurs: makers of organic herb breads, handmade sausages, honey, maple syrup, European-style cheeses, smoked fish, and free-range beef, veal, lamb, turkey, and chicken.

GREENS IN BASIC VINAIGRETTE

MAKES 1 CUP

*T*o prepare salads, wash the greens first, then dry them thoroughly so the dressing will stick. Ripped lettuce leaves will not rust as quickly as those that are cut. Always use fresh herb dressings right away; otherwise the herbs will turn rancid after about a day in the refrigerator. Never wash wooden salad bowls; simply wipe them clean and rub them with a clove of garlic and a little oil.

Here is a Basic Vinaigrette recipe, with numerous variations.

> *¼ cup lemon juice or vinegar*
> *Any of the ingredients listed below, alone or in combination*
> *¾ cup oil (vegetable, olive, and nut oils are best)*
> *Salt and freshly ground pepper to taste*

*V*inaigrettes may be tart, smooth, rough, or tangy-sweet, depending on the ingredients you are dressing.

- 1 tablespoon mustard (Dijon or any flavored mustard)
- 1 shallot, peeled and chopped, or 1 tablespoon chopped scallion
- 1 clove garlic, crushed
- 1–2 tablespoons chopped fresh herbs
- 1 tablespoon chopped capers
- 2 tablespoons sour cream, Thickened Cream (page 87), or yogurt

Greens in Basic Vinaigrette (continued)

🌱 1 tablespoon white wine

🌱 1 tablespoon tomato paste with 1 tablespoon sherry

🌱 For a sweet-tart taste, add 1 tablespoon honey, brown or white sugar, or maple syrup.

🌱 On a diet? Cut the oil by ¼ cup and add ¼–½ cup buttermilk.

Combine the lemon juice or vinegar and the other ingredients with a whisk or by pouring them into a jar and shaking, then slowly add the oil. For an emulsified texture, make the dressing in a blender or food processor fitted with a steel blade. Always adjust the seasoning after you've tossed your greens.

Buying vegetables at an open-air market in 1935

ROSEMARY-BALSAMIC VINAIGRETTE

MAKES 1½ CUPS

*T*his flavorful dressing doubles as a marinade and basting sauce. It is delicious as a finishing touch drizzled over grilled meat or poultry just before serving.

> *½ cup balsamic vinegar*
> *4 cloves garlic*
> *2 teaspoons cracked pepper*
> *Dash of Tabasco sauce and Worcestershire sauce*
> *2 tablespoons chopped fresh rosemary*
> *1 cup olive oil*
> *Few drops water, as needed*

*W*hisk together the ingredients or process in a blender. The mixture should be emulsified.

Use this dressing as:

- Marinade for beef, chicken, or shrimp before grilling
- Dressing for a grilled steak or turkey salad
- Dressing for cooked, chilled white beans

SHALLOTS

The mild, sweet shallot is perhaps the most enticing member of the onion family. Shallots cook quickly because they are so tender, infusing simple sauces and dressings with their delicate flavor. While a little more expensive than onions, shallots can make a difference in special recipes. They will keep in a dry, cool place about a month.

To prepare shallots, peel and mince or chop as you would garlic or onions. They tend not to be as juicy as onions and are also easily minced in the food processor.

If you can't get shallots, use the white parts of a young green onion or scallion instead. Onions are too tough as a substitute, and garlic is too strong.

SHALLOT VINAIGRETTE

MAKES 1 CUP

In this recipe the vinegar marinates and tenderizes the shallots, giving the vinaigrette a light, distinctive flavor.

¼ cup peeled, sliced shallots
½ cup good-quality white wine vinegar
2 teaspoons Dijon mustard
¾ cup good-quality olive oil
Salt and freshly ground pepper to taste

Put the shallots into a medium-sized bowl and add the vinegar. Allow to sit for about 2 hours at room temperature. Whisk in the mustard, then add the oil in a slow, steady stream. Season with salt and pepper to taste.

Try the dressing on:

- Blanched asparagus with toasted pine nuts
- Shredded baby bok choy with chopped sweet red pepper
- Sliced red and yellow tomatoes with chopped fresh chives and chive flowers

MAPLE-MUSTARD VINAIGRETTE (AND BASTING SAUCE)

MAKES 2 CUPS

*T*his sweet, rough vinaigrette is wonderful tossed with bitter greens or used to baste grilled pork, chicken, or steak. The recipe makes two cups and may be cut in half. It keeps well in the refrigerator, and is nice to have on hand.

⅓ cup cider vinegar
3 cloves garlic, peeled and crushed
2 shallots, peeled and diced
1 teaspoon freshly ground pepper
1 tablespoon smooth Dijon mustard
1 tablespoon coarse mustard
⅔ cup maple syrup
1 cup vegetable oil

*P*ut all the ingredients *except the oil* into a blender. Blend on high, then pour in the oil in a slow stream and process until thick.

Try the dressing on:

- A salad of grilled chicken, turkey, or duck with wild rice
- Tossed bitter greens with chopped apples and Spicy Nuts (page 296)
- Roast or grilled pork, chicken, turkey, duck, or other game birds, brushing it on the meat during the last 10 minutes to glaze the meat and add flavor

Farmhouse garden in Minnesota, 1910

WALNUT OIL VINAIGRETTE

MAKES 1½ CUPS

*W*alnut oil is expensive but so flavorful the thrifty cook needs only a little to jazz up a simple vinaigrette or sauté. It will keep indefinitely in the refrigerator, but it turns rancid quickly if left at room temperature.

> *Juice of 1 large lemon*
> *2 tablespoons cider vinegar*
> *1 teaspoon Dijon mustard*
> *Dash of Worcestershire sauce*
> *¾ cup walnut oil**
> *Salt and freshly ground pepper to taste*
>
> **This vinaigrette is also delicious made with hazelnut oil.*

*I*n a small bowl, whisk together the lemon juice, vinegar, mustard, and Worcestershire sauce. Whisk in the oil in a slow, steady stream and then add salt and pepper to taste.

Try the dressing on:
- Composed salad of chicken, apples, and walnuts
- Wild rice, cranberry, and hazelnut salad

CILANTRO-LIME VINAIGRETTE

MAKES 1 CUP

*T*hanks to the influence of Hmong and Vietnamese immigrants, cilantro is almost as available as parsley in grocery stores throughout the Northern Heartland. It is also known as coriander and Chinese parsley.

> *1 tablespoon seeded, chopped jalapeño pepper*
> *1 tablespoon grated lime zest*
> *⅓ cup freshly squeezed lime juice*
> *⅔ cup vegetable oil*
> *1 bunch fresh cilantro, chopped (about ¼ cup)*
> *1 teaspoon sugar or to taste*
> *Dash of salt and freshly ground pepper to taste*

*C*ombine the jalapeño pepper, lime zest, and lime juice, and then whisk in the oil. Add the cilantro and sugar to taste, then season with salt and pepper.

Try the dressing on:
- Grilled tuna or salmon
- Blanched sweet peas mixed with fresh sweet corn kernels
- Salad of roasted sweet peppers and navy beans
- Steamed cauliflower, carrots, and broccoli

CREAMY MUSTARD-HERB DRESSING

MAKES 1½ CUPS

2 tablespoons Dijon mustard
2 tablespoons chopped fresh tarragon or sage
¼ cup lemon juice
2 tablespoons water
⅓ cup vegetable oil
⅔ cup olive oil
Salt and freshly ground pepper to taste

*I*n a blender or food processor fitted with a steel blade, combine all of the ingredients *except the oils, salt and pepper.* Add the oils in a slow, steady stream and process until emulsified. Season with salt and pepper to taste.

Try the dressing on:
- Seasoned Flank Steak for Summer and Winter (page 120)
- Shrimp and hard-boiled egg salad
- Steamed cauliflower, carrots, and broccoli

LEMON, THYME, AND MINT VINAIGRETTE

MAKES 1¾ CUPS

½ cup lemon juice
Grated rind of a lemon (no pith)
¼ cup chopped fresh thyme leaves
¼ cup chopped fresh mint leaves
1 clove garlic, peeled and minced
2 teaspoons sugar
1¼ cups vegetable oil
Few grinds white pepper to taste

*P*ut all of the ingredients, *except the oil and white pepper,* into a blender or food processor fitted with a steel blade and process until smooth. Add the oil in a slow, steady stream. (If the dressing is too thick, add a few drops of hot water.) Season to taste with white pepper.

Try the dressing on:
- Diced, mixed cucumbers and chopped tomatoes
- Fresh Succotash Salad with Wilted Greens (page 260).

Field of peas in blossom

BLUE CHEESE DRESSING

MAKES 1 GENEROUS CUP

*T*his tangy, smooth dressing doubles as a dip for fresh, raw vegetables.

1 tablespoon peeled, chopped onions
1 clove garlic, peeled and crushed
2 tablespoons chopped fresh parsley
1 tablespoon white wine vinegar
½ cup Basic Mayonnaise (page 259) or good-quality pre-
*   pared mayonnaise*
¼ cup sour cream or yogurt
Dash of Tabasco sauce
¼ cup crumbled blue cheese
Salt and freshly ground pepper to taste

*I*n a food processor fitted with a steel blade, or in a blender, whirl together the onions, garlic, parsley, and vinegar; turn into a bowl, and fold in the mayonnaise, sour cream, and Tabasco. Fold in the blue cheese, then season with salt and pepper to taste.

Try the dressing on:

- Bitter greens, walnuts, and diced pears or apples
- Steamed new potatoes and chopped scallions
- Smoked trout and watercress

BASIC MAYONNAISE

MAKES 3 CUPS

*T*o avoid using raw eggs, we've devised this simple homemade mayonnaise, which is made by cooking the yolks. It is far better-tasting than most commercial varieties and will keep one week, covered, in the refrigerator.

> *3 egg yolks*
> *Dash of Tabasco sauce*
> *1–2 teaspoons Dijon mustard*
> *¼ teaspoon each, salt and freshly ground pepper*
> *1 tablespoon lemon juice or vinegar*
> *2 cups vegetable oil*

*P*ut the eggs into the top of a double boiler and bring the water to a low simmer, whisking the eggs constantly. As the eggs begin to thicken, add the Tabasco sauce, mustard, salt, pepper, and lemon juice, and continue whisking about 20 to 30 seconds, or until the mixture is thick and glossy and the eggs are cooked through to 130°F. Remove from the heat and whisk in the oil in a slow, steady stream. If the mixture is too thick, thin with a few drops of lemon juice, vinegar, hot water, or stock.

SUMMER CORN

"**S**ummer ripens the fields golden with wheat and rye; on a warm night, when the bright moon is up after a shower has fairly wet the earth and waked up the drowsy corn, I will swear that you can see the stalk stretch and swell in its new sheath, rise through the contracted lips of the upper blade to crack and burst and murmur in green-tongued speech. You hear the green cry of growth and the potatoes murmur to each other 'move over.' "

—MERIDEL LE SUEUR, *NORTH STAR COUNTRY*

FRESH SUCCOTASH SALAD
WITH WILTED GREENS

SERVES 4

*I*n the Northern Heartland succotash came to mean a plate of corn and beans, sometimes sweetened with maple syrup or flavored with salt pork or dressed with cream.

In this light, fresh-tasting dish, we quickly sauté red peppers, corn, and beans in a little olive oil until just tender-crisp and serve them garnished with fresh herbs and bright red cherry tomatoes and, if we have them, a few nasturtium blossoms from the garden.

> *1 cup uncooked corn kernels (preferably fresh)*
> *1 medium red bell pepper, cored, deveined, seeded, and*
> *   diced into pieces the size of corn kernels*
> *1 cup fresh lima beans or peas*
> *1 tablespoon olive oil*
> *3 tablespoons Lemon, Thyme, and Mint Vinaigrette (page*
> *   256)*
> *Salt and freshly ground pepper to taste*
> *2 cups freshly washed and dried salad greens*
> *4–6 red and yellow cherry tomatoes, cut in half, for garnish*
> *Nasturtium flowers for garnish, if available*

*I*n a large skillet, lightly sauté the corn, pepper, and beans in the olive oil over medium-high heat for about 2 minutes, or until they are bright but still crisp. While the vegetables are still warm, toss with the vinaigrette, season with salt and pepper to taste, and place on a bed of salad greens. Garnish with cut cherry tomatoes and nasturtium flowers, if you've got them.

RADISH AND CUCUMBER SALAD
IN YOGURT DRESSING

SERVES 4 TO 6

*T*his recipe tosses together bright red radishes with cool cucumbers in a refreshing, light yogurt-based dressing. It's best served ice-cold.

2–3 cucumbers, peeled, sliced, and seeded
3 scallions or young onions, chopped
12 radishes, trimmed and sliced

DRESSING

3 tablespoons chopped fresh dill
Grated zest of 1 lemon
Juice of 1 lemon
1 cup plain yogurt
2 teaspoons sugar
Salt and freshly ground pepper to taste

*I*n a large bowl, toss together the chopped vegetables. In a small bowl, make the dressing. Whisk together the dill, lemon zest and juice, yogurt, sugar, and salt and pepper to taste. Toss with the vegetables and chill about 15 to 30 minutes before serving.

Corn-eating champions, Sweet Corn Festival, Ortonville, Minnesota, 1933. (Winner on left, age twenty-two, ate 44 ears; winner on right, age seventy-one, ate 45 ears.)

FRESH CORN PUDDING

SERVES 8

*O*ur version of this old-fashioned favorite is more like a timbale. It will bake up puffy and light and sink as it cools. Scrape the corn kernels from the cob into a bowl to catch the corn milk, which you will add to the pudding.

> *1 tablespoon butter*
> *¼ cup fresh bread crumbs*
> *3 cups corn kernels (from about 12 ears)*
> *2 shallots, peeled and minced*
> *1 cup heavy cream, warmed*
> *Dash of Tabasco sauce*
> *Dash of Worcestershire sauce*
> *1 teaspoon salt*
> *¼ teaspoon freshly ground pepper*

6 eggs, lightly beaten
1 tablespoon chopped fresh dill
½ cup grated Monterey Jack cheese

*B*utter an 8-cup soufflé or baking dish and sprinkle with the bread crumbs. In a food processor fitted with a steel blade, blend together *1 cup* of the corn kernels with the shallots and the warm cream, Tabasco and Worcestershire sauces, salt, and pepper until creamy. Turn into a large bowl and add the lightly beaten eggs, the remaining 2 cups corn, the dill, and the cheese.

Pour the corn mixture into the prepared dish and loosely cover with heavily buttered aluminum foil. Put the dish in a baking pan and fill the pan with boiling water two thirds of the way up the sides of the baking dish. Put the pan in a preheated 350°F oven and bake for 45 minutes. Remove the aluminum foil and continue baking another 15 minutes, or until a knife inserted in the center comes up clean.

THE MAGIC OF CORN

The Indians taught the early settlers to place beans between the sprouting corn plants, allowing the vines to curl up the cornstalks. They believed that corn possessed magical powers that protected beans and other vegetables.

"Now the corn, as we believe, has an enemy—the sun who tries to burn the corn. But at night, when the sun has gone down, the corn has magic power. It is the corn that brings the night moistures—the early morning mist and fog, and the dew—as you can see yourself in the morning from the water dripping from the corn leaves. The corn grows and keeps on until it is ripe.

"The sun may scorch the corn and try hard to dry it up, but the corn takes care of itself, bringing the moistures that make the corn and also the beans, sunflowers, squashes, and tobacco grow."

—BUFFALO BIRD WOMAN, *BUFFALO BIRD WOMAN'S GARDEN*

OVERNIGHT COLESLAW

SERVES 4 TO 6

*W*e like to make this the night before a day of fishing, then tote it in the cooler with beer and Homemade Tartar Sauce (page 215), so that it's ready for a North Shore Lunch of just-hooked walleye, pan-fried over an open fire on the sandy lakeshore (page 214).

DRESSING

1 bay leaf
1 cup red wine vinegar
3 tablespoons brown sugar, light or dark
Dash of Tabasco sauce
1 clove garlic, crushed
1 tablespoon caraway seeds, toasted in a 350°F oven for
  about 5 minutes
1 tablespoon Dijon mustard
½ cup vegetable oil
Salt and freshly ground pepper to taste

½ head red or green cabbage (or a combination of both),
  thinly sliced
1 red onion, peeled and thinly sliced

*I*n a small saucepan, combine the bay leaf, vinegar, sugar, Tabasco sauce, and garlic, and bring to a boil. Remove from the heat and allow to cool. Remove the bay leaf. Whisk the toasted caraway seeds, mustard, and vegetable oil into the vinegar mixture and season with salt and pepper to taste. Put the sliced cabbage and onion in a large bowl and toss with the dressing. Adjust the seasoning. Cover and refrigerate overnight.

SUMMER TOMATO, POTATO, AND EGGPLANT BAKE

SERVES 6 AS AN ENTRÉE OR 10 AS A SIDE DISH

*T*his simple recipe makes a vegetarian main course or hearty side dish, combining garden fresh zucchini and bright red, green, and yellow peppers with juicy tomatoes and eggplant. We arrange the vegetables in rows across a wide, flat casserole dish to show off the fresh summer colors.

> *1 pound boiling potatoes (about 4–6 potatoes), peeled and*
> *   cut into ⅛-inch slices*
> *Salt and freshly ground black pepper*
> *½ cup olive oil*
> *1 large unpeeled eggplant, cut into ½-inch slices, then cut*
> *   in half*
> *1 pound zucchini (about 3–4 small), cut into ½-inch slices*
> *1 each, yellow, red, and green bell peppers, halved, seeded,*
> *   and cut into ½-inch strips*
> *2 red onions, peeled and cut into ½-inch strips*
> *3 cloves garlic, peeled and crushed*
> *4 big tomatoes, cut into 1-inch chunks*
> *20 calamata olives, pitted*
> *1 cup chunks of feta cheese (optional)*

*A*rrange the potatoes in a single layer on the bottom of an ovenproof glass baking pan (about 9 × 12 inches). Sprinkle lightly with salt and pepper and drizzle with *a little* of the oil.

Toss the vegetables with the remaining oil and spread them over the potato layer. Scatter the olives and feta cheese, if you are using it, over the vegetables and cover tightly with aluminum foil. Place in a preheated 375°F oven for 30 minutes. Remove the aluminum foil and continue baking another hour to 1½ hours, or until all the vegetables are cooked through. Brush with additional oil if the vegetables seem to be getting dry.

GRATIN OF PUMPKIN
AND LEEKS

SERVES 8 TO 10

*Y*ears ago pumpkins were an important food, not just for jack-o'-lanterns and pie. They were baked with maple syrup, mashed with butter, tossed into soups and stews, cooked into "butter," pressed for syrup, and even roasted and ground for coffee.

Here we roast the pumpkin with carrots and leeks, then bake them all together in a casserole, sprinkled with cheese. This hearty dish is delicious with grilled chicken or served as a simple supper with a salad and bread.

> *1 pumpkin (about 4½–5 pounds), peeled, seeded, and cut into ½-inch chunks*
> *2 leeks, slit horizontally, trimmed, washed under cold running water, and cut into 2-inch chunks*
> *4 carrots, peeled and cut into ½-inch chunks*
> *3 small onions, peeled and cut into ½-inch chunks*
> *4 tablespoons olive oil*
> *½ teaspoon freshly ground nutmeg*
> *2 tablespoons chopped fresh rosemary or 2 tablespoons dried*
> *Salt and freshly ground pepper to taste*
> *¼ cup white wine or chicken stock*
> *¼ cup grated Parmesan cheese*
> *½ cup toasted bread crumbs*
> *½ stick (4 tablespoons) butter*

*P*ut the pumpkin, leeks, carrots, and onions into a large roasting pan, drizzle with the oil, and sprinkle with the nutmeg. Roast the vegetables in a preheated 375°F oven for 30 to 40 minutes, or until tender.

Add the rosemary, salt and pepper, and the wine to the pan and gently toss together. Sprinkle the vegetables with the Parmesan cheese and bread crumbs, then dot with butter. Bake in a 350°F oven for about 20 minutes, or until the cheese is melted, the bread crumbs are browned, and the vegetables are very soft.

Prizewinning vegetables of the Minnesota State Fair, 1926

SQUASH DOLLS

"When I was a little girl, about ten years old, my friends and I would go to the pile and pick out squashes for dolls. We used to pick out the long ones that were parti-colored—squashes whose tops were white or yellow and the bottoms of some other color. I carried my squash about in my arms and sang for it as for a babe and carried it on my back in my calfskin robe."

—BUFFALO BIRD WOMAN, *BUFFALO BIRD WOMAN'S GARDEN*

COUNTRY SAUERKRAUT

SERVES 4 TO 6

Served on top of bratwurst, sausage, and hot dogs, alongside spareribs and braised pork chops, with potatoes and over dumplings, homemade sauerkraut was once as common in many German and East European homes as bottled ketchup and relish are today.

This recipe combines sauerkraut with sweet apples, cider, and caraway seeds for an easy, quick side dish.

> *1 medium white onion, peeled and sliced*
> *2 tablespoons bacon fat or vegetable oil*
> *1 pound sauerkraut, drained*
> *2 tart apples, peeled, cored, and cut into 1-inch slices*
> *½ cup apple cider*
> *1 teaspoon caraway seeds*
> *2 tablespoons brown sugar, light or dark, or to taste*
> *Salt and freshly ground pepper to taste*

In a large, deep skillet, sauté the onion in the fat until brown. Add the sauerkraut, apples, cider, and caraway seeds, and stir to combine. Simmer, uncovered, for about 20 minutes. Add the brown sugar, taste, and adjust the seasoning.

BRUSSELS SPROUTS
WITH TOASTED ALMONDS

SERVES 6 TO 8

*T*he farmers at market sell fresh Brussels sprouts on the stalk. The miniature cabbages, tiniest on top, spiral down and become as big as plums at the bottom. Brussels sprouts are ready as early as late September, but frost sweetens them. They develop a bitter taste, however, when stored too long.

Brussels sprouts turn gray and mushy when overcooked. They should be lightly steamed, blanched, or braised until just tender to preserve their lovely bright green color and delicate flavor. The brown butter in this recipe adds a distinctly nutty taste.

> *¼ cup slivered blanched almonds*
> *1 pound Brussels sprouts*
> *½ stick (4 tablespoons) butter*
> *Salt and freshly ground pepper to taste*
> *2 tablespoons chopped fresh parsley*

*S*pread the almonds on a baking sheet and lightly toast them in a preheated 350°F oven for about 7 to 10 minutes, shaking the pan occasionally, until they are golden brown. You'll smell them when they're done.

Trim the sprouts of dead outer leaves, score the bottom end with an X, and wash in warm water. Cut the sprouts in half and steam or blanch the sprouts until just tender and bright green (3 to 5 minutes, depending on size). Be careful not to overcook. Drain and quickly rinse the sprouts in ice water to set the color.

Melt the butter in a large skillet and cook over medium heat until it begins to brown and smell nutty. Be careful. If it goes too long, the butter will burn, but if it is not cooked long enough, it will lack the nutty flavor characteristic of brown butter. Add the Brussels sprouts to the pan and heat through, tossing to coat with the butter. Season with salt and pepper and toss in the almonds and chopped parsley. Serve immediately.

FALL INTO WINTER

"There was great excitement in the fall, the terror of the winter coming on. In the winter we didn't have what we did not can, preserve, ferment, or bury in the sand. We had to hurry to cut the wood and to get the tomatoes, beans, and piccalilli canned before frost in the garden. It was like preparing for a battle. My mother wrapped the apples in newspaper and put them cheek by jowl in the barrels. Cabbage was shredded and barreled for sauerkraut. Even the old hens were killed. I was always surprised to see my gentle grandmother put her foot on the neck of her favorite hen and behead her with a single stroke of a long-handled ax."

—MERIDEL LE SUEUR, *NORTH STAR COUNTRY*

RAMPS

Much prized by today's cooks, ramps (wild leeks) were an important food of the early Ojibway tribes, who lived in northern Wisconsin and Minnesota. These nomadic hunters would combine ramps and other wild greens with game in birch-bark containers, which they hung over an open fire to cook.

Resembling scallions with lilylike leaves, the ramp is more flavorful than the mild-mannered leek. Both thrive in hostile climates and are virtually pest-free. Their flavor cannot be duplicated by using onions, garlic, or shallots. When a recipe calls for leeks, use leeks (or ramps).

Cultivated leeks may be substituted for ramps. Ramps should be treated like scallions, simply rinsed, trimmed, and then added to a recipe. Leeks are a bit trickier to clean. The broad, tightly packed leaves collect and hide grit and soil. Trim off the "whiskers" at the bulb's base and then slit the bulb horizontally and wash under cold running water.

BRAISED RED CABBAGE
WITH APPLES AND BACON

SERVES 6

*T*o keep red cabbage crisp in this recipe, toss it with the vinegar before cooking—an old German trick. Slowly simmered with apples, onions, and a few cloves, this dish makes a pretty accompaniment to pork, veal, and chicken and is also good the next day, served at room temperature.

> *3 strips bacon or 2 tablespoons butter or vegetable oil*
> *1 small yellow onion, peeled and thinly sliced*
> *1 medium head red cabbage, shredded*
> *½ cup cider vinegar*
> *2 tart apples, peeled, cored, and thinly sliced*
> *½ cup apple cider*
> *4 whole cloves*
> *⅓ cup sugar*
> *Salt and freshly ground pepper to taste*

*I*n a large, deep skillet or kettle, fry the bacon (or if using oil or butter, heat over medium heat). Leave the drippings in the pan and drain the bacon on paper towels. Crumble the bacon and set it aside for garnish. Sauté the onion in the fat until limp and brown. Toss the shredded cabbage with the vinegar, then add this, along with the remaining ingredients *except the salt and pepper,* to the pot and simmer, uncovered, until the cabbage is bright and tender (it should not get soggy), about 20 minutes. Season with salt and pepper to taste and serve garnished with the crumbled bacon.

PERFECT MASHED POTATOES

SERVES 8

*I*t's hard to go wrong with these easy mashed potatoes. We like to leave in a few lumps for texture. Sometimes, we'll throw in a few turnips, parsnips, or rutabagas for a vegetable whip (see variation below). Try adding a sprinkling of sharp grated cheese. Serve alongside a slice of Swedish Meat Loaf (page 125) or with a dinner of Holiday Roast Wild Turkey (page 190). Double the recipe so you'll have extra to make Potato Bread (page 21).

> *3½–4 pounds russet potatoes*
> *Water*
> *1 teaspoon salt*
> *1 stick (8 tablespoons) butter*
> *1 cup light cream or whole milk*
> *Salt and freshly ground pepper to taste*

*P*eel the potatoes and cut them into equal-sized chunks; then put them into a large pot and cover with cold water and add the salt. Bring the water to a boil and cook the potatoes until they are very tender, about 20 to 30 minutes. Drain the potatoes, return them to the pot, and mash with a masher, adding the remaining ingredients as you mash, until the potatoes are as smooth as you like.

Vegetable Whip: Add to the pot approximately ½ pound peeled and cut turnips, parsnips, or rutabagas (alone or in combination). When mashing the potatoes and roots, you may need more cream and butter.

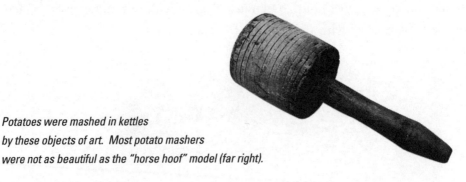

Potatoes were mashed in kettles
by these objects of art. Most potato mashers
were not as beautiful as the "horse hoof" model (far right).

ROASTED SWEET POTATO PURÉE

SERVES 6 TO 8

*I*n the Northern Heartland the sweet potatoes that grow best have a drier flesh and are less sweet than those that grow down South. You may use any variety of the over forty kinds now sold across the United States; adjust the amount of honey to taste. The purée is delicious alongside Iowa Chops with Savory Rub (page 115).

> *6–8 sweet potatoes (about 3 pounds)*
> *3 tablespoons butter*
> *2 tablespoons half-and-half or milk*
> *1 tablespoon honey or to taste*
> *¼ teaspoon freshly ground nutmeg, plus more for garnish*
> *Salt and freshly ground pepper to taste*

*S*crub the potatoes and poke them several times with a fork; bake in a preheated 400°F oven for about 1 hour, or until they are very soft. Slit them open and scrape the meat into a medium bowl or into a food processor fitted with a steel blade. Add the remaining ingredients and process the potatoes on high for about 3 minutes, or process, adding more half-and-half or milk as needed, until they reach the consistency you like. Add salt and pepper to taste. Serve warm with a sprinkling of nutmeg.

CHIPPEWA GLOSSARY
FOR NAMES OF THE MONTH

- GITCIMANIDO GIZIS—big-spirit month (January)

- ONA BINIGI ZIS—snow-crusted month (February)

- BOBA KWUDAGIME GIZIS—broken-snowshoe month, so-called because the crusted snow broke the netting on the snowshoes (March)

- I CKIGAMI SIGEGI ZIS—maple-sugar-making month, literally boiling month (April)

- WA BIGWUN IGI ZIS—flower (May)

- ODE IMIN IGI ZIS—strawberry (June)

- MIN IGI ZIS—indicates blueberry or seeds (July)

- MANO MINIGI ZIS—rice (August)

- WASE BUGOGI ZIS—shining leaf (September)

- BINAKWE GIZIS—rake / comb (October)

- GUCKU DINOGI ZIS—it freezes (November)

- MANIDO GIZISONS—spirit month (December)

BASIC WILD RICE

A low-fat, high-fiber carbohydrate, wild rice supplies appreciable amounts of protein, minerals, and vitamins and contains only seventy calories per half-cup serving.

Wild rice may seem pricey compared with brown or white rice, but because it swells up to four times its size as it cooks, it is a good value when the cost per serving is considered. Scandinavian homesteaders called wild rice "pocket money," because just a little would expand to easily feed a family of five.

One full pound of wild rice will yield about ten to twelve cups, or enough for twenty to twenty-four servings. One cup of wild rice increases to four cups when cooked, enough for six servings.

Wild rice should be cooked until it puffs and the inner, lighter part is visible. Overcooking increases the volume but leaves the rice mushy. For salads we sometimes undercook the rice so that it is chewy and nutty.

Uncooked wild rice can be stored in a tightly covered container set in a cool place for several months; after that, it should be kept in the refrigerator. Cooked, well-drained rice will keep in the refrigerator in a tightly covered container for a week. It may also be stored frozen for up to three months. For mail-order sources for wild rice, see Sources, page 372.

> *1 cup wild rice*
> *4 cups water*
> *1 teaspoon salt*

*W*ash the rice thoroughly by putting it in a colander and running it under cold water. Turn the wild rice, water, and salt into a large, heavy saucepan and bring to a boil. Reduce the heat, cover, and simmer about 45 minutes to 1 hour, or until the rice has puffed and most of the liquid has been absorbed. Fluff the rice with a fork and let it stand a few minutes before serving.

WILD RICE

In dreams we have learned how everything given to us is to be used; how the rice is harvested and the animals hunted.
—BILL JOHNSON OF NETT LAKE, MINNESOTA

Wild rice, the seed of the aquatic grass that grows along the shallow shores of the deep northern lakes in Wisconsin, Minnesota, and neighboring Canada, has always been immensely important to the Ojibway tribe of the area. Years ago at harvesttime, the entire village would move to its rice camp on the lakeshore. Families worked together; the men poled the canoe with two women aboard, who would knock the stalks to fill the boat with rice. On shore, the rice was sun-dried or parched on screens set over low fires.

To thresh, the men, with moccasin-shod feet, would tread on the dried rice, which was placed in a small skin-lined hole in the ground. The chaff was then separated by pouring the rice from one basket to another, allowing the light breezes to carry it away. The rice was bagged and buried deep in the cool earth for winter.

Wild rice remains a Native American staple throughout the Northern Heartland, and it is still hand-harvested with canoes. The rice is eaten for breakfast with maple syrup, popped like popcorn for snacks, and tossed into stews, casseroles, and breads. A mother unable to nurse her infant might give the baby wild rice boiled with broth. A gruel of crushed rice is strained and mixed with herbs to become a salve for poison ivy and other skin rashes.

The rice also has a spiritual significance apart from its medicinal and nutritional value. Girls abstain from all foods except wild rice during puberty rites, pregnant women eat rice at the end of their term for easy labor, and the dying are fed wild rice for strength on their journey into the afterlife.

The sacred nature of wild rice is expressed in the Ojibway's reluctance to propagate it for commercial sale. While they recognize their responsibility for reseeding the rice, they shun the idea of actually sowing a rice crop. Each year's reappearance is attributed to the spirit of the lake. "Any attempt to sow the rice as whites sow corn would curse the lake, and rice would never grow in it again," said Charlie Day, an elder of the Ojibway tribe. The Ojibway believe that if the Great Spirit so desires, the rice will always grow.

—*WILD RICE AND THE OJIBWAY PEOPLE*

WILD RICE, CRANBERRY, WALNUT, AND VEGETABLE SALAD

SERVES 4

*T*his crunchy, nutty combination makes a colorful addition to a holiday buffet table and, with the addition of leftover roast turkey, is a simple lunch entrée.

> *½ cup cranberries, rinsed*
> *¼ cup water*
> *1 medium carrot, coarsely chopped*
> *2 cups cooked wild rice*
> *1 stalk celery, coarsely chopped*
> *1 small red onion, peeled and coarsely chopped*
> *1 small tart apple, cored and coarsely chopped*
> *¼ cup Walnut Oil Vinaigrette (page 254)*
> *Salt and freshly ground pepper to taste*
> *Salad greens*

*I*n a small saucepan, cook the cranberries in the water just until they have popped. Blanch the chopped carrot in enough rapidly boiling water to cover for 2 minutes. Drain and rinse in ice water. Turn the carrot and the cranberries (in their juice) into a large bowl, along with the wild rice and the chopped celery, onion, and apple. Add the dressing and toss to coat the ingredients. You may want to add more dressing to taste. Season with salt and freshly ground pepper and serve on a bed of greens.

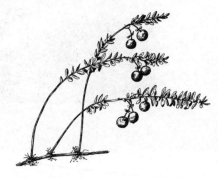

WILD RICE PILAF
WITH DRIED CHERRIES
AND WALNUTS

SERVES 4 TO 6

*T*his tangy pilaf is delicious with wild game, turkey, or chicken. It may be made ahead and reheated, covered, in a low oven.

> *1 cup wild rice, rinsed*
> *4 cups water (enough to cover the rice by an inch or so)*
> *1 teaspoon butter*
> *2 shallots, peeled and minced*
> *Grated zest of 1 orange*
> *¼ cup dried cherries, currants, or chopped dried apricots*
> *¼ cup toasted chopped hazelnuts (for toasting directions,*
>   *see page 216)*
> *Salt and freshly ground pepper to taste*

*P*ut the wild rice and water into a medium-sized saucepan and bring to a boil. Reduce the heat, cover, and simmer until the rice is tender (see general cooking instructions on page 275), about 45 minutes. Uncover the pot, toss in the remaining ingredients, and add salt and pepper to taste.

Old-fashioned Apple Butter

Sweet and Hot Pepper Jelly

Spiced Blueberry-Lemon Preserve

Vanilla Poached Fruit

Cranberry-Leek Compote

Our Very Best Pickles

Sweet Corn Relish

Pickled Beets

Rhubarb Chutney

Green Tomato Mincemeat

Chive Flower Vinegar

Spicy Nuts

PRESERVES
AND PICKLES

SWEET AND SAVORY EMBELLISHMENTS

"Putting up" pickles, conserves, preserves, jams, jellies, and butters with the bounty of a Midwestern garden is still done by many home cooks today. Years ago the only fruit and vegetables available in January were those that had been preserved in October. Nothing was wasted—rose petals, watermelon rind, green tomatoes, or less than perfect apples—all were turned into sweet or sour condiments. Come frost, the pantry shelves were lined with canned tomatoes, corn relish, pickled beets, beans, carrots, and cucumbers. Attic rafters were strung with slices of drying mushrooms. A faint odor of fermenting kraut permeated the dark root cellar, where apples were stored wrapped in newspaper, and turnips, parsnips, and carrots were packed in sawdust-filled wooden barrels.

Today's cooks are more apt to enjoy preserving for its simple creative satisfaction; we are no longer driven by pure necessity. We gather friends to share in the making of Spiced Blueberry-Lemon Preserve, for instance, with berries picked in the north woods; a fragrant blend of fruit and spices, it's delicious on corn bread and with grilled meat. Such condiments make welcome gifts and embellish simple, home-cooked meals.

"APPLE PEELIN' AND STIRRIN'"

In the apple-growing areas of Minnesota, Wisconsin, and northern Iowa, an "apple peelin'" (and the related "stirrin'") were good reasons for a party. Upon arriving at the host's farm, guests would be handed a paring knife and a crock of apples to peel and core. Competition among bachelors to finish the most apples was fierce because the winner could kiss any girl he chose.

Work done, the men would prepare the parlor for dancing, moving out furniture, taking up rugs, and sprinkling cornmeal over the floor. The fiddler would call out, "Partners to your places, hook up your back bend and tighten your braces."

The next day neighbor ladies would return for a "stirrin'." The apples, cider, and spices were dumped into a big copper kettle set on rocks over a log fire. A dozen scrubbed stones "the size of a silver dollar" were added to help keep the butter from sticking to the bottom of the pot. The women took turns stirring the butter with a long wooden paddle, and if it was not ready by supper, the fire was allowed to go out, the kettle was covered with a cloth, and the work resumed early the next morning.

Some cooks canned their apple butter. Others kept it frozen in the winter on the outdoor back porch. When the cook needed a fresh supply, she would chip some out of the cask to thaw.

OLD-FASHIONED APPLE BUTTER

MAKES ABOUT 12 TO 13 PINTS (RECIPE IS EASILY CUT IN HALF.)

*W*e make this late in the fall when the apples are especially sweet. It fills the house with a spicy apple aroma as it cooks. It is delicious on toast, muffins, pancakes, and waffles, stirred into plain yogurt, spooned over ice cream, and served alongside ham and grilled chicken. We always make enough to give to friends.

> 5 cups apple cider (dark is best)
> 10 pounds apples (about 30 cups), peeled, cored,
>   and quartered
> 4 cups sugar
> 1 cup dark corn syrup
> 1 tablespoon ground cinnamon
> 2 teaspoons ground cloves

*I*n a large, 10-quart kettle, bring the cider to a boil, add the apples, reduce the heat, and simmer for about 1 hour. Add the sugar, corn syrup, and the spices. Continue simmering, stirring frequently, for about 3 hours, or until the butter becomes dark brown and very thick. Fill hot sterilized canning jars with the butter and process according to the manufacturer's instructions.

SWEET AND HOT PEPPER JELLY

MAKES 3 PINTS

*H*ot peppers give this sweet, pretty jelly a light kick. Use either red or green peppers, depending on what's in season. Spread it on crackers with cream cheese, use it to glaze grilled meat, stir it into sour cream to make a sauce for fish, chicken, or steamed vegetables, or eat it right out of the jar.

Sweet and Hot Pepper Jelly (continued)

> *2 red or green bell peppers*
> *3 red or green Habañero, or 6 hot Hmong, or 6 jalapeño*
>   *peppers**
> *1½ cups cider vinegar*
> *6 cups sugar*
> *6 ounces liquid pectin*

> **Use caution handling hot peppers. Wear rubber gloves and do*
> *not touch your eyes with your hands before washing with soap.*

*R*emove the veins and seeds from the peppers. Chop coarsely, then put them into a blender with the vinegar and blend to a purée. Pour the purée into a pot, add the sugar, and bring to a boil. Add the pectin and boil for 1 minute. (Watch that the mixture doesn't boil over.) Turn off the heat and skim the foam from the top. Pour the liquid into sterilized jars and process according to the manufacturer's directions. The jelly will keep in the refrigerator at least a month.

SPICED BLUEBERRY-LEMON PRESERVE

MAKES 6 TO 8 ½ PINTS

*W*ild blueberries are especially delicious in this recipe, but cultivated berries also work well. Try this mild, spiced preserve on breakfast toast; it is also good alongside wild game.

> *2 teaspoons allspice berries*
> *4 cinnamon sticks*
> *8 teaspoons whole cloves*
> *2 quarts rinsed, picked over blueberries*
> *2 tablespoons grated lemon rind*
> *½ cup lemon juice*
> *2 cups sugar*

*T*ie the spices into a cheesecloth bag and put them in a large saucepan, along with the remaining ingredients. Bring the preserve to a boil, lower the heat, and cook until it starts to thicken. This will take from 20 to 45 minutes, depending on how juicy the berries are. Frozen berries tend to take longer. (To test, put a small spoonful of the boiling preserve onto a refrigerated plate, then put the plate back into the refrigerator until the sample is cool to the touch. The preserve is ready if it holds its shape.) Remove the spice bag and spoon the preserve into hot, sterilized jars and process according to the manufacturer's instructions.

VANILLA POACHED FRUIT

MAKES 5 TO 6 CUPS

*W*hen the peaches, plums, and pears are ripe, we make this sauce to put away and then serve through the winter. It's great over ice cream, on the German Oven Pancake (page 44), with Rich Bread Pudding (page 359), and on top of White Cake (page 318).

> *1 cup mixed dried fruit (dates, prunes, currants, cherries,*
> *golden raisins, figs, dried cherries, chopped apricots)*
> *½ cup orange juice*
> *¼ cup port*
> *2 teaspoons vanilla extract or one large vanilla bean, split*
> *4–5 cups peeled, sliced, and cored peaches, plums, or pears*
> *(alone or in combination)*

*P*ut the dried fruit, orange juice, port, and vanilla into a medium-sized saucepan and simmer over low heat for about 5 minutes, or until the dried fruit becomes soft. Add the fresh fruit and gently stir a few times. (Be careful, the fruit should be coated with the sauce but not really cook and become mushy.) Turn off the heat, remove the vanilla bean, spoon the fruit and liquid into canning jars, and process according to the manufacturer's directions.

CRANBERRY-LEEK COMPOTE

MAKES 5 TO 6 CUPS

A surprising side dish of cranberries and leeks, this makes a wonderful accompaniment to roast poultry, game, and the Thanksgiving turkey. It can be made up to five days ahead and kept in the refrigerator, or frozen. It's best served at room temperature.

> *½ cup currants or dried cranberries*
> *1 cup apple cider*
> *4 cups cranberries, rinsed and sorted*
> *¾ cup sugar*
> *6 tablespoons butter*
> *2½ pounds leeks (white and light green parts), rinsed and*
> *   sliced into rounds*
> *Salt and freshly ground pepper to taste*

*I*n a small saucepan, soak the currants or dried cranberries in *¼ cup* of the cider for 30 minutes to plump; then add the fresh cranberries and the remaining cider and cook over medium heat until the berries pop, about 5 minutes. Add the sugar and stir to dissolve. Set aside.

In a large, deep skillet, melt the butter and cook the leeks over low heat until they become very soft and begin to brown, stirring frequently, about 25 minutes. Add the cranberries and liquid to the skillet and cook about 2 to 3 minutes, stirring occasionally. Allow to cool and add salt and pepper to taste.

SUMMER'S BLESSING (OR CURSE?)

"The pressure cooker has been running full blast for days. Ralph is out of Kerr lids but vegetables fill up the fridge, the kitchen counter—quarts of tomatoes have been canned, still more tomatoes move in. The Mister reaches for the razor in the morning. He picks up a cucumber. Picks up the paper, underneath it are three zucchini. They crawled in under there to get some shade, catch a few Z's, maybe read the comics. Pumpkins are moving in to live with them. At night they check the bed for kohlrabi. Turn out the lights, they hear rustling noises downstairs: a gang of cauliflower trying the back door. Go to sleep, dream about watermelon vines reaching out and wrapping their spiny little fingers around your neck. The Big Berthas, the forty-pounders. Those tomatoes they planted, the Dauntless Dukes: why did they plant twelve hills? Why not two?

" 'I like to have extra just in case and it's also nice to have some to give away,' says Mrs. Luger, her hair melted to her head from an afternoon of canning. *But everyone else has some to give away.*"

—GARRISON KEILLOR, *LAKE WOBEGON DAYS*

OUR VERY BEST PICKLES

MAKES 12 QUARTS

*J*ust about every vegetable from the garden used to be pickled: green tomatoes, carrots, beans, cabbage, cauliflower, broccoli. The measure of every proud canner was the perfect pickle. These pickles come from Beth Fisher, a chef at Lucia's Restaurant. She makes them at her farm on Lake Pepin in southern Wisconsin. To spice things up, try the variations listed at the end of the recipe.

> 10 pounds pickling cucumbers (about 2–3 inches long)
> 13½ cups white vinegar
> 13½ cups water
> 2¼ cups pickling or kosher salt
> 1½ cups pickling spices
> 12 cloves garlic, peeled and sliced
> 15 stems fresh dill

*W*ash the cucumbers. Make a brine of vinegar, water, salt, and pickling spices, and bring it to a boil in a large saucepan. Pack the cucumbers, garlic, and dill into sterilized 1-quart jars. Cover the cucumbers with the hot brine, leaving ½ inch at the top. Seal, wiping the rims carefully. Process the jars according to the manufacturer's directions.

- Add 1 tablespoon curry powder to each jar.
- Substitute sprigs of rosemary, tarragon, or thyme for the dill.
- Add 2 tablespoons each, sweet corn kernels and chopped red bell peppers, to each jar for color.
- Add 1 fresh jalapeño or chili pepper to each jar for kick.
- Add a few baby carrots to each jar with the cucumbers.

SWEET CORN RELISH

MAKES 8 TO 9 CUPS

*F*resh, sweet relish is as much a part of backyard barbecues as are homemade pickles. Lulu's recipe (Lucia's grandmother) called for thirty "striped" (or partially ripened) tomatoes and "green" corn, using up vegetables that were plucked not quite ripe, but before the frost. We've made some changes, cutting back the quantity and adding more spices. It tastes best when made with really ripe tomatoes and sweet golden corn, and it is delicious on hot dogs and alongside grilled salmon.

> *1 large cucumber, peeled, seeded, and finely chopped*
> *3 medium onions, peeled and finely chopped*
> *1 green pepper, seeded, deveined, and finely chopped*
> *4 cups sweet corn kernels (cut from about 12 large cobs)*
> *2 tomatoes, peeled, seeded, and chopped*
> *½ cup sugar*
> *1 tablespoon salt*
> *½ teaspoon freshly ground pepper*
> *½ cup cider vinegar*
> *½ teaspoon turmeric*
> *2 teaspoons mustard seed*
> *½ teaspoon celery seed*

*P*ut all of the ingredients into a large kettle. Bring the mixture to a boil, lower the heat, and simmer, stirring occasionally, for about 15 to 20 minutes, or until the corn is just tender. Spoon into hot, sterilized jars and process according to the manufacturer's directions.

PICKLED BEETS

MAKES 2 QUARTS

*N*o smörgåsbord is complete without a salad of pickled beets and herring. These vibrant pickled beets make a pretty accent on an appetizer tray or a platter of cold meat, and they're a low-calorie snack as well.

> *2 pounds beets (about 4 large beets), trimmed, scrubbed,*
> *   and peeled*
> *1 medium onion, peeled and sliced*
> *1 clove garlic, peeled and sliced*
> *1 cup cider vinegar*
> *¼ cup sugar or to taste*
> *1 tablespoon cardamom seeds*
> *1 tablespoon whole cloves*
> *Pinch of salt*

*P*ut the beets into a medium-sized saucepan and cover with cold water. Bring the water to a boil, reduce the heat, and simmer the beets, partially covered, for about 25 to 30 minutes, or until they are tender. *Save 2 cups of the cooking liquid.*

   Slice the beets and put them, along with the onion and garlic, into a quart-size jar. In a separate saucepan, stir together the vinegar, 2 cups of the beet juice, sugar, and the spices, and heat just long enough to dissolve the sugar. Pour this over the beets, onion, and garlic. Cool to room temperature, cover, and refrigerate at least overnight before serving. These will keep a week in the refrigerator.

RHUBARB CHUTNEY

MAKES 7 TO 8 CUPS

*T*art and spicy, this chutney embellishes grilled meat and poultry, roast turkey, and curries of all kinds.

> *2 pounds rhubarb (about 8 cups), cut into 1-inch pieces*
> *1 whole lemon, chopped and seeded, with peel on*
> *1 whole orange, chopped and seeded, with peel on*
> *½ cup cider vinegar*
> *2 cloves garlic, peeled and crushed*
> *1 medium onion, peeled and chopped*
> *1 cup brown sugar, light or dark, or more to taste*

¼ cup grated fresh gingerroot
1 tablespoon mustard seed
1 tablespoon whole cloves
1 teaspoon ground cumin
1 teaspoon ground coriander
2 cups golden raisins

*I*n a large pot, mix together all the ingredients *except the raisins* and simmer, uncovered, stirring occasionally, for about an hour to 1½ hours. Toward the last 30 minutes, stir the mixture frequently. The chutney should start to get brown and stick to the bottom of the pot. Add the raisins 15 minutes before pulling the chutney from the stove. Spoon into hot, sterilized canning jars and process according to manufacturer's directions. This chutney will also keep in the refrigerator for about 3 months, or frozen.

SAUERKRAUT

Making sauerkraut was a traditional fall ritual for many Eastern European families. Women and children would harvest the easily grown green cabbages and slice them with a cabbage cutter set between two chairs. "By the end of the day, our knuckles were bloody from the blade and stinging from the coarse salt," recalls Jim Kwitchak.

The barrel was packed with layers of cabbage sprinkled with salt (and sometimes, caraway seeds), then covered with a clean cloth, a board, and heavy stone. It took about six weeks to cure, and was ready when the smell and taste mellowed from pungent to sour and salty. "We ate kraut through the winter," remembers Jim. "At least once a week we had it with spareribs, pork, or bacon, and other times in dumplings or with potatoes. When the barrel was almost empty, we fought over who got to drink the juice."

MRS. GEORGE COLLING'S SAUERKRAUT*
(IN AN OPEN CROCK)

FILLS A VERY LARGE CROCK

Sauerkraut takes a strong, steady arm to shred the cabbage, and a lot of patience—more time and patience than most people have today. It must be stored in a cool, dark place, or the cabbage will get moldy before it's soured. While the cabbage is curing, the smell can be very pungent, so it's best kept away from central living areas.

40 pounds cabbage, cleaned and shredded
1 pound or about 1½ cups kosher salt
½ pound or 1 cup sugar

Mix well in enamel or plastic tub. Pack firmly in an open crock. If too much juice accumulates, dip some off with a saucer or ladle and discard. Cover with some clean cabbage leaves and sprinkle with salt. Then cover with a clean cloth and a plate to fit the crock closely and add a clean weight (a smooth stone will do on top). Tie a clean towel or a piece of plastic wrap over the crock and let set about 3 weeks. Keep it clean and keep saltier water over the top of the plate. The sauerkraut may be canned or frozen.

* This recipe comes from a very reliable source, but we have not tested it.

GREEN TOMATO MINCEMEAT

MAKES ABOUT 5 PINTS

*T*his spicy-sweet vegetarian mincemeat makes a wonderful, old-fashioned pie and is also good served as a relish for grilled pork or chicken.

To peel the green tomatoes, blanch them by dropping them into a big pot of boiling water and cooking them about a minute, then quickly plunging them into ice water. The skin should pull off easily with a knife.

> *6 cups chopped apples*
> *6 cups chopped green tomatoes*
> *4 cups brown sugar, light or dark*
> *1⅓ cups cider vinegar*
> *3 cups raisins*
> *1 cup currants*
> *3 teaspoons ground cinnamon*
> *1 teaspoon ground cloves*
> *1 teaspoon ground allspice*
> *1 teaspoon ground mace or nutmeg*
> *1 teaspoon freshly ground black pepper*
> *2 teaspoons salt*
> *1 stick (8 tablespoons) butter*

*T*oss together the apples and tomatoes in a large colander and drain well. Turn them into a large kettle, along with the remaining ingredients except the butter. Bring the mixture to a boil over high heat, then lower the flame and simmer, uncovered, for about 3 hours, stirring often.

Add the butter and fill sterilized canning jars with the hot mincemeat. Seal and process the jars according to the manufacturer's instructions. Store in a cool place. Allow a few days for the spices to marry before using.

CHIVE FLOWER VINEGAR

MAKES 1 QUART

*V*inegar has always been important not only for its flavor but as the key to making pickles. Before the turn of the century, cooks brewed their own vinegars from apple cider, apple peels and cores, molasses or maple syrup, and yeast. They often added fruit, spices, or the petals of flowers.

In this recipe the chive flowers add color as well as a mild onion flavor to the vinegar. Use similar quantities to make opal basil vinegar, rose petal vinegar, or nasturtium vinegar. Strain the vinegar into bottles and add a chive flower or herb sprig before corking.

> *1 quart white wine vinegar*
> *12 chive flowers*
> *2 cups chopped chives*

*W*arm the vinegar in a saucepan. Put the flowers and chives into a large glass jar. Pour the vinegar over the flowers and chives and cover. Keep the jar in a cool, dark place for about 1 week (or longer if the flavor is not strong enough). Strain the vinegar, pour into bottles, and seal with a cork.

SPICY NUTS

MAKES 3 CUPS

*T*hese spicy-sweet nuts are hard to resist. They are delicious with beer and dry white wine, tossed in a salad, blended into butter (see page 95), and used in cookies and cakes. Make a double batch to have some on hand and give away. The nuts will keep two weeks in an airtight container.

3 cups pecan or walnut halves
½ stick (4 tablespoons) butter
1 tablespoon ground cinnamon
1 teaspoon cayenne pepper
2 teaspoons freshly ground pepper (white is best)
1 teaspoon ground allspice
½ teaspoon salt
2 teaspoons sugar

*S*pread the nuts on a cookie sheet and toast in a preheated 350°F oven for about 15 minutes, stirring occasionally, until lightly browned and crunchy. Rely on your nose. The nuts will begin to smell nutty and toasty.

Melt the butter over low heat. Turn the nuts into a large bowl and toss with the butter and the remaining ingredients until the nuts are coated. Spread out on the cookie sheet to dry before storing in airtight containers.

COME FOR
COFFEE

CAKES, COOKIES, AND BARS

When my mother got lonesome, she would bake and invite people in for coffee.

—DAISY SAMUELSON, OXLIP COUNTY, MINNESOTA

"Come for coffee" is an invitation full of tempting prospects. A coffee promises something sweet, fresh from the oven, friends and lively conversation, sure to warm the spirit on a bleak January afternoon.

Through baking, especially at holiday time, we connect with our past. Lucia recalls, "We knew how close Christmas Day was by what my grandmother baked. She'd begin in early December with Swedish Gingersnaps (*Pepparkakor*) because they kept so well, and by Christmas Eve was finishing off delicate *Spritz*. Hatboxes full of cookies were tucked in the attic rafters. Special cakes were kept frozen on the back porch."

Delicate cakes have always been the yardstick of a cook's skills. Since the 1880s, Home Arts judges in the Minnesota, Iowa, and Wisconsin state fairs have been awarding blue ribbons for all categories of baked goods. Corporations such as Pillsbury have been paying handsomely for contest-winning recipes. The prize cakes suggest emerging trends. Will this year's be higher and lighter or denser and richer?

Both of us learned to cook by first learning how to bake. Guided by grandmothers whose recipes called for a handful of this and a teacup of that, as children we loved the rhythm and magic of a busy kitchen and the reward of something sweet. Rolling out *Lebkuchen* (German spice cookies) and frosting the Minnesota Fudge Cake takes us back to the pleasure of simpler days.

Fourth of July party, 1908

BEST SUGAR COOKIES

MAKES 2 TO 3 DOZEN COOKIES

*T*hese delicate cookies are pale in the center with a pretty brown rim.

1 stick (8 tablespoons) butter
1 cup sugar
1 egg
1 teaspoon vanilla or almond extract
1½ cups unbleached all-purpose flour
½ teaspoon salt
1 teaspoon baking powder

*C*ream together the butter and sugar until light and fluffy. Beat in the egg and vanilla or almond extract. Sift together the flour, salt, and baking powder, then stir into the butter mixture to make a soft dough. Scoop up teaspoonfuls of the dough and place them on a lightly greased cookie sheet, about 3 inches apart. To shape each cookie, dip the bottom of a flat juice glass in water, then in sugar, and press each mound of dough. Bake in a preheated 375°F oven for about 8 to 10 minutes, or until the edges are light brown and the center is golden. Remove the cookies from the sheet and cool on a wire rack.

BUCKWHEAT

Buckwheat is not a grain at all, but a distant cousin of the rhubarb plant. It grows like a weed in the most hostile climates, and in the Midwest it was nicknamed "whisk broom," "umbrella," and "spotted turban" (referring to its pink-and-white flowers). It is a magnet for honeybees, who, after feasting on its papery blossoms, create a dark, rich, perfumed honey.

Buckwheat has also been known as "pigweed," grown to feed the pigs when the supply of flour was low. It was planted as a "catch crop" in the area between different crops where nothing else would grow. Today it is prized by bakers for its high-protein content and nutty flavor.

KEN GOFF'S BUCKWHEAT COOKIES

MAKES 4 DOZEN COOKIES

*T*hese unusual, delicate, sweet, nutty-tasting cookies were created by Ken Goff, chef at the Dakota Restaurant, St. Paul, which features nationally acclaimed jazz musicians and fine regional cuisine.

> *2 cups sugar*
> *1 stick plus 2 tablespoons (10 tablespoons) butter*
> *⅓ cup unbleached all-purpose flour*
> *¼ cup buckwheat flour*
> *⅔ cup buckwheat groats (also known as kasha)*

In a large bowl, mix together all of the ingredients to make a stiff dough. Cover and chill at least 1 hour. Scoop up small pieces of the dough and form into 1-inch balls. Place the balls about 2½ to 3 inches apart on a lightly greased baking sheet. (They will spread and form 3-inch cookies.) Flatten the balls lightly with your fingers. Bake the cookies in a preheated 325°F oven for about 15 to 20 minutes; they should be golden. These cookies are very fragile, so use care in removing them from the sheets and placing on a wire rack to cool.

LACE COOKIES

MAKES 3 DOZEN COOKIES

Sometimes called "broom-handle cookies," these toffee-like confections were often draped over a broom handle so that they cooled into crisp rolls. To make cookie bowls, drape the warm cookies over inverted custard cups or juice glasses so they will assume the bowl-like shape as they cool. Then fill the bowls with fresh fruit, sorbet, ice cream, or chocolate whipped cream.

> *½ cup ground blanched almonds*
> *1 stick (8 tablespoons) butter*
> *½ cup sugar*
> *1 tablespoon unbleached all-purpose flour*
> *1 tablespoon milk*

Combine all the ingredients in a saucepan and heat over low until the butter melts. Drop the dough by teaspoonfuls onto a lightly greased and floured cookie sheet, about 4 inches apart. Bake in a preheated 375°F oven for about 6 minutes. Gently remove the cookies from the sheet and wrap them around a clean broom handle or drape them over a custard cup and allow to cool into that shape. If the cookies aren't removed from the baking sheet quickly enough, they begin to harden and become difficult to shape. If that happens, return them to the oven for a minute or so and then try again. If you want a flat cookie shape, simply set the cookies on a wire rack to cool.

SWEDISH GINGERSNAPS (PEPPARKAKOR)

MAKES 5 TO 6 DOZEN COOKIES

*T*he name *Pepparkakor* is derived from a medieval term that refers to the spices—ginger and pepper—often used together in holiday baking. *Pepparkakor* are so popular that the American Swedish Institute's *Var Sa God* cookbook gives twelve recipes for making them, each just a little different.

Here we offer a basic recipe, plus lemon, orange, and triple ginger variations.

> *1½ sticks (12 tablespoons) butter*
> *1 cup brown sugar, light or dark*
> *2 tablespoons plus 1 teaspoon molasses*
> *1 tablespoon boiling water or strong, hot coffee*
> *2¾–3 cups unbleached all-purpose flour (approximately)*
> *1 teaspoon baking soda*
> *½ teaspoon ground cloves*
> *1 teaspoon ground cardamom*
> *2 teaspoons ground ginger*
> *¼ teaspoon freshly ground black pepper (optional)*

*C*ream together the butter and sugar until light. Mix in the molasses and water. Sift together the dry ingredients and stir them into the wet ingredients to make a soft, smooth dough. (Add a little more flour if the dough is gooey.) Knead the dough three times on a lightly floured board.

If you are planning to roll the dough out flat to be cut with cookie cutters, wrap it in plastic wrap and place it in the refrigerator for at least 1 hour first. Then with a lightly floured rolling pin on a lightly floured board, roll the dough very thin (about ⅛ inch thick) and cut into shapes. Place these on lightly greased baking sheets. *Or* shape the dough into 3 logs (about 8 inches long), wrap in plastic wrap, and refrigerate at least 1 hour or overnight. Slice the logs into thin circles (less than ⅛ inch thick) and place on lightly greased baking sheets.

Bake the cookies in a preheated 350°F oven for about 8 to 10 minutes. Be careful not to overbake. Remove from the sheets and cool the cookies on a wire rack.

Lemon Gingersnaps: Omit the boiling water and add 1 tablespoon lemon juice and 1 tablespoon finely grated lemon rind to the wet ingredients. Omit the cloves and cardamom.

Orange Gingersnaps: Substitute 1 tablespoon orange juice for the boiling water and add 1 tablespoon finely grated orange rind to the wet ingredients. Omit the cardamom and add 2 teaspoons cinnamon to the dry ingredients.

Ginger-Ginger Gingersnaps: Add 1 tablespoon finely grated fresh ginger-root and 2 tablespoons finely chopped crystallized ginger to the wet ingredients. Omit the cardamom and cloves from the dry ingredients and increase the ground ginger by ¼ teaspoon, if desired.

HIS MOTHER'S *PEPPARKAKOR* (SWEDISH GINGERSNAPS)

"I remember making Christmas cookies the first year I was married. My husband wanted me to use his mother's recipe for *Pepparkakor,* his favorite. Walter tasted the first cookie; he said, 'This is good, but it just doesn't taste like Mother's.' So I made another batch with a little more ginger and a little more butter. He said, 'It's still not like Mother's.' I tried again, adding more cardamom. By now I was getting tired and not paying much attention. Walter grabbed a cookie from the sheet and said, 'This is it! Just like Mother's!' Well, the cookie was burned on the bottom. His mother probably gave him her burned and broken cookies, saving the best for company and gifts, you know, and that was the taste he remembered."

—GRETA OLSON OF AMES, IOWA

SPRITZ
(DELICATE PRESSED
BUTTER COOKIES)

MAKES ABOUT 4 DOZEN COOKIES

Spritz are the first Christmas cookies we learned to make as children, and they are still the most fun. Almost all *Spritz* recipes start with a base of ground nuts, and then they are shaped into wreaths, trees, teddy bears, flowers, and stars. Most cooks use a special cookie press available in supermarkets throughout the region (see Sources, page 372).

Lacking a cookie press, you may simply drop the dough with a spoon onto the cookie sheet and flatten each cookie with a fork to make a crosshatch pattern, or using your thumb, make a slight well to fill with Old-fashioned Lemon Curd (page 369) or your favorite jam.

2 sticks (16 tablespoons) butter
⅔ cup confectioners' sugar
1 egg yolk
1 teaspoon almond extract or 1 tablespoon grated lemon
  rind
1 teaspoon vanilla extract
½ cup finely ground blanched almonds
2 cups unbleached all-purpose flour

Cream the butter and sugar, then add the egg yolk and beat until the mixture is light and fluffy. Beat in the almond and vanilla extracts and then gradually stir in the ground almonds and the flour to make a soft dough. Do not overmix.

Pack the dough into a cookie press and force it onto an ungreased cookie sheet, leaving about 1½ inches between cookies. Or use a tablespoon to drop the dough onto an ungreased cookie sheet, about 1½ to 2 inches apart. Flatten these cookies lightly with the back of a fork or use your thumb to make a shallow well in the center of each cookie. Bake the cookies in a preheated 375°F oven for about 7 to 10 minutes. Watch that they don't overbake—they should remain pale. Remove from the sheet and cool on a wire rack. Fill the "thumbprint" cookies with a dollop of jam or Old-fashioned Lemon Curd (page 369).

OATMEAL-MOLASSES COOKIES

MAKES 2 TO 4 DOZEN COOKIES
(DEPENDING ON HOW LARGE YOU LIKE THEM)

*T*hese were called "logger's cookies" or "thresher's cookies," depending on who was eating them. The molasses and spices keep them fresh-tasting for a long time. (They actually taste better a few days after they are made.)

> *2 sticks (16 tablespoons) butter*
> *1 cup brown sugar, light or dark*
> *¼ cup molasses*
> *1 egg*
> *1 teaspoon vanilla extract*
> *1½ cups unbleached all-purpose flour*
> *1 teaspoon baking soda*
> *¼ teaspoon salt*
> *2 teaspoons ground cinnamon*
> *1 teaspoon ground nutmeg*
> *3 cups oatmeal (not instant)*
> *½ cup raisins*

*I*n a large bowl, cream together the butter, sugar, and molasses. Beat in the egg and vanilla. Sift together the flour, baking soda, salt, and spices, and mix into the butter. Stir in the oatmeal and the raisins.

Drop the dough by the tablespoonful onto a lightly greased cookie sheet, about 2 to 3 inches apart, and bake in a preheated 375°F oven for 9 to 11 minutes, depending on how chewy or crispy you like your cookies. Remove the cookies from the sheet and cool on a wire rack.

LEBKUCHEN
(GERMAN SPICE COOKIES)

**MAKES BETWEEN 25 AND 30 COOKIES
(RECIPE IS EASILY DOUBLED.)**

*T*he German name for these spicy, chewy cookies is derived from the Latin term for a consecrated cake. Today they are especially popular at Christmas in German-American homes.

Ann Burckhardt, who grew up outside Ames, Iowa, remembers: "My grandmother started making her Christmas *Lebkuchen* in October. These cookies taste better as they age; the spices mellow and they become softer. My grandmother never quit her baking even after she turned ninety. She sent me care packages of *Lebkuchen* right up until she died."

If you have the time, allow the dough to ripen overnight (or up to three days), covered, in a cool place. Traditionally, the baked cookies should age and mellow at least two weeks, wrapped in plastic wrap or stored in an airtight container. They are delicious right out of the oven, too. They will keep several months at room temperature and indefinitely in the freezer.

1 cup honey
¾ cup brown sugar, light or dark
1 tablespoon strong coffee or water
2 tablespoons butter
1 egg
2¾ cups unbleached all-purpose flour
½ teaspoon baking soda
¼ teaspoon salt
1 teaspoon ground cloves
1 teaspoon ground allspice
2 teaspoons ground cinnamon
2 teaspoons ground nutmeg
2 tablespoons grated orange or tangerine rind, or
   ¼ cup finely chopped candied citron for a more
   traditional cookie

1 tablespoon grated lemon rind
½ cup blanched slivered almonds

GLAZE

1 tablespoon sherry or orange or lemon juice
1 cup confectioners' sugar

*I*n a large saucepan, combine the honey, sugar, coffee or water, and butter, and bring to a boil. Remove from the heat and cool to room temperature. Beat in the egg. Sift together the dry ingredients and stir that into the honey mixture. Add the orange rind or candied citron, lemon rind, and almonds. It's best (if you have the time) to cover the bowl with plastic wrap and allow the dough to ripen a day or two in a cool place.

Turn the dough out onto a lightly floured board and roll out to about ⅓ inch thick. Cut the dough into squares or triangles about 2 inches × 3 inches and place on a greased cookie sheet. Bake in a preheated 325°F oven for about 12 to 15 minutes, or until the cookies are a light brown. Be careful not to overbake.

Mix together the glaze ingredients. Remove the cookies from the sheet while still warm and brush with the glaze before they've cooled. When the cookies are completely cool, store them between sheets of waxed paper in cookie tins or wrapped in plastic wrap to age about 2 weeks.

HILDA'S (ALMOND RING CAKES) KRANSEKAKE

MAKES 18 RINGS OR 4 TO 5 DOZEN COOKIES

*N*o Norwegian celebration is complete without the traditional *Kransekake,* a tower of almond-cookie rings. Garnished with roses and tiny paper Norwegian flags, it often stands beside the bridal cake in Norwegian-American weddings.

Hilda Kringstad of Minneapolis has been making *Kransekake* for almost twenty years. She uses special ring pans found in Scandinavian import stores (see Sources, page 372). The rings may also be pressed from a pastry tube into circles.

For a simpler presentation, shape the dough into small balls or finger-size logs, bake, and serve as cookies.

DOUGH

1¼ pounds almonds
5 cups confectioners' sugar
4 large egg whites, lightly beaten

ICING

2 cups confectioners' sugar
1 egg white
1 teaspoon almond extract

*I*n a food processor fitted with a steel blade, grind the nuts fine, then add the sugar and egg whites and continue processing until you have a stiff, sticky dough.

To make the circles for a cake, spoon the dough into well-greased *Kransekake* ring forms of graduating size. Traditionally, there are about 21.

To make cookies, lightly butter your hands and shape the dough into small balls or finger-size logs and place them onto a lightly greased cookie sheet.

Bake the cake rings in a preheated 300°F oven for about 15 minutes. Allow the rings to cool completely before removing from the pans. Bake the cookies about 8 minutes (be careful they do not brown), remove them from the baking sheet, and allow them to cool on a wire rack. Store the rings or cookies in an airtight tin with a slice of bread to keep them fresh and slightly chewy.

To make the icing, stir together the ingredients, thinning it with water, a teaspoon at a time, if necessary.

Build the *Kransekake* on the day it is to be used. Put the icing into a cake-decorating bag and use it to cement the rings together, beginning at the bottom or largest circle and working up to the smallest circle on top. Decorate the sides of the cake with scallops of icing as you build up. To serve, begin from the bottom, lifting the *Kransekake* by loosening the largest ring first, and breaking it into pieces.

Norwegian Kransekake

MAPLE SUGARING

In northern Minnesota and Wisconsin, maple sugaring begins just as the pussy willows are popping out in April. Members of the Chippewa tribe build camp in the sugarbush, collect the sap, and boil it down in great iron kettles set over open fires. When the sap really starts flowing, buckets are emptied every forty-five minutes. It takes forty-three gallons of sap to make one gallon of syrup. During the exhausting two-to-three-week season, wood piles must be restocked, and the fires tended and watched constantly.

Betty Gruno, a Chippewa born in 1913, teaches sugaring to area schoolchildren. "When we're out in the camp, we make *zembagooda-gooanenbish.* That's maple-sap tea. You take maple sap, put it in a kettle, and hang it over an open fire. When it comes to a boil, drop in two tea bags. It's just a little sweet and delicious. We cook our [wild] rice in this sap. Every year we have a feast to give thanks for the maple syrup. We take a cup of syrup from the kettle and a cup of rice and pour them on earth. If Mother Earth sees fit to give us more, we take. We don't ask questions.

"We sugar according to the pussy willows. They get a fuzzy, fluffy look on them, and a yellow tip, and a coat right over the top. That's the end of it, and the syrup gets stronger. The last of the sap is real black and bitter-sweet."

MAPLE NUT BARS

MAKES 6 TO 7 DOZEN SQUARES

*M*aple sugaring remains a cottage industry throughout the Northern Heartland. Jean Housey "sugars" with a group of friends each year in the woods behind her home in Grand Marais, northern Minnesota. "The children like to snap off icicles from the trees; they taste like maple Popsicles," she says.

This old-fashioned recipe may be made with honey if real maple syrup is unavailable. If the distinctive flavor of black walnuts is too strong for you or the nuts are not readily available, substitute pecans, almonds, or walnuts.

BOTTOM LAYER

2 cups unbleached all-purpose flour
⅔ cup confectioners' sugar
2 sticks (16 tablespoons) butter

TOP LAYER

1 stick plus 3 tablespoons (11 tablespoons) butter
½ cup maple syrup
½ cup brown sugar, light or dark
2 tablespoons sour cream
2 tablespoons grated orange rind (optional)
2 cups chopped black walnuts

*S*ift the flour and sugar together and cut in the butter using two knives, your fingers, or a food processor fitted with a steel blade, to form crumbs the size of small peas. Pat the crust into a lightly greased 9 × 13-inch baking pan and bake in a preheated 350°F oven for about 20 minutes. (It should be firm and golden, but not too brown.) Remove the pan from the oven and prepare the top layer.

In a small saucepan, stir together all the ingredients *except the nuts*. Cook over low heat until smooth. Bring the mixture to a boil and cook for about 1 to 2 minutes more, until the syrup begins to thicken. Stir in the nuts, then spread over the crust. Put the bars back into the oven and bake another 20 to 25 minutes. Cool and then cut them small—they are very rich.

MRS. MACINE'S BROWNIES

MAKES ABOUT 20 BROWNIES

*M*rs. Macine of International Falls, Minnesota, used to bake these for company. Everyone begged for the recipe. It was saved in Lulu's (Lucia's grandmother's) cookbook.

> *Three 1-ounce squares unsweetened chocolate*
> *1 stick (8 tablespoons) butter*
> *2 eggs*
> *1 cup sugar*
> *1 teaspoon vanilla extract*
> *½ cup unbleached all-purpose flour*
> *½ cup chocolate chips or chopped dark chocolate (optional)*

*M*elt together the chocolate and butter in the top part of a double boiler set over low heat, then allow to cool. Beat together the eggs and sugar, then add the chocolate mixture along with the vanilla. Stir in the flour and pour the batter into a lightly greased 9-inch-square baking pan. Bake in a preheated 375°F oven for about 12 to 18 minutes. The brownies are done before the sides begin to pull away from the pan. Do not overbake. Remove the pan from the oven and scatter chocolate chips over the top while the brownies are still hot. Allow the brownies to cool to room temperature before cutting them into squares with a sharp knife.

I love you dearly

ANN HESKINS' MATRIMONIAL DIAMONDS

MAKES 6 TO 7 DOZEN BARS

*V*ariations on this cookie recipe can be found in almost every Midwestern church cookbook published after 1920. None tells us the reason for calling these "Matrimonial Diamonds." Ann Heskins, a friend of Lucia's grandmother, used to bring these simple bars to bridal showers for good luck. Helen Myhre, owner of the Norsk Nook in Osseo, Wisconsin, and author of a cookbook by the same name, says, "These are as fundamental on the farm as the tractor."

> *1½ cups unbleached all-purpose flour*
> *1½ cups oatmeal (not instant)*
> *¾ cup brown sugar, light or dark*
> *½ teaspoon baking soda*
> *⅛ teaspoon salt*
> *1 stick (8 tablespoons) butter*
> *1 pound dates, chopped*
> *Juice of 1 lemon (2 tablespoons)*
> *Grated rind of 1 lemon*
> *1 cup water*

*I*n a large bowl, combine the flour, oatmeal, brown sugar, baking soda, salt, and butter, and rub together with your fingers to make a soft crumb. Spread a little more than half of this over the bottom of a lightly greased 9 × 13-inch pan and press down to form a soft crust.

In a medium saucepan, cook the dates with the lemon juice, rind, and water until thick, then spread the mixture over the crust. Top with the remaining crumbs, patting them down lightly. Bake in a preheated 400°F oven for 25 to 30 minutes, or until lightly browned. When cool, cut into diamonds or bars.

KMA COOKIE SWAP

Once a year the KMA Radio Homemakers, who broadcast such shows as "Home Hour" and "Stitch and Chat Club" from their homes, would invite their Midwestern listeners to a "cookie swap." At the height of their popularity the Homemakers drew over eight hundred "friends in radio land" to Shenandoah, Iowa, the station's home. Over 120,000 cookies were consumed at the "world's largest cookie swap," and the event was recorded in the *Guinness Book of World Records 1959*.

CHOCOLATE PEANUT BUTTER BARS

MAKES 4 TO 5 DOZEN BARS

*D*ouble this recipe and freeze more for later, but be warned—these delicious bars are almost too good to have around.

CRUST

⅓ pound graham crackers (1 pack of a 3-pack box)
1 cup peanut butter
2 sticks (16 tablespoons) butter
3 cups confectioners' sugar

TOPPING

3 tablespoons butter
3 tablespoons brown sugar, light or dark
3 tablespoons milk
1 cup chocolate chips
1 teaspoon vanilla extract

*I*n a food processor fitted with a steel blade, grind the graham crackers into crumbs; then add the remaining ingredients and process until a ball of dough forms. Turn the crust into a 9 × 13-inch pan and spread it smooth with a spatula. Bake in a preheated 350°F oven for about 5 to 10 minutes. In a medium saucepan, stir together the ingredients for the topping over low heat until the chocolate is melted. Pour this chocolate over the crust while it is still warm, then chill and, when firm, cut into squares.

WHITE CAKE,
PLAIN AND FANCY

MAKES TWO 9 × 1½-INCH ROUNDS OR ONE 9 × 13-INCH PAN

*T*his cake is a classic that can be dressed up or down depending on the occasion. Use the leftover egg yolks to make a filling of Old-fashioned Lemon Curd (page 369), or use it in place of shortcake and top it with strawberries and whipped cream. Frost it with Chocolate Buttercream Frosting (page 331). Soak it with Blueberry-Honey Sauce (page 367), and top it with fresh blueberries and whipped cream. Bake it into cupcakes and top with Chocolate Sauce (page 365) or Caramel Sauce (page 366) or both, and serve with Easy Vanilla Ice Cream (page 364).

When cut into two-inch cubes and covered with white frosting and rolled in chopped peanuts, the cake is called "Blarney Stones."

Children love this warm from the oven, spread with butter and sprinkled with confectioners' sugar.

> 2¾ cups cake flour
> 3 teaspoons baking powder
> ½ teaspoon salt
> 1½ sticks (12 tablespoons) butter
> 1½ cups sugar
> 1 teaspoon vanilla extract
> 1 teaspoon almond extract
> 1 cup milk
> 6 egg whites, at room temperature

*S*ift together the flour, baking powder, and salt, and set aside. In a large bowl, cream the butter with *1 cup* of the sugar, then add the vanilla and almond extracts, beating until light and fluffy. Add the flour mixture, alternating with the milk. In a large bowl, beat the egg whites until they are foamy, then gradually add the remaining *½ cup* sugar and continue to beat until soft peaks form. With a spatula, gently mix the egg whites into the batter until it is smooth.

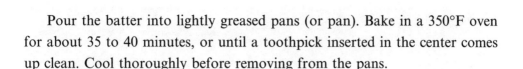

Pour the batter into lightly greased pans (or pan). Bake in a 350°F oven for about 35 to 40 minutes, or until a toothpick inserted in the center comes up clean. Cool thoroughly before removing from the pans.

LUCIA'S HALF-POUND CAKE

MAKES ONE 9 × 3-INCH LOAF CAKE

*L*ucia created this recipe remembering her grandmother's simple, unwritten formula: a pound of flour, a pound of sugar, a pound of butter, and a pound of eggs. Lucia cut the quantities in half and added lemon for flavor. In the summer she folds fresh blueberries into the batter, and in the winter, cranberries tossed with sugar. The cake is especially good served with Blueberry-Honey Sauce (page 367).

> *2 cups unbleached all-purpose flour*
> *¾ teaspoon baking powder*
> *¼ teaspoon salt*
> *2 sticks (16 tablespoons) butter*
> *Grated rind of 1 lemon*
> *1½ teaspoons vanilla extract*
> *1 cup sugar*
> *4 eggs, well beaten*
> *1 cup blueberries*

*S*ift the flour, baking powder, and salt together into a large bowl. In a small bowl, cream the butter and beat in the lemon peel and vanilla. Beat in the sugar until the butter looks light and fluffy, then beat in the eggs. The mixture will look separated. Fold in the dry ingredients, quickly and gently. The batter will be thick. Fold in the blueberries and pour the batter into a greased and lightly floured 9 × 3-inch loaf pan. Bake in a preheated 325°F oven for about 1 hour, or until a toothpick inserted in the center comes up clean. Cool about 10 minutes in the pan, then remove and cool completely on a wire rack.

CHOCOLATE ANGEL FOOD CAKE

MAKES ONE 10-INCH CAKE

*W*hen Lulu made angel food cake, she'd beat the egg whites with a whisk, her arm moving so fast it seemed a blur. Often she'd plan to make this cake on the day she made Old-fashioned Lemon Curd (page 369) or noodles, both of which called for lots of egg yolks.

We top slices of this light cake with Mocha Ice Milk (page 363) and Chocolate Sauce (page 365) for a dessert that is surprisingly low in fat. When leftover slices are toasted, the outside caramelizes into a crust and the center stays soft. We serve these with berries and whipped cream.

The egg whites will whip more successfully if they are at room temperature.

⅓ cup unsweetened cocoa powder
⅓ cup hot coffee
1¾ cups sugar
1 cup cake flour

½ *teaspoon salt*
16 egg whites, at room temperature
1½ teaspoons cream of tartar

*I*n a small bowl, dissolve the cocoa powder in the coffee and let cool to room temperature. Sift together ¾ *cup* of the sugar, the flour, and salt. In a large mixing bowl, beat the egg whites until frothy, then add the cream of tartar and continue beating until soft peaks form. Gradually add the remaining *1 cup* sugar and beat until stiff. Do not overbeat. Sprinkle the dry ingredients, little by little, over the whites while folding them in with a rubber spatula. Stir 1 cup of the batter into the chocolate-coffee-egg-white mixture, then fold this back into the batter, gently mixing everything together until it is a uniform color.

Pour the batter into an ungreased 10-inch tube pan. Run a small spatula or knife through the batter to remove air pockets. Bake in a preheated 350°F oven for about 55 minutes, or until a cake tester inserted in the middle comes up clean and the cake springs back when lightly touched. Remove the pan from the oven, invert it, and allow the cake to cool completely before loosening it with a knife to remove it from the pan.

THE BAKE-OFF

The Pillsbury Company, headquartered in Minneapolis, hosted the first organized national baking competition in 1949. Originally called the "Grand National Recipe and Baking Contest," it was quickly dubbed the "Bake-Off."

The winning recipes were published by Pillsbury in a series of Bake-Off cookbooks that have shaped American baking. For example, a Tunnel of Fudge Cake, the 1966 winner, popularized the little-known bundt-cake pan to kitchen prominence. Pillsbury received over 200,000 requests for help in locating these three-quart, fluted, round cake pans. Often the publication of winning recipes sent grocers scrambling for special ingredients. In 1950, after the Starlight Mint Surprise cookie placed second in the Bake-Off, the Rockwood Candy Company ran out of Mint Wafers within a day.

LUCIA'S DEVIL'S FOOD CAKE WITH MILK-CHOCOLATE SOUR CREAM ICING

MAKES TWO 8-INCH LAYER CAKES

*I*n contrast to the preceding Chocolate Angel Food Cake, this dense chocolaty cake is rich and filling. It's best served by itself or with fruit.

THE CAKE

½ cup sifted unsweetened cocoa powder
1 cup boiling water
2¼ cups unbleached all-purpose flour
½ teaspoon baking soda
1 teaspoon baking powder
½ teaspoon salt
1 stick (8 tablespoons) butter
1½ cups light brown sugar
3 eggs
1 teaspoon vanilla extract
½ cup buttermilk

MILK-CHOCOLATE SOUR CREAM ICING

6 ounces milk chocolate, cut into pieces
½ stick (4 tablespoons) butter
1 tablespoon light brown sugar
1 teaspoon vanilla extract
½ cup sour cream

*M*ix together the cocoa and water and set aside to cool. Sift together the flour, baking soda, baking powder, and salt and set aside. In a large bowl, cream the butter and brown sugar until light and fluffy. Add the eggs and vanilla and continue beating until smooth. Add the dry ingredients alternately with the cocoa mixture and the buttermilk and beat until smooth.

Pour the batter into two 8-inch greased and floured pans and bake in a preheated 350°F oven about 25 to 35 minutes, or until the cakes spring back when gently touched with your fingers. Take the cakes from the oven and cool on a wire rack about 10 minutes before removing from the pan.

Prepare the icing: In a small saucepan, melt the chocolate over low heat, stirring constantly. Set aside to cool. In a medium bowl, beat together the remaining ingredients until light and fluffy. Gradually beat in the chocolate and continue to beat until fluffy. Spread some of the icing over one layer for a filling; place the other layer over and spread the rest of the icing over the top and sides.

THREE-CITRUS CHIFFON CAKE

MAKES ONE 10-INCH TUBE CAKE (SERVES ABOUT 14)

*I*n 1947 General Mills purchased the recipe for the Three-Citrus Chiffon Cake from Harry Baker, a Los Angeles insurance salesman, who also baked elegant desserts for Hollywood stars. Betty Crocker billed it as "the first new type of cake in one hundred years, as glamorous as the angel food cake but easier to make."

Chiffon cakes combine the moist richness of butter cakes with the lightness of sponge cakes. They keep well and are relatively low in cholesterol and saturated fat.

Tightly wrapped in plastic wrap, the cake will keep up to three days at room temperature, ten days in the refrigerator, and two months in the freezer.

Three-Citrus Chiffon Cake (continued)

> 2¼ cups cake flour
> 1½ cups sugar
> ½ teaspoon baking soda
> ½ teaspoon salt
> ½ cup vegetable oil
> 7 eggs, separated, plus 3 egg whites
> ⅔ cup water
> 2 tablespoons lemon juice
> 1 tablespoon grated lemon zest
> 1 tablespoon grated orange zest
> 1 tablespoon grated lime zest
> 1 teaspoon vanilla extract
> 1¼ teaspoons cream of tartar

*S*ift together the flour, sugar, baking soda, and salt in a large bowl. Make a well in the center, then add the oil, *egg yolks,* water, lemon juice, the lemon, orange, and lime zests, and the vanilla. Beat until smooth, about 1 minute.

In another large bowl, beat all 10 egg whites until frothy; then add the cream of tartar and continue beating until soft peaks form. Gently fold the egg whites into the batter with a spatula.

Pour the batter into an ungreased 10-inch tube pan and bake the cake in a preheated 325°F oven for 55 minutes, or until a toothpick inserted in the center comes up clean and the cake springs back when lightly pressed in the center. Invert the pan, placing the tube opening over the neck of a bottle to suspend it well over the counter, and cool the cake completely in the pan, about 1½ hours, before loosening it with a knife and removing from the pan.

BURNT SUGAR CAKE

MAKES TWO 8-INCH OR 9-INCH LAYER CAKES

*T*his old-fashioned, one-bowl cake is delicious served with the Caramel Sauce (page 366) and sliced apples, or iced with the Cardamom-Coffee Icing (page 326).

THE SYRUP

½ cup sugar
½ cup boiling water

THE CAKE

2¼ cups unbleached all-purpose flour
¾ cup sugar
3 teaspoons baking powder
¼ teaspoon salt
1 stick (8 tablespoons) butter, softened
2 eggs
1 teaspoon vanilla extract

*M*ake a syrup by melting the ½ cup sugar in a small heavy saucepan over very low heat. Shake the pan slightly as the sugar melts and becomes lumpy. When it begins to melt, stir constantly until it becomes a dark gold color. Remove the sugar from the heat. Gradually stir in the boiling water. Be careful, it will sizzle and spatter; it may seize up into a ball. Place the pan back on the burner and cook the mixture, stirring constantly until the lumps are dissolved. Pour the syrup into a measuring cup and add water to make 1 cup. Set aside to cool.

Sift together the flour, ¾ cup sugar, baking powder, and salt into a large mixing bowl. Add the butter and ¾ *cup* of the syrup. Beat about 2 minutes, scraping down the sides of the bowl a few times. Add the eggs, vanilla, and the remaining syrup and continue beating another 2 minutes until smooth.

Pour the batter into two greased and floured cake pans and bake in a pre-heated 350°F oven about 30 to 35 minutes, or until the surface springs back when gently pressed with your fingers. Remove the cakes from the oven and place on wire racks to cool for about 10 minutes. Remove the cakes from the pans and continue to cool thoroughly before icing.

SPICE CAKE WITH
CARDAMOM-COFFEE ICING

MAKES TWO 8-INCH LAYER CAKES OR ONE 13 × 9-INCH SHEET CAKE

*B*aking this cake fills the kitchen with a lovely spicy scent. It is delicious served with strong coffee.

> *2¼ cups unbleached all-purpose flour*
> *1 teaspoon baking powder*
> *1 teaspoon baking soda*
> *½ teaspoon salt*
> *1 teaspoon ground cinnamon*
> *½ teaspoon ground cloves*
> *⅛ teaspoon ground pepper*
> *¼ teaspoon ground cardamom*
> *1 stick (8 tablespoons) butter*
> *½ cup dark brown sugar*
> *1 cup sugar*
> *2 eggs*
> *1 teaspoon vanilla extract*
> *1¼ cups buttermilk*

CARDAMOM-COFFEE ICING

> *¼ cup milk*
> *1 tablespoon instant coffee or espresso*
> *1 teaspoon ground cardamom*
> *1 teaspoon vanilla extract*
> *2 sticks (16 tablespoons) butter*
> *¾ cup confectioners' sugar*

*S*ift the flour with the baking powder, baking soda, salt, cinnamon, cloves, pepper, and cardamom. In a large bowl, beat together the butter, sugars, eggs, and vanilla until light and fluffy (about 5 minutes), scraping the sides down with a spatula.

Seventy-two-year-old Arthur Schlegel of Blakeley, a farmer, preparing to compete for the 1952 spice cake prize, Minnesota State Fair

Beat in the flour mixture alternately with the buttermilk, beginning and ending with the flour mixture. Beat just until smooth (about 1 minute). Pour the batter into two 8-inch greased and floured cake pans or a 13 × 9-inch pan and bake in a preheated 350°F oven about 30 to 35 minutes for the layers, and 40 to 50 minutes for the oblong cake, or until the surface springs back when gently touched with your fingers. Remove the cake(s) from the oven and cool on wire racks about 10 minutes, then remove from the pans and continue cooling.

Spice Cake with Cardamom-Coffee Icing (continued)

Meanwhile, prepare the icing: Heat the milk and dissolve the instant coffee or espresso in it and allow it to cool. Beat together the remaining ingredients, then add the coffee mixture and continue beating until fluffy. Spread a little of the icing over one of the layers, cover with the second layer, and spread the remaining icing over the top and sides.

SUSAN'S OLD-FASHIONED PRUNE CAKE

MAKES ONE 9 × 13-INCH CAKE

Susan Poupore, who runs a catering business in Duluth that is known for its baked goods, shared this recipe. "Whenever I bake this cake, I recall practicing the piano as a child. Mother would place a piece on top of the piano to encourage me to complete my entire lesson," she said.

Dense and spicy, this cake is topped with a mixture of buttermilk, sugar, and butter boiled together and poured over the top just as it comes from the oven. It's best served warm.

THE CAKE

2 cups unbleached all-purpose flour
1 teaspoon baking soda
1 teaspoon salt
1 teaspoon ground cinnamon
1 teaspoon ground nutmeg
¼ teaspoon ground allspice
2 cups sugar
1 cup vegetable oil
1 cup buttermilk
1 teaspoon vanilla extract
3 eggs

1 cup seedless prunes, cut in quarters*
1 cup chopped walnuts

**If the prunes are very dry, plump them first in a little hot water
to cover, then drain.*

BUTTERMILK TOPPING

¾ cup sugar
¾ cup buttermilk
6 tablespoons butter
½ teaspoon baking soda

*M*ix all of the dry ingredients together in a large bowl. Then stir in the oil, buttermilk, and vanilla. Beat in the eggs, one at a time. Fold in the prunes and nuts. Pour the batter into a greased 9 × 13-inch cake pan. Bake in a pre-heated 350°F oven for 45 to 55 minutes, or until a toothpick inserted in the center comes up clean.

In a small saucepan, bring all of the topping ingredients to a boil. Remove the cake from the oven and place it on a cooling rack. Pierce the cake all over with a long-tonged fork or wooden pick. Slowly pour the topping evenly over the cake. Serve warm or cool.

For a lighter dessert, omit the topping and serve warm cake slices with Vanilla Poached Fruit (page 286) or Old-fashioned Lemon Curd (page 369) and whipped cream.

MINNESOTA FUDGE CAKE

MAKES A TWO-LAYER 10-INCH CAKE

*T*his five-egg, two-layer cake is the pride of Minnesota's cooks and professional bakers, who frost it with Chocolate Buttercream Frosting (page 331). Wisconsin cooks split the layers in half and make a towering four-layer cake, each layer spread with a different filling. Try with Milk-Chocolate Sour Cream Icing (page 322) and Cardamom-Coffee Icing (page 326).

> *2½ cups sugar*
> *Five 1-ounce squares unsweetened chocolate*
> *1¾ cups milk*
> *5 eggs*
> *1½ sticks (12 tablespoons) butter*
> *2 teaspoons vanilla extract*
> *1½ teaspoons baking soda*
> *½ teaspoon salt*
> *3 cups cake flour*

*I*n a double boiler set over simmering water, stir together *1 cup* of the sugar with the chocolate and *¾ cup* of the milk and *1* of the eggs. Keep stirring while the chocolate melts, and cook, stirring, until the mixture becomes thick and glossy. (This will take about 5 minutes.) Remove from the heat and allow to cool to room temperature.

In a large bowl, cream together the butter and the remaining sugar, then beat in the remaining eggs and the vanilla. Sift together the dry ingredients and add them alternately with the remaining milk to the butter mixture. Beat in the chocolate mixture. Pour the batter into two lightly greased and floured 10-inch cake pans and bake in a preheated 350°F oven for 25 to 35 minutes, or until a sharp knife or toothpick inserted in the center comes up clean. Cool the cakes for about 10 minutes, then remove from the pans and cool thoroughly on a wire rack before frosting.

CHOCOLATE BUTTERCREAM FROSTING

ENOUGH TO FROST A 2-LAYER CAKE

1½ cups chopped milk chocolate
1½ cups chopped semisweet chocolate
1½ sticks (12 tablespoons) butter

*I*n the top of a double boiler, slowly melt the milk chocolate and the semisweet chocolate over simmering water. Remove from the heat and allow to cool to room temperature. In a bowl, beat the butter until light and fluffy. Continue beating while adding the chocolate mixture.

COFFEE GROUNDS

Lucia's aunt, Elinor, claims that stale chocolate cake is the best, for it can be made into Coffee Grounds. "Up on Rainy Lake, we only went to town every other week," she says. "So when the supplies ran low, Lulu would take her stale leftover chocolate cake, crumble it into a bowl, add some milk to soften it, and an egg or two, then a tablespoon of baking powder. She'd pour the mixture into a cake pan and bake it in a moderate oven for about a half hour. It looked a little like coffee grounds, and we ate it with whipped cream. Boy, was that ever good!"

> ## "A RECEIPT FOR THE MANUFACTURE OF SUNSHINE ON A DARKSOME DAY."
>
> "Take a good handful of industry, mix it thoroughly with family love, season well with good nature and mutual forbearance, gradually stir in smiles, jokes and laughter to make it light; take care these ingredients do not run over or it will make a cloud instead of what you wish; follow this receipt carefully and you will have an excellent supply of sunshine, warranted to keep in all weather."
>
> —*A COOK BOOK COMPILED BY THE LADIES OF DAYTON AVENUE PRESBYTERIAN CHURCH,*
> ST. PAUL, 1892

POPPY SEED CAKE

MAKES ONE 9-INCH BUNDT CAKE

Serve this moist, flavorful cake with Old-Fashioned Lemon Curd (page 369). It freezes well and will keep several days, wrapped in plastic, in the refrigerator. We soak the poppy seeds overnight to be sure they are tender.

> 1 cup poppy seeds
> ¾ cup milk
> 1½ sticks (12 tablespoons) butter
> 1¼ cups sugar
> 3 eggs
> 1 teaspoon vanilla extract
> 1 tablespoon grated orange rind
> 2 cups unbleached all-purpose flour
> 2 teaspoons baking powder
> ½ teaspoon salt

Soak the poppy seeds in the milk overnight.

Cream the butter and sugar in a large bowl. Add the eggs one at a time, beating well after each addition. Add the vanilla, orange rind, and the milk with the poppy seeds. Sift together the dry ingredients and add to the wet, mixing well. Pour the batter into a well-buttered bundt pan and bake in a preheated 375°F oven for 30 to 40 minutes, or until the cake springs back when lightly pressed with your fingers. Take the cake out of the oven and allow to cool on a wire rack about 10 minutes before removing from the pan and cooling completely.

RHUBARB-SOUR CREAM CAKE

MAKES ONE 10-INCH BUNDT CAKE OR 2 LOAF CAKES

*S*erve slices of this rich, moist cake with fresh strawberries.

> *6 tablespoons butter*
> *2¼ cups brown sugar, light or dark*
> *2 eggs*
> *1½ teaspoons vanilla extract*
> *3½ cups unbleached all-purpose flour*
> *¾ teaspoon ground nutmeg*
> *1½ teaspoons baking soda*
> *½ teaspoon salt*
> *¼ teaspoon freshly ground pepper*
> *1½ cups sour cream*
> *6 cups chopped rhubarb*

*I*n a large mixing bowl, cream the butter and sugar. Beat in the eggs and vanilla. Sift together the dry ingredients and fold them into the wet ingredients alternately with the sour cream. Fold in the rhubarb. Turn the batter into a greased bundt pan or two greased 9 × 3-inch loaf pans. Bake in a preheated 350°F oven for 1 hour to 1 hour 15 minutes for the bundt cake, and 50 minutes to an hour for the loaf cakes. Remove the cake(s) from the oven and allow to cool 15 minutes on wire racks before removing from the pans.

ALICE HOOLIHAN'S SOUR CREAM COFFEE CAKE (POTICA CAKE)

MAKES ONE 10-INCH BUNDT CAKE

*T*his rich cake is to coffee what brownies are to milk. Some call it *Potica* Cake after the Slavic delicacy (see Box). "I always like to have one on hand in case neighbors stop by or when our children bring the grandchildren home," says Alice Hoolihan of Grand Rapids, Minnesota. "It's one I bring to wedding and baby showers, Christmas coffees, and bake as a gift for friends."

STREUSEL

⅓ cup brown sugar, light or dark
2 tablespoons sugar
1 cup chopped walnuts
2 teaspoons ground cinnamon
½ cup unbleached all-purpose flour
½ stick (4 tablespoons) butter, softened

BATTER

2 sticks (16 tablespoons) butter, softened
1¼ cups sugar
2 eggs
1 cup sour cream
2 teaspoons vanilla extract
2 cups unbleached all-purpose flour
½ teaspoon baking soda
1 teaspoon baking powder

*I*n a small bowl, cut together the streusel ingredients with two knives or your fingers to make a soft, crumbly mixture. This may also be done in a food processor fitted with a steel blade.

In a large bowl, make the batter. Cream the butter and sugar, then beat in the eggs, sour cream, and vanilla. Sift together the dry ingredients and stir into the batter, mixing until smooth. Pour half of the batter into a lightly greased and floured 10-inch bundt pan and sprinkle with half of the streusel mixture; pour the rest of the batter over the streusel and sprinkle with the remaining mixture. Bake in a preheated 350°F oven about 55 minutes to 1 hour, or until a toothpick inserted in the middle comes up clean. Check the cake halfway through baking, and if it is browning too quickly, cover it with a piece of lightly buttered aluminum foil. Allow the cake to cool slightly before removing from the pan. It's great served warm.

POTICA (OR POTIVTICA)

A Slavic version of strudel, *potica* (pronounced *po-tee-cia*) is a specialty of Iron Range bakeries in northern Minnesota and of skilled home cooks. *Potica* is made with a yeast dough that is pulled out to fit over a large kitchen table and stretched so thin that a newspaper may be read though it. A gooey filling of brown sugar, butter, ground walnuts, cream, and dates is slathered over the dough, which is then rolled up, baked, and brushed with lots of melted butter.

Making *potica* is time-consuming and fussy, requiring more patience and practice than today's cooks have. For those who want to enjoy this classic from the Old World, Sunrise Bakery of Hibbing, Minnesota, makes *potica* with fresh butter, eggs, and cream, and ships it frozen (see Sources, page 372).

THE COFFEE BREAK

How is it that Northern Heart-landers can drink an average of six cups of "Swedish Gasoline" per day without ill effect? Afi-cionados of Egg Coffee credit the following brewing method.

To make a big pot, fill an old-fashioned ten-cup metal coffeepot with water, and bring to a boil. Mash together ten tablespoons of ground coffee with one egg yolk, making a paste. When the water boils, add the mash to the pot and simmer it until the grounds sink to the bottom—about five min-utes. Let the brew rest a few minutes and then pour. Egg cof-fee is not bitter and seems less acid than most brews. It holds well on the back of the stove, long after other brews have turned thick and black.

Northern Heartlanders take coffee drinking quite seriously. Stanton, Iowa, hosts the "World's Largest Coffeepot," a water tower, fashioned with spout and handle, and painted with Swedish rosemaling (reputed to hold 640,000 cups). It is a symbol of the town's Scandinavian pride.

But it is Stoughton, Wisconsin, Norse Capital of the United States, that claims to be the "home of the coffee break." Local companies relied on Norwegian-born women for much of their labor. Given short time periods off to check on children and slow-simmering meals, these women would go home and grab a quick cup of coffee from the back of the stove. Thus the phrase "coffee break" was born.

ZUCCHINI BREAD

MAKES 2 LOAVES (9 × 3-INCH LOAF PANS)

*T*his bread is sweet enough to be considered a cake and is best served with a cup of coffee or cold glass of milk late on a summer's day. It makes good use of all those zucchini that take over the vegetable patch come early August—a bounty that often drives gardeners to such desperate measures as leaving a grocery sack of zucchini on a stranger's porch or on the backseat of a car.

> *3 cups unbleached all-purpose flour*
> *1 teaspoon baking soda*
> *3 teaspoons ground cinnamon*
> *¼ teaspoon baking powder*
> *1 teaspoon salt*
> *2 cups sugar*
> *1 cup vegetable oil*
> *3 eggs, beaten*
> *3 teaspoons vanilla extract*
> *3 cups unpeeled, grated zucchini*
> *1 cup chopped nuts or Spicy Nuts, page 296*

*S*ift together the flour, baking soda, cinnamon, baking powder, and salt. In a large bowl, beat together the sugar, oil, eggs, and vanilla. Mix the dry ingredients into the wet ingredients. Stir in the grated zucchini and then the nuts. Turn the batter into 2 well-greased 9 × 3-inch bread pans and bake in a preheated 350°F oven for about 1 hour, or until a toothpick inserted in the center comes up clean. Allow to cool slightly before removing from the pans.

PUMPKIN SPICE ROULADE

SERVES 12

*T*his spicy, fragrant rolled cake, with a cream cheese filling, is great for holiday entertaining. There is no butter in this cake. The mashed pumpkin keeps it moist.

THE CAKE

¾ cup unbleached all-purpose flour

1 teaspoon baking powder

2 teaspoons ground cinnamon

2 teaspoons pumpkin pie spice

½ teaspoon salt

½ teaspoon ground nutmeg

3 eggs

1 cup sugar

⅔ cup cooked and mashed pumpkin or winter squash

1 cup chopped walnuts

FILLING

1 cup confectioners' sugar

8 ounces cream cheese

6 tablespoons butter

1 teaspoon vanilla extract

Confectioners' sugar

*S*ift together the dry ingredients. In a large bowl, beat the eggs with the sugar until lemon colored and thick, then beat in the pumpkin. Stir in the dry ingredients to make a smooth batter and add in the nuts. Line a jelly-roll pan with waxed paper or parchment paper, grease lightly, and sprinkle with flour. Pour the batter into the pan and bake in a preheated 375°F oven for about 15 minutes, or until a toothpick inserted in the center comes up clean.

Just after you pull the cake from the oven, cover a dish towel with confectioners' sugar. Turn the jelly-roll sheet upside down onto the towel.

Quickly peel off the waxed paper from the bottom of the cake and roll the cake up, starting from the shortest side, using the towel as a guide. (Do not roll the towel into the cake.) Wrap the towel around the rolled cake and set it on a wire rack to cool.

While the cake is cooling, make the filling by beating together all the filling ingredients in a small bowl.

Remove the towel. Place the cake on a serving plate and gently unroll it. Spread the filling over the top of the unrolled cake, then gently roll it back up and sprinkle with confectioners' sugar, if desired.

PRIDE OF THE HEARTLAND

PIES, PUDDINGS, AND SWEETS

"**W**e came upon bushes of wild and spicy blackberries, as large as the joint of a man's thumb," wrote one early Wisconsin settler in the 1850s. Blackberries, raspberries, blue, red, and yellow plums, apples and pears, cultivated and wild, thrive in the Northern Heartland's rich soil.

The German, Scandinavian, and East European settlers, who left behind meager farms, delighted in the area's plentiful fruit, and the rich butter and cream produced on dairy farms. They created the splendid tortes, strudels, pastries, and puddings of their homeland with the area's bountiful ingredients. Fruit pies with tender, flaky crusts and rich, smooth ice cream have long been the pride of Northern Heartland cooks of all backgrounds.

In this chapter we've selected a variety of recipes that run the gambit from homey to spectacular—such as a simple Gingered Fruit Crisp with Rum Whipped Cream and elegant Almond-Stuffed Poached Pears.

The recent interest in lower-fat meals hasn't dampened our enthusiasm for luscious creations, just broadened our range. Our Mocha Ice Milk is deliciously light, while Chocolate Bread Pudding, made with wholesome ingredients, is worth every rich bite.

341

DEEP-DISH
BLUEBERRY-RASPBERRY PIE

MAKES ONE 9-INCH PIE

*I*ntrepid Northland berry pickers often tell tales of intruding on a bear's favorite patch. Lucia's mother, Ann, recalls a morning when she looked up from her berries and stared right at a cub not far away. "Luckily, he was as scared as I," she recalls. "We both turned tail and ran back to our mamas, fast as we could."

This pie calls for sweet, tiny wild blueberries and raspberries. If you're not near a patch, the domesticated or frozen berries will do.

1 Sweet Cornmeal Piecrust recipe (page 343), well chilled
3–4 cups blueberries, sorted, rinsed, and drained
2 cups raspberries, sorted, rinsed, and drained
¾ cup sugar or to taste
3 tablespoons unbleached all-purpose flour
1 teaspoon grated lemon zest

*R*oll half of the well-chilled dough out on a floured pastry cloth or waxed paper and cut to fit a 9-inch-deep pie tin. In a large bowl, gently toss together the blueberries and raspberries with the remaining ingredients. Turn the fruit into the prepared tin. Roll out the remaining dough and cut to fit the top of the pie tin. Crimp the edges together to form a border, sealing the pie. Make four 2-inch slashes in the pastry starting near the edge and going toward the center of the pie.

Bake the pie in a preheated 350°F oven for about 50 minutes to 1 hour, or until the crust is golden brown and firm and the juices have bubbled up through the slashes.

SWEET CORNMEAL PIECRUST

**MAKES TWO 9-INCH PIECRUSTS
(OR A DOUBLE-CRUST PIE)**

*T*his crust has a delicious flavor and sturdy texture that works well with any of our fruit pie recipes. Use it for a double-crust pie, or roll it into a rectangle or circle and arrange sliced pears or apples on top for a free-form country tart.

>   *1 cup cornmeal*
>   *1 cup flour*
>   *½ teaspoon salt*
>   *3 tablespoons sugar*
>   *2 teaspoons baking powder*
>   *3 tablespoons butter*
>   *½ cup milk*

*I*n a large bowl, stir together the dry ingredients. Cut in the butter with two knives or your fingers until the consistency is that of small peas. Add the milk and toss the mixture together lightly until just combined, then gather into a large ball. Cover and refrigerate about 30 minutes.

Divide the dough into two balls (or make one large ball for a large, open-faced tart). On a lightly floured surface with a lightly floured rolling pin, roll out the dough slowly and evenly (be gentle).

GINGERED FRUIT CRISP
WITH RUM WHIPPED CREAM

SERVES 6 TO 8

*B*eginning with rhubarb in the late spring, strawberries and sour cherries by the Fourth of July, wild blueberries and raspberries in July and August, and then fall raspberries in September, plus apples and pears, the possibilities for fruit crisps are endless.

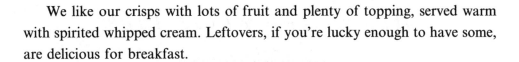

We like our crisps with lots of fruit and plenty of topping, served warm with spirited whipped cream. Leftovers, if you're lucky enough to have some, are delicious for breakfast.

> *2 cups unbleached all-purpose flour*
> *1 cup brown sugar, light or dark*
> *2 teaspoons ground cinnamon*
> *1½ sticks (12 tablespoons) butter*
> *1 cup lightly toasted, chopped walnuts*
> *1 tablespoon grated fresh gingerroot*
> *Juice of 1 lemon*
> *Grated rind of 1 lemon*
> *1–2 teaspoons cornstarch, depending on how juicy the fruit*
>   *is (optional)*
> *¾–1 cup sugar to taste, depending on how sweet the fruit is*
> *4–6 cups chopped fresh fruit or berries*

RUM WHIPPED CREAM

> *1 cup heavy cream*
> *1 tablespoon sugar*
> *1 tablespoon dark rum*
> *1 teaspoon vanilla extract*

*I*n a medium bowl, mix together the flour, brown sugar, and cinnamon, then work in the butter and walnuts to make a coarse meal to be used as topping. In another bowl, mix together the ginger, lemon juice and rind, cornstarch, sugar, and fruit. Turn the fruit mixture into a 2-quart baking dish, or a 9-inch-square baking pan, or 6 to 8 individual ovenproof serving dishes, and cover with the topping mixture. Bake in a preheated 350°F oven for about 20 to 35 minutes, or until the topping is crisp and brown and the fruit is bubbly.

To make the Rum Whipped Cream, beat together the cream, sugar, rum, and vanilla. Serve on the crisp while it's still warm.

HEARTLAND FRUIT PIES

MAKES ONE 9-INCH PIE

*S*erved with midmorning and midafternoon coffee, as well as for dessert, seasonal fruit pies are a staple throughout the Northern Heartland. Here we offer a basic recipe with several variations to spark your imagination. Serve slices of warm pie with Rum Whipped Cream (page 345) or Easy Vanilla Ice Cream (page 364).

> *1 Sweet Cornmeal Piecrust (page 343) or Rich Tart Crust*
> *(page 353)*
> *4–4½ cups chopped fruit or berries*
> *¾–1 cup sugar, depending on how sweet the fruit is*

*R*oll half of the well-chilled dough out on a floured pastry cloth or waxed paper and cut to fit the pie tin. In a large bowl, gently toss together the fruit with the sugar and turn into the prepared tin. Roll out the remaining dough and cut to fit the top of the pie tin. Crimp the edges together to form a border, sealing the pie. Make 2-inch slashes in the pastry starting near the edge and going toward the center of the pie.

Bake the pie in a preheated 350°F oven about 50 minutes to 1 hour, or until the crust is golden brown and firm and the juices have bubbled through the slashes.

FRUIT FILLING VARIATIONS

Apple Black Walnut: Toss together 4–4¼ cups chopped apples with ¼ cup black walnuts and 1 tablespoon grated lemon rind. Substitute light or dark brown sugar for the white sugar.

Strawberry Rhubarb: Toss together 2 cups rhubarb and 2 cups strawberries. Increase the amount of sugar to 1 cup. Brush the top of the crust with a glaze made with 1 egg beaten with 1 tablespoon water and sprinkle with blanched slivered almonds before putting the pie in the oven.

Pear Ginger: Toss 4 cups chopped pears with 1 tablespoon grated ginger-root.

Sour Cherry: Use 4 cups sour cherries and increase the sugar to 1 cup. Toss with toasted slivered almonds.

Plum and Early Apple: Toss together 2 cups chopped apples and 2 cups plums with 1 tablespoon grated orange rind.

Apple Cranberry: Increase the amount of sugar to 1 cup and toss together 2 cups cranberries and 2 cups chopped apples.

MICHIGAN'S CHERRIES

Around Traverse City, Michigan, on the Old Mission Peninsula, nearly a thousand cherry growers produce about 75 percent of the nation's sour cherry crop. First planted by a Presbyterian missionary named Peter Dougherty in the mid-1800s, the trees thrive in the unusually moderate climate created by the big lake. Rolling orchards now boast over four million trees, making Traverse City the Cherry Capital of the World.

For one short, magical week in mid-May the fifteen-foot trees, blooming with fragrant white flowers, span the rolling hills to the pure blue lake. The harvest begins in early July. After that, only the dried and canned varieties are available.

Fresh sour cherries are wonderful tossed into muffins, quick breads, and cakes. Remember to up the amount of sugar in the recipe, for they are quite tart. They also make a marvelous pie (page 347).

Dried sour cherries make a delicious substitute for raisins or chopped dried apricots in any recipe.

For more information about cherry products, see Sources (page 372).

APPLE STRUDEL

SERVES 6 TO 8

Making strudel dough is still best learned at the side of a patient German grandmother who can show you just how to adjust the amount of flour on a rainy day, who can tell by its feel when the dough is the right temperature for stretching (neither too cold nor too warm), and who can patch your holes with leftover scraps and melted butter.

These days making a strudel dessert requires only a package of frozen phyllo dough and this simple filling. While the results will not yield the glorious flavor and endearing imperfections of homemade, it's still plenty good with whipped cream or Easy Vanilla Ice Cream (page 364).

> 4 cups diced fruit or berries (apples, peaches, plums, straw-
>   berries, raspberries, blueberries—alone or in combination)
> Grated zest of 1 orange
> Juice of 1 orange
> ¼ cup brown sugar, light or dark
> 1 teaspoon vanilla extract
> 1 teaspoon ground cinnamon
> ½ teaspoon ground nutmeg
> ½ cup raisins (optional)
> 2 sticks (16 tablespoons) butter, melted
> 1 package phyllo dough

In a large bowl, toss together the fruit with the orange zest and juice, brown sugar, vanilla, spices, and raisins. Working quickly, lay 2 sheets of phyllo dough down on a large piece of waxed paper, long side toward your waist. Brush the dough with melted butter, lay a single sheet of dough on top of this, and brush it with melted butter. Continue laying down the sheets of dough, brushing them with butter, until you've used 8 sheets of dough. (A good tip is to keep the stack of sheets covered with a lightly dampened cloth so they don't dry out while you are working.)

Mound the filling down the long center of the dough, from left to right, leaving about 2 inches of dough as a border all around. Fold in the border closest to you so that it flaps over about 1 inch of the filling. Fold in the outer 2 borders about 1 inch also. Roll the dough up, using the end of the waxed paper as a guide. (Be careful not to roll the waxed paper into the strudel.) Brush the top and sides of the strudel with the remaining melted butter. Place on a parchment-lined or buttered baking sheet and bake in a preheated 350°F oven about 40 minutes, or until brown and crispy. This is best served warm.

Apples of the
Northern Heartland

Variety	Available	Characteristics	Uses
Dutchess	August–September	Smaller, purple-red; earliest appearing apple	Pie, sauce, baking
Red Free	August–September	Smaller, red, slightly sweet early season apple	Fresh eating, pie, sauce
Early Blush	August–September	Large, yellow with rosy blush, attractive, formerly called Douglas 1692; a recent U of M hybrid	Excellent all-purpose
Paula Red	August–October	Large, red with green showing; respectable keeper (sometimes available until Thanksgiving)	Fresh eating, pie, sauce; excellent for freezing
State Fair	August–September	Medium-sized, white flesh, round, smooth, bright red and glossy, crisp and juicy	Fresh eating, pie, sauce
Burgandy	August–September	Medium-sized, red/green; crisp, dense, tart, juicy	Fresh eating, salads
Wealthy	August–September	Medium/large, green with red blush; good keeper; first apple grown in MN (1869)	Excellent all-purpose
Nova Mac	September–November	Organic disease-resistant version of standard Macintosh	Excellent all-purpose
McIntosh	September–November	Medium-sized red apple with some green; crisp eating, cooks up soft	Excellent all-purpose
Cortland	September–November	Solid red; stays white when sliced	Excellent for salads; fresh eating, sauce
Sweet Sixteen	September–December	Red-striped, sweet, crisp; cross between MN 447 and Northern Spy	Fresh eating, pie, sauce
Spartan	September–late December	Medium-sized, deep red; crisp, white, juicy flesh; cross between McIntosh and Newtown	Fresh eating, pie, sauce

Variety	Available	Characteristics	Uses
Empire	September–late December	Smaller, nice eating apple; disease resistant; very popular on the East Coast; cross between McIntosh and Red Delicious	Excellent all-purpose
Priscilla	October–November	Organic variety, blush red, firm; a very sweet, spicy-tasting apple	Excellent all-purpose
Liberty	October–November	Organic variety; deep red, medium-sized, very hard, crunchy; lightly tart, mellows with storage	Excellent all-purpose
Ida Red	October–December	Medium-sized, pink to light red, not glossy; firm but not crisp flesh, mildly tart	Excellent in pies and sauce, good fresh eating
Mutsu	October–January	Very large, light green to yellow; crisp, sweet, fresh and juicy; excellent keeper.	Excellent all-purpose
Haralson	October–March	Medim-sized, striped red with freckles; crisp, tart, juicy and coarse; very popular; sometimes prone to russeting	Excellent for fresh eating, pie, sauce, baking, freezing
Jonathan	October–February	Smaller, bright red; tart; often the choice for lunch boxes and carameled apples	Fresh eating, pie, sauce
Honeygold	October–February	Large yellow-green; crisp, yellow, juicy flesh; flavor similar to Golden Delicious	Fresh eating, pie, sauce
Prairie Spy	October–April	Large, striped red; dense, hard flesh; slightly tart; long keeper; slices hold shape when cooked	Fresh eating, pie, sauce, baking
Regent	October–April	Medium-sized, bright red with dark striping; dense, crisp, slightly tart flesh; cross between Duchess and Delicious	Fresh eating, pie, sauce, baking
Fireside	October–April	Large, red with yellow/orange, slightly larger and more tart than its cousin, the Connell Red; crisp and flavorful; good keeper	Fresh eating, baking, salads
Connell Red	October–April	Medium-large, solid red hybrid of Fireside, slightly less tart than its cousin; good keeper	Fresh eating, baking, salads

APPLE HARVEST FRUIT TART

MAKES ONE 10-INCH TART

*E*nriched with nuts and dried fruit, this tart makes the best of late harvest apples. A little of this tart goes a long way. Cut the slices thin and serve with a bit of Rum Whipped Cream (page 345) or Thickened Cream (page 87).

> *Rich Tart Crust (page 353)*
> *1 cup chopped dried prunes*
> *1 cup chopped dried apricots*
> *½ cup golden raisins*
> *1 cup peeled, chopped apples*
> *⅓ cup sugar*
> *½ cup chopped walnuts*
> *¼ cup melted butter*
> *⅔ cup Grand Marnier, or orange juice*

*R*oll out half of the tart-crust dough to line a 10-inch tart pan and refrigerate. Place the dried fruit in a medium-sized saucepan and add just enough water to cover the fruit. Bring to a boil, cover the pan, and cook for about 20 minutes, or until the filling is very soft. Drain the fruit and cool slightly. Add the remaining ingredients and stir until the sugar is melted. Heap the filling into the tart pan. Roll out and cut the remaining dough into strips and make a lattice top, crimping the edges. Bake in a preheated 350°F oven for about 30 to 35 minutes. Remove from the oven and cool slightly before serving.

RICH TART CRUST

MAKES TWO 10-INCH TARTS

3 cups unbleached all-purpose flour
2 tablespoons sugar
2 sticks (16 tablespoons) butter
2 egg yolks
6–7 tablespoons ice water

*I*n a large bowl, mix together the flour and sugar. Cut in the butter to make a soft, small crumb. Stir in the egg yolks and then add the water, 1 tablespoon at a time, to make a soft dough. Gather the dough into a ball, wrap in plastic wrap, and refrigerate for at least 1 hour.

SCHAUM TORTE
(MERINGUE)

**MAKES ONE 9-INCH TART OR ONE 9-INCH,
FREE-FORM SHELL (RECIPE IS EASILY DOUBLED.)**

A traditional German summer dessert, this light meringue shell is usually filled with strawberries and whipped cream. It's also delicious filled with ice cream or sorbet.

¼ teaspoon salt
1 cup sugar
1 tablespoon cornstarch
4 egg whites, at room temperature
½ teaspoon vanilla extract
½ teaspoon white vinegar

*M*ix together the salt, sugar, and cornstarch. In a large bowl, beat the egg whites until soft peaks form. Gradually add the sugar mixture, 1 tablespoon at a time, beating well after each addition. Beat in the vanilla and vinegar. Pour into a lightly greased and floured 9-inch spring pan, or mound the meringue onto a lightly greased and floured cookie sheet and, using a rubber spatula, spread it into a 9- or 10-inch circle. Bake in a preheated 225°F oven for about 1 hour. Allow to cool, then fill with any of the following:

- 1 cup cream, whipped, topped with 1 cup fresh berries
- 1 cup cream, whipped with 1 tablespoon sugar and 1 tablespoon crystallized ginger, topped with fresh berries
- 1 cup cream, whipped and folded into 1 cup Old-fashioned Lemon Curd (page 369), topped with fresh berries
- 1 cup cream, whipped with 2 tablespoons coffee liqueur and topped with ¼ cup shaved semisweet chocolate and toasted slivered almonds

CREAMY WILD RICE PUDDING

SERVES 6

*W*ild rice adds a nutty taste and texture to this rich, creamy pudding. Serve warm with Blueberry-Honey Sauce (page 367). If you have cooked wild rice on hand, use it in lieu of the uncooked wild rice. For traditional rice pudding, use all-white rice (see the footnote), and bake an almond into the center of it.

> *3 cups whole milk*
> *½ cup long-grain white rice**
> *¼ cup wild rice*
> *2 tablespoons butter*
> *3 egg yolks*
> *¾ cup sugar*
> *2 teaspoons vanilla extract*
> *½ teaspoon almond or maple extract (optional)*
> *½ cup heavy cream*
> *¼ teaspoon ground cinnamon*
> *1 tablespoon sugar*
>
> **For traditional rice pudding, increase the white rice to ¾ cup and omit the wild rice. Bury an almond in the center of the rice after turning it into the casserole.*

*P*ut the milk, rice, and butter in the top of a double boiler, then cover and cook over simmering water for about 1½ hours. In a small bowl, beat the egg yolks with the sugar, extracts, and cream, and slowly add to the rice mixture, stirring rapidly to combine. Pour the mixture into a 2-quart buttered casserole or baking dish. Mix together the cinnamon and sugar and sprinkle it over the rice. Bake in a preheated 350°F oven for about 15 minutes, or until the pudding is thick. Serve warm.

THE *GRØT* OF LIFE

*R*ommegrøt, Norwegian cream porridge, like lutefisk and lefse, has become a traditional holiday food, cherished for its historical significance. In Scandinavian churches and clubs across the Northern Heartland, these foods are served in tribute to ancestors who overcame the harsh frontier conditions, and they have become symbols of ethnic heritage and pride.

True *rommegrøt* can no longer be made in the United States because it requires unpasteurized sour cream. Years ago, when raw milk was available from local dairies, the untreated cream was allowed to stand a few days to sour. The *grøt* was cooked for several hours over low heat and stirred constantly with a *tvare* made from the top of an evergreen tree, the end branches clipped to form tines. *Rommegrøt* was served as the first course of a traditional holiday meal, topped with the butter that surfaced during its long cooking time.

Today's version is made with heavy whipping cream, lemon juice, and flour. At Scandinavian heritage luncheons it is served with sandwiches of cheese and spicy sausage, along with coffee and Christmas cookies.

Rommegrøt figures heavily in Norwegian folklore as a gift to the *nisse* (barn spirits) or as a bribe for the trolls. It was believed that *rommegrøt* helped new mothers recover from delivery and provided strength for nursing. It was served to field hands to celebrate a rich harvest.

Sigrid Stordalen, a Norwegian immigrant in southern Minnesota, wrote in a letter to his family over one hundred years ago, "The soil here is so rich, one can make *rommegrøt* of it!"

Here is a recipe from *The Best of the Old Church Cookbooks*, by Florence Ekstrand.

ROMMEGRØT

2 parts of cream to 1 part milk

Cook cream 15 minutes before adding flour, adding enough flour to make real thick; cook until butter comes and take off as much butter as possible. Have milk boiling hot and add gradually to thickened cream mixture. Salt to taste.

ROMMEGRØD (CREAM MUSH)

Sour cream boiled and stirred constantly. Sift in flour until mush gets thick. Stir steadily till butter comes out. Skim off part of butter to be used as gravy. Add more flour and boiling milk until thick.

STEVEN HOWARD'S
BREAD PUDDINGS

Steven Howard, former pastry chef at D'Amico Cucina, Minneapolis, credits his great-grandmother, Bertha Ellison, for his dessert-making talent. "She was a wonderful farm woman who cooked for the threshers and, later, owned the only café in town. She served fruit pies and cobblers with homemade ice cream and rich puddings. Of course, she always made her own bread and rolls."

These two bread pudding recipes will transform any old bread into wonderfully rich desserts. We often use our leftover Honey Cracked Wheat Bread (page 8); dry, not too sweet breads work best.

Steven Howard's Bread Puddings (continued)

CHOCOLATE BREAD PUDDING

SERVES 6 TO 8

½ loaf unsliced homemade-type bread, cut into 1-inch
squares (about 4–5 cups)
1¼ cups heavy cream
1¼ cups whole milk
¾ pound semisweet chocolate, shaved, or chocolate chips
3 eggs
½ cup sugar
2 teaspoons vanilla extract
½ teaspoon almond extract

*P*ut the bread cubes into a large bowl. In a medium-sized saucepan, bring the cream and milk to a boil, turn off the heat, and stir in the chocolate until it has melted. Pour this over the bread and let it sit for 10 to 15 minutes so that the bread absorbs the mixture. Beat the eggs and sugar with the vanilla and almond extracts. Pour over the bread, tossing gently. Dump the bread mixture into a large, greased 2-quart pan or an 8 × 8-inch cake pan. Cover with aluminum foil. Bake in a preheated 350°F oven for about 35 to 45 minutes, or until the edges are firm but the inside is still soft and moist. The pudding should seem underbaked. Serve hot with Easy Vanilla Ice Cream (page 364) or whipped cream.

RICH BREAD PUDDING

SERVES 6 TO 8

½ *loaf unsliced homemade-type bread, cut into 1-inch*
  squares (about 5 cups)
2 *cups whole milk*
3 *eggs*
¾ *cup sugar*
2 *teaspoons vanilla extract*
½ *teaspoon almond extract*
Grated rind of ½ *orange (optional)*
½ *cup berries or chopped fruit (optional)*

*P*ut the bread cubes into a large bowl. In a medium-sized saucepan, bring the milk to a boil, pour over the bread, and allow to sit for about 10 to 15 minutes so the bread absorbs the milk. Beat the eggs and sugar with the vanilla and almond extracts and pour over the bread. If desired, add the orange rind and fruit and toss all the ingredients together. Dump the bread mixture into a large, greased 2-quart pan or an 8 × 8-inch cake pan. Cover the pan with aluminum foil. Bake in a preheated 350°F oven for about 35 to 45 minutes, or until the edges are firm but the inside is still soft and moist. The pudding should seem underbaked. Serve hot with warm Blueberry-Honey Sauce (page 367).

For a richer bread pudding, substitute 2 cups heavy cream for 2 cups whole milk.

Men collecting maple sap, 1940

MAPLE-GLAZED BAKED APPLES

SERVES 4

*T*his simple recipe works particularly well with the tart, crisp Haralson and Fireside apples that grow here. It makes a simple, low-fat dessert. For those who don't count calories, serve with Rum Whipped Cream (page 345), Caramel Sauce (page 366), or Easy Vanilla Ice Cream (page 364).

> *4 tart apples*
> *4 tablespoons maple syrup*
> *¼ cup dried cherries or raisins*
> *Dark apple cider*

*C*ore the apples to about ½ inch of their bottoms. Peel each apple down about to its middle. Place the apples, bottoms down, in a baking dish and fill each of the apples with equal amounts of syrup and dried cherries. Fill the dish with ¼ inch of cider. Bake the apples in a preheated 350°F oven for about 35 to 45 minutes, depending on the apple, until they are tender but not mushy. Serve the apples warm.

MAPLE FRANGO

SERVES 6 TO 8

*T*his dessert was made popular in the 1950s by the Skyroom Restaurant of Dayton's Department Store, Minneapolis. Creamy and sweet, Maple Frango deserves to make a comeback. It's delicious topped with fresh blueberries or toasted chopped nuts—and it's a snap to make.

> *1 cup maple syrup*
> *4 eggs, separated*
> *2 cups heavy cream*

*I*n a medium-sized saucepan, warm the syrup, then whisk in the egg yolks, one at a time. Bring the mixture to a simmer and cook over low heat, stirring constantly, until it begins to thicken. (It will just coat the back of a spoon.) Allow to cool. Beat the egg whites until they hold stiff peaks. Whip the cream. Fold both egg whites and cream into the maple mixture; don't overmix so that they are completely blended—there should be some white streaks. Pour into a 9-inch-deep pie dish or an 8 × 8-inch cake pan or into individual serving goblets. Put in the freezer until it becomes very firm but not frozen solid. (If it gets too hard, remove from the freezer to soften before serving.)

CHRISTMAS RICE PUDDING

Rice pudding is the traditional Christmas Eve dessert in many Swedish and Norwegian-American homes. The recipes vary greatly among families, as does the accompanying folklore. Whether baked in the oven or simmered on the back of the stove, made with eggs or without, studded with raisins, or dusted with cinnamon sugar, Christmas Eve rice pudding is always served in a fancy dish with a blanched almond hidden somewhere inside it. Whoever finds the almond will have good luck throughout the year: the unmarried will find a mate; a married couple will have a child; a young family will prosper; and the older couple will live comfortably.

Agnes Dahlein of Stratford, Iowa, recalls: "Our mother always made this pudding for our Christmas Eve family dinner. If any was left, it was carefully saved to coax sleeping children out of warm beds for early Christmas services. It always worked!"

ALMOND-STUFFED POACHED PEARS

SERVES 8

*I*n the days when everyone had at least two apple trees and one pear tree in the backyard, pear butter, pear pie, pickled pears, along with poached pear desserts, were turn-of-the-century favorites.

> *1 cup blanched almonds*
> *2 cups sugar*
> *2 tablespoons rosewater or orange juice*
> *¼ teaspoon almond extract*
> *8 pears*
> *Water to cover pears*
> *2 tablespoons lemon juice*

*I*n a food processor fitted with a steel blade or in a blender, grind the almonds fine, then add *1 cup* of the sugar, the rosewater, and almond extract to make a thick paste. Set aside.

Peel the pears with a vegetable scraper and trim the bottoms to make a flat surface. Place the pears in a large pot and add the remaining ingredients. Bring the liquid to a simmer and poach the pears. Cooking time will vary greatly, from 10 to 25 minutes, depending on the variety and how ripe the pears are. Don't overcook; the pears shouldn't be mushy. Remove the pears and reserve the poaching liquid.

Cool the pears and remove the cores with a melon baller. Pack the cavity of each pear with the almond stuffing. Place the pears in a 9 × 13-inch baking dish with about 2 inches of the poaching liquid and cover with aluminum foil. Put the dish in a preheated 350°F oven for about 10 minutes, or until the pears are warm. Serve with whipped cream.

M O C H A I C E M I L K

SERVES 8

*W*e serve this with the Chocolate Angel Food Cake (page 320) and Chocolate Sauce (page 365). It has a rich, dense flavor and is light and refreshing.

> *¼ cup sugar*
> *½ cup water*
> *½ cup strong coffee*
> *2 cups milk*
> *6 ounces semisweet chocolate*
> *1 teaspoon vanilla extract*

*I*n a heavy saucepan, bring the sugar and water to a boil. Add the coffee and boil about 2 minutes. Add the milk and stir in the chocolate until it melts. Remove the pan from the heat and stir in the vanilla, then strain the mixture into a metal bowl to chill. Pour the mixture into an ice-cream maker and process according to the manufacturer's directions.

EASY VANILLA ICE CREAM

MAKES 1½ QUARTS
(RECIPE IS EASILY DOUBLED OR CUT IN HALF.)

*I*s there anyone who doesn't like ice cream? Most people associate it with summer and Fourth of July celebrations and, if they're old enough, taking turns at the hand crank of the big wooden barrel freezer—a chore everyone shared. In the Northern Heartland homemade ice cream is also associated with Christmas and special occasions throughout the winter, when ice was easily gotten from the yard and the freezer was the back porch.

Today Minnesotans consume the largest amount of ice cream per capita in the nation, with the amount actually increasing a bit through the winter months. Wisconsin is second.

This recipe belongs to Stephen Howard and is wonderful alongside his Chocolate Bread Pudding (page 358). It's rich, yet light, made with cream but not eggs, and it doesn't need to be cooked.

> *3 cups heavy cream*
> *1½ cups milk*
> *1 cup sugar*
> *¼–½ vanilla bean or 1 teaspoon vanilla extract*

*C*ombine all of the ingredients in a large bowl. If using a vanilla bean, scrape the inside into the cream-milk mixture: cut the bean in half lengthwise with a small, sharp knife. Place the side of a knife at one end and press down to flatten the bean as you move the knife away from you, toward the pot. Scrape the seeds into the bowl. Refrigerate the mixture for 1 to 2 hours or overnight, until it reaches about 40°F.

Pour the mixture into an ice-cream maker and process according to manufacturer's directions.

Ice cream cone party, 1908

CHOCOLATE SAUCE

MAKES ABOUT 1 CUP

*W*e drizzle this over Chocolate Angel Food Cake (page 320) with Mocha Ice Milk (page 363), on top of Minnesota Fudge Cake (page 330) with whipped cream, and, of course, on Easy Vanilla Ice Cream (page 364).

6 ounces semisweet chocolate, chopped, or chocolate chips
½ cup strong coffee
½ teaspoon vanilla extract

*I*n the top of a double boiler set over simmering water, melt the chocolate with the coffee, stirring frequently. Remove the pan from the heat, then stir in the vanilla. Serve the sauce warm or at room temperature.

THE SUNDAE

E.B. (Ed Berners), the proprietor of a modest ice cream parlor in Two Rivers, Wisconsin, created the first ice cream sundae in the summer of 1881. In an interview before his death he recalled: "One night, a regular customer, George Hauller, dropped in and ordered a dish of ice cream. As I was serving it, he spied a bottle of chocolate syrup on the snack bar, which I used for making sodas.

" 'Why don't you put some of that chocolate on the ice cream?' he asked.

" 'You don't want to ruin the flavor of the ice cream,' I protested. But he answered, 'I'll try anything once,' and I poured on the chocolate. Hauller liked it, and the ice cream sundae was born." The chocolate-topped ice cream became a rage, and Berners began creating delicious concoctions with names like Flora-Dora, Mudscow, and Chocolate Peany with peanuts.

The name sundae, however, originated in neighboring Manitowoc, when George Giffy began serving his ice cream specialties once a week, on Sunday, after church services. One weekday a little girl ordered a dish of ice cream "with that stuff on it." George told her we only serve those on Sunday, and the child replied, "Why then, this must be Sunday, for it's the kind of ice cream I want." Giffy acquiesced and named the dish "sundae," changing the spelling to avoid seeming sacrilegious.

CARAMEL SAUCE

MAKES 2 CUPS

*A*t the Apple Festival in Bayfield, Wisconsin, the local ice cream parlor features Caramel Apple Sundaes: a scoop of vanilla cream, surrounded by fresh slices of tart, crisp Haralson or Fireside apples, topped with plenty of caramel sauce.

The only trick to making this sauce is in cooking it to just the right color.

If removed from the heat too soon, it will lack flavor and body; if left on too long, it will taste burned. We pull the pan from the heat as the sugar turns a deep golden color—not quite amber—and then add the cream. Remember that the syrup will continue to cook after it is pulled from the heat. *Be careful.* This is hot stuff, so do not taste it until after it has cooled.

> *1½ cups heavy cream*
> *1⅓ cups sugar*
> *⅓ cup water*
> *1 teaspoon vanilla extract*

*I*n a small saucepan, scald the cream by bringing it just to a boil, then removing it from the heat. In a medium-sized saucepan, stir together the sugar and water, bring to a simmer, and cook, stirring occasionally and scraping the crystals that form on the side of the pan back down into the liquid. Remove the pan from the heat when the color is dark golden, not quite amber. (One trick to keep the crystals from developing on the side of the pan is to cover the pan for a few minutes at a time.) The cooking will take about 5 minutes, and the caramel should register about 245°F on a candy thermometer.

Slowly add the warm cream, stirring constantly. Be careful. The cream will sizzle, bubble, and splash. Return the pan to the stove, bring the mixture to a boil, then reduce the heat and simmer about 2 to 3 minutes. Stir in the vanilla and it's ready to serve.

BLUEBERRY-HONEY SAUCE

MAKES ABOUT 2 CUPS

*I*f you can, make this sauce when the tiny wild blueberries are at their peak. Serve it over Lucia's Half-Pound Cake (page 319), with more fresh berries and whipped cream or Easy Vanilla Ice Cream (page 364). Try it on Pancakes (page 42), French Toast (page 38), and Creamy Wild Rice Pudding (page 355). Vary the berries with the season.

Blueberry-Honey Sauce (continued)

> 2 cups blueberries
> ½ teaspoon ground cinnamon
> ¼ teaspoon ground nutmeg
> ¼ cup honey
> 2 tablespoons butter

*I*n a medium-sized saucepan, combine all the ingredients and bring to a boil. Reduce the heat and simmer for 5 minutes. (If you are using other berries that are particularly seedy, such as raspberries, you may want to strain before serving.)

IN THE CLOVER (BUCKWHEAT, SOYBEANS, ALFALFA)

In the frontier days, settlers and Indians would collect honey from hollow trees where bees swarmed. Later farmers began capturing and keeping swarms in just about whatever they could find—hollow logs, overturned baskets, and old crates—to harvest honey, provide beeswax, and pollinate crops.

Today small family-run apiaries in Minnesota, Wisconsin, and Iowa produce more than half of the nation's honey. Most of our commercial light, mild-tasting honey comes from bees fed on clover. Buckwheat honey (dark, amber-colored, strong, almost nutty-tasting), soybean honey (light and nutty), and alfalfa honey (just a bit darker than clover) are all becoming popular in food co-ops throughout the region.

OLD-FASHIONED LEMON CURD

MAKES ABOUT 1 CUP

*W*e often make this just to have on hand for a quick dessert. Fold it into whipped cream and spoon it into a tall glass. Serve it in a lightly baked and cooled Rich Tart Crust (page 353) or into a piecrust topped with meringue for lemon meringue pie, or on top of Lucia's Half-Pound Cake (page 319) or on the German Oven Pancake (page 44). Serve with muffins for brunch or as a topping for a dish of fresh raspberries.

> *Grated rind of 4 lemons*
> *½ cup lemon juice (about 4 lemons)*
> *2 eggs plus 2 egg yolks*
> *1 cup sugar*
> *6 tablespoons butter*

*I*n a medium-sized saucepan, beat together the lemon rind, lemon juice, whole eggs, egg yolks, and sugar. Cook over low heat, stirring constantly, until the mixture becomes thick and translucent, about 5 to 10 minutes. Remove from the stove and strain the mixture into a separate bowl to remove the bits of rind and any strands of cooked egg white. Add the butter and stir until it is melted. Cover and store in the refrigerator. It will keep about 1 week.

CARAMELS

MAKES 120 CARAMELS

*P*astry chef Gene Zarling teaches candy-making classes throughout the Twin Cities. This recipe is one of her favorites.

> *6 cups granulated sugar*
> *2¼ cups light corn syrup*
> *3 sticks unsalted butter*
> *6 cups heavy cream*

*L*ine a 12 × 16-inch pan with aluminum foil and butter it well. In a large, 3-quart saucepan, stir together the sugar, corn syrup, butter, and *5½ cups* of the heavy cream. Bring the mixture to a rolling boil over medium heat and cook for 1 minute. Stir in the remaining cream but be careful: the mixture may bubble up. Continue cooking over medium-high heat, stirring occasionally. Have a glass of ice water ready. When the mixture reaches 245°F on a candy thermometer and ½ teaspoon of it becomes a firm ball when dropped into the glass of ice water, it is ready. Remove from the stove and immediately pour the mixture into the prepared pan. Let it cool before cutting into bite-size squares.

SATURDAY NIGHT TAFFY PULLS

"**W**hen we were kids, my older brother and his wife lived with us for a while; so did my older sister and her husband. Saturday nights we always had oyster stew. And Saturday night we used to play 'matches'; it was a card game, and we used farm matches. Afterwards, mother made taffy. She made it with sorghum that she would cook in the cast-iron frying pan with some butter. She would let it cool; then we put butter on our hands and pulled it. We'd stretch it into crazy shapes, then throw it in the snow to cool."

—DAISY SAMUELSON OF OXLIP COUNTY, MINNESOTA

INDEX

Numerals in **boldface** indicate recipe titles. Numerals in *italics* indicate illustrations.

Alfalfa honey, 368
Alice Hoolihan's Sour Cream Coffee
    Cake (*Potica* Cake), **334–5**
almond(s), 4, 362
    Brussels Sprouts with Toasted, **269**
    Kransekake, Hilda's, **310–11**
    Lace Cookies, **303**
    -Maple-Pecan Butter, **95**
    -Stuffed Poached Pears, **362–3**
Amana Colonies, *122*, *145*
American Swedish Institute,
    Minneapolis, 304
Amidon, Tom, 10
Angel Food Cake, Chocolate, **320–1**
anise, 4
Ann Heskins' Matrimonial Diamonds,
    315
apple(s), 281, 282, *349*, 350–1
    Braised Red Cabbage with Bacon
        and, **271**
    Butter, Old-Fashioned, **283**
    Chicken Salad with Apples,
        Walnuts, and Maple-Mustard
        Vinaigrette, **74**
    Harvest Fruit Tart, **352**
    Maple-Glazed Baked, **360–1**
    "peelin' and stirrin'," 282

apple(s) *(continued)*
    Pork Loin with Apples and Cider
        Sauce, **110–11**
    Strudel, **348–9**
    types of, 350–1
Asian immigrants, 151, 239, 248, 255
asparagus:
    and Fiddlehead Ferns, Baked
        Walleye with, **213**
    Morels, and Sunchokes in Brown
        Butter with Toasted Hazelnuts,
        245
Austrian Vanocka, **31**

Bacon:
    Braised Red Cabbage with Apples
        and, **271**
    Hazelnuts, and Lemon-Sage Butter,
        Pan-Fried Trout with, **216–17**
Bailly (Alexis) Winery, 203
Baked Apples, Maple-Glazed, **360–1**
Baked Wisconsin Goat Cheese on
    Croutons, **98**
Bake-Off, 321
baking and milling, 2–53
Balsamic Vinaigrette, Rosemary, **251**
bar(s), 298–300
    Ann Heskins' Matrimonial
        Diamonds, **315**
    Chocolate Peanut-Butter, **317**
    Maple Nut, **313**

373

PHOTOGRAPHIC CREDITS

The photographs and illustrations reproduced in this book were provided with the permission and courtesy of the following:

Minnesota Historical Society, St. Paul, Minn.: 5, 17, 63, 67, 85, 86, 88, 97, 113, 121, 135, 155, 164, 172, 197, 205, 212, 221, 225, 235, 244, 250, 254, 257, 262, 267, 276, 285, 288, 292, 300, 320, 349, 353, 360, 365

General Mills: 11

State Historical Society of Wisconsin, Madison, Wisc.: 13, 43, 127, 150, 179

Vesterheim Norwegian American Museum, Decorah, Iowa: 25, 40, 41, 272

Superbly Swedish: Recipes and Traditions, Penfield Press, Iowa City, Iowa: 35

Susan Puckett's *A Cooks Tour of Iowa*, University of Iowa Press, Iowa City, Iowa: 52, 336

Karal Ann Marling's *Blue Ribbon*, Minnesota Historical Society Press, St. Paul, Minn.: 92, 327

Lisa Fourre: 100

Amana Heritage Society, Amana, Iowa: 122, 145

Edward S. Curtis, collection of Christopher Cardozo, from *Native Nations*, a Bulfinch Press Book, Little, Brown & Company and Callaway Editions, Inc.: 193, 344

Tom Jenz: 209

Henry F. Zeman and *In-Fisherman* magazine, Brainerd, Minn.: 228

Lief Dahl, Sons of Norway, Minneapolis, Minn.: 311

KMA Radio, Shenandoah, Iowa: 316

BETH DOOLEY is a writer and teacher whose books include *The Heartland: New American Cooking, Prevention's Quick and Healthy Pasta,* and *Peppers Hot and Sweet*. She is a contributing editor for *Mpls/St.Paul* magazine, and her work has appeared in *Fine Cooking, City Pages,* the Minneapolis *Star Tribune,* and National Public Radio's *The Splendid Table*. She lives in Minneapolis with her husband and three sons and teaches English at the Lake Country School.

LUCIA WATSON is the well-known chef and owner of Lucia's, one of Minneapolis's top restaurants. She teaches cooking throughout the Midwest and has written for *Fine Cooking* and *In-Fisherman*. She served on the board of the Chef's Collaborative and currently serves as board chair for Youth Farm & Market Project. Her family has deep roots in Minnesota, and both her grandmothers passed down their recipes, talent, and passion for cooking to Lucia, who uses them in her own cooking.